CW01497331

TEACHING DESIGN AND TECHNOLOGY CREATIVELY

Packed full of practical ideas, *Teaching Design and Technology Creatively* is a stimulating source of guidance for busy trainee and practising teachers. Grounded in the latest research, it offers a wealth of suggestions to foster creative development in D&T and supports teachers in providing their students with more authentic, enjoyable experiences.

Providing a wealth of ready-to-use ideas for creative lessons, key topics covered include:

- Understanding links between D&T and creativity
- Creating a foundation for D&T in the early years
- Using objects, books and real-life contexts as imaginative starting points
- Developing designerly thinking
- Making the most of construction kits
- Helping children draw to develop their ideas
- Encouraging dialogic talk in D&T to drive learning
- Exploring food as a creative resource
- Practical approaches to embedding IT and programming in the curriculum
- Taking learning outside the classroom.

Teaching Design and Technology Creatively provides practical teaching suggestions to ensure teachers of all levels understand how to teach *for* creativity. It shows how learning experiences in D&T have the potential to extend children's technological knowledge, and to promote problem-solving and evaluation skills. Drawing on examples from real-world projects, this text is invaluable for all those who wish to engage students in D&T and encourage creative classroom practice.

Clare Benson is Professor of Primary Education, specialist D&T, Birmingham City University, UK.

Suzanne Lawson is Senior Lecturer and the PGCE Secondary Course Leader, University of Worcester, UK.

THE LEARNING TO TEACH IN THE PRIMARY SCHOOL SERIES

Series editor: Teresa Cremin, The Open University, UK

Teaching is an art form. It demands not only knowledge and understanding of the core areas of learning, but also the ability to teach these creatively and foster learner creativity in the process. *The Learning to Teach in the Primary School Series* draws upon recent research which indicates the rich potential of creative teaching and learning, and explores what it means to teach creatively in the primary phase. It also responds to the evolving nature of subject teaching in a wider, more imaginatively framed twenty-first-century primary curriculum.

Designed to complement the textbook *Learning to Teach in the Primary School*, the well-informed, lively texts in this series offer support for students and practising teachers who want to develop more creative approaches to teaching and learning. Uniquely, the books highlight the importance of the teachers' own creative engagement and share a wealth of research-informed ideas to enrich pedagogy and practice.

Titles in the series:

Teaching Music Creatively, 2nd Edition
Pam Burnard and Regina Murphy

Teaching Design and Technology Creatively
Edited by Clare Benson and Suzanne Lawson

Teaching Outdoors Creatively
Edited by Stephen Pickering

Teaching History Creatively, 2nd Edition
Edited by Hilary Cooper

Teaching Geography Creatively, 2nd Edition
Edited by Stephen Scoffham

Teaching Science Creatively, 2nd Edition
Dan Davies and Deb McGregor

Teaching English Creatively, 2nd Edition
Teresa Cremin

Teaching Mathematics Creatively, 2nd Edition
Linda Pound and Trisha Lee

Teaching Religious Education Creatively
Edited by Sally Elton-Chalcraft

Teaching Physical Education Creatively
Angela Pickard and Patricia Maude

TEACHING DESIGN AND TECHNOLOGY CREATIVELY

Edited by
Clare Benson and
Suzanne Lawson

Routledge
Taylor & Francis Group

LONDON AND NEW YORK

First published 2017
by Routledge
2 Park Square, Milton Park, Abingdon, Oxon OX14 4RN

and by Routledge
711 Third Avenue, New York, NY 10017

Routledge is an imprint of the Taylor & Francis Group, an informa business

British Library Cataloguing in Publication Data
A catalogue record for this book is available from the British Library

Library of Congress Cataloging in Publication Data
A catalog record for this book has been requested

ISBN: 978-1-138-65457-0 (hbk)
ISBN: 978-1-138-65459-4 (pbk)
ISBN: 978-1-315-62315-3 (ebk)

Typeset in Times New Roman and Helvetica Neue
by Florence Production Ltd, Stoodleigh, Devon, UK

MIX
Paper from
responsible sources
FSC
www.fsc.org   FSC® C013056

Printed and bound in Great Britain by
TJ International Ltd, Padstow, Cornwall

CONTENTS

CONTRIBUTORS

James Archer

James is Senior Lecturer in Primary Education at Leeds Beckett University where he teaches on some of the primary D&T provision. James has worked in initial teacher education in two other institutions including Bradford College, where he held the management responsibility for Primary Science, and Canterbury Christ Church University, where he taught science and D&T. James has been an advisor in primary science and has taught in both the primary and secondary phases in the UK and South Africa. He loves making things and is passionate about exploring the links between science and D&T.

Clare Benson

Clare is Professor of Primary Education at Birmingham City University. She has taught in primary schools in this country and overseas, and has been an advisory teacher for D&T before moving into teacher education and research. Over 1000 students have registered on an MA Ed primary D&T programme that Clare developed. She has chaired the Primary Working Group for the D&T Association since its inception. She has written numerous curriculum and research publications, presented her work at many international conferences and supported a wide range of National Curriculum developments in England and overseas. Her current interests include the development of early years D&T and teaching D&T creatively.

Caroline Colfer

Caroline has taught in primary schools in Germany, Spain and England, co-ordinating both science and D&T. Her passion for D&T ignited when she saw how responsive children were, particularly when she planned other subjects to link with D&T. She is convinced that exploratory and dialogic talk not only enhances children's learning in D&T but equips them with communication skills in many aspects of life. Caroline is now a Senior Lecturer at the University of St Mark and St John. She has spoken at international conferences in Dublin, London, Berlin and Sydney, written curriculum materials and published her research into the types of talk children use when problem-solving.

Wendy Fox-Turnbull

Wendy is currently a Senior Lecturer at the University of Canterbury's College of Education, New Zealand. She lectures in Technology Education and Professional Education Studies and Inquiry Learning across a range of programmes in the initial teacher education sector. Her special research interests include authentic learning in D&T education, the role and nature of effective conversation in learning, and teaching and learning approaches for the twenty-first century. She has presented regularly at PATT conferences and is published in a range of technology education journals. Wendy is the current chair of the Technology Education New Zealand (TENZ) Council and was recently awarded the Outstanding Contribution to Technology Education Award.

Sally Hardman

Sally is a Senior Lecturer in Primary Education at the University of Winchester. Her expertise is in science and D&T education in the primary sector. She teaches on the undergraduate and postgraduate initial teacher education programmes and has been actively involved in several small-scale research projects associated with children's curiosity and developing understanding of the world. She is particularly interested in creative approaches to teaching and learning.

Gill Hope

Gill has recently retired from Canterbury Christ Church University where she was a Senior Lecturer for 14 years, teaching D&T education across both undergraduate and postgraduate initial teacher education courses. Prior to this, she was a primary school teacher in Kent for more years than she cares to consider! Gill is the author of three books on teaching D&T in the primary school, as well as of several journal articles and book chapters. Her main research interest is in how young children can be enabled to use drawing to generate and develop creative design ideas.

Steve Keirl

Steve has taught D&T in primary and secondary schools in London and Australia. He lectured in D&T and Curriculum Studies in Australian universities for 17 years and is currently Reader in Design Education at Goldsmiths, University of London. Steve researches and writes about D&T curriculum and pedagogy. He believes that all children in the world should receive a rich D&T education – one that advances technological and design literacy in ways that are critical, ethical and democracy-serving. Steve has published extensively and delivered conference papers, workshops and keynote addresses internationally. He collects washing-up brushes.

Remke Klapwijk

Remke is a Senior Researcher at the Science Education and Communication group of the Delft University of Technology and an educational consultant at the Hobéon Group. Her research is practice-driven and focuses on the facilitation of creative thinking processes in primary D&T education. She has published several scientific articles including a study on the future of D&T education, partly published in English as 'Career orientation of secondary school students (m/f) in the Netherlands'. Her interests are, among others, design methodology, creativity, user-oriented and real-life design projects, teacher training, children in disadvantaged neighbourhoods and formative evaluation of creative design.

Suzanne Lawson

Suzanne is the PGCE Secondary Course Leader at the University of Worcester, teaching on the postgraduate and MA programmes. Before this, she worked as a Senior Lecturer at Birmingham City University where she was the PGCE D&T Programme Leader and also a member of the Centre for Research in Primary Technology (CRIPT). She has 14 years of teaching experience working in a range of schools in the UK, with a further 13 years' experience working in teacher training. Suzanne's main research interests are food technology and calculated risk-taking in teacher education.

Pam Maunders

Pam is a Senior Lecturer in Primary Education at the University of Winchester and is actively involved in initial teacher education at undergraduate and postgraduate levels in ICT and computing. Her research projects have included using audio feedback for assessment at higher education level and using blogging as an assessment tool. One of her current research projects is the implementation of iPads in initial teacher education in the Department of Teacher Development at the University of Winchester.

Sue Miles-Pearson

Sue is a Senior Lecturer and module convenor for Primary Design and Technology Education at the University of Roehampton, London, teaching on both undergraduate and postgraduate programmes. She is just completing her tenth year at the university. Before this, she worked in primary schools in the east end and north of London, where she coordinated both science and D&T, before spending 5 years as a special educational needs coordinator. She is interested in CAD/CAM and has jointly written articles, including one on design concepts, that have been presented at national D&T conferences.

Louise Milne

Louise is a Senior Lecturer in Technology Education at the University of Waikato. She teaches primary pre-service teachers in both graduate and undergraduate papers. She has a background in primary teaching with a particular interest in junior primary students. She worked as a facilitator and director of professional development contracts implementing the technology curriculum. She has also worked on a number of Ministry of Education contracts including Technology Education for Year 7 & 8 specialist teachers, planning and assessment contracts and the development of resources for technology. Louise's PhD investigated the EOTC (Education Outside the Classroom) environment and how this supports 5-year-old students studying technology education.

Eric Parkinson

Eric initially taught geography and geology in the West Indies and then began a career as a primary teacher in Kent when primary science and technology were evolving as new curriculum elements. A move into science teacher education at Canterbury

Christ Church University led to consultancy work in Jamaica, South Africa, India and Nigeria. International links increasingly directed his attention beyond science into primary D&T education. His research interests have revolved around issues concerning technological literacy and the evolution of the construction kit.

Marion Rutland

Marion began teaching at the University of Roehampton, London, in 1993, where she was the Course Leader for D&T, the PGCE Secondary D&T tutor and GTP tutor for D&T students on school-based courses. She taught on the Primary D&T modules, the MA programme for D&T and supervised PhD students. Currently she is an honorary research fellow. Marion taught food-related subjects and textiles in secondary schools in England, and for a short period in Australia, for 22 years and was an ICT Advisory Teacher in London. Research interests include teaching and learning in D&T, creativity and food technology.

Sue Wood-Griffiths

Sue is the PGCE Secondary Design and Technology Subject Leader at the University of Worcester. The course prepares trainees to teach food and textiles. She also contributes to the primary undergraduate route teaching D&T. Before working in higher education, she taught for 21 years in schools across the UK and overseas. As Subject Leader at the university, Sue aims to develop confident, capable and creative teachers who can inspire their pupils to engage with exciting and relevant D&T activities. Throughout the course, she models good teaching practice and encourages and supports trainees to develop innovative teaching strategies, to share ideas and to take 'intelligent' risks.

PREFACE

Over recent decades, teachers working in accountability cultures across the globe have been required to focus on raising standards, setting targets and 'delivering' prescribed curricula and pedagogy. The language of schooling (Mottram and Hall, 2009: 109) has predominantly focused upon 'oversimplified, easily measurable notions of attainment', which, they argue, has had a homogenising effect, prompting children and their development to be discussed 'according to levels and descriptors', rather than as children, as unique learners. Practitioners, positioned as passive recipients of the prescribed agenda, appear to have had their hands tied, their voices quietened and their professional autonomy both threatened and constrained. At times, the relentless quest for higher standards has obscured the personal and affective dimensions of teaching and learning, fostering a mindset characterised more by compliance and conformity than curiosity and creativity.

However, creativity too has been in the ascendant in recent decades; in many countries, efforts have been made to re-ignite creativity in education, since it is seen to be essential to economic and cultural development. This impetus for creativity can be traced back to the National Advisory Committee on Creative and Cultural Education (NACCCE, 1999), which recommended a core role for creativity in teaching and learning. Primary schools in England were encouraged to explore ways to offer more innovative and creative curricula (DfES, 2003), and new national curricula in Scotland also foregrounded children's critical and creative thinking. Additionally, initiatives such as Creative Partnerships, an English government-funded initiative to nurture children's creativity, inspired some teachers to reconstruct their pedagogy (Galton, 2010). Many other schools and teachers, encouraged by these initiatives and determined to offer creative and engaging school experiences, have exercised the 'power to innovate' (Lance, 2006). Many have proactively sought ways to shape the curriculum responsively, appropriating national policies in their own contexts and showing professional commitment and imagination, despite, or perhaps because of, the persistent performative agenda (e.g. Woods and Jeffrey, 1996; Neelands, 2009; Cremin et al., 2015a).

Schools continue to be exhorted to be more innovative in curriculum construction, and national curricula afford opportunities for all teachers to seize the space, exert their professionalism and shape their own curricula in collaboration with the young people with whom they are working. Yet for primary educators, tensions persist, not only because the dual policies of performativity and creativity appear contradictory, but also perhaps because teachers' own confidence as creative educators, indeed as creative individuals, has been radically reduced by the constant barrage of change and challenge. As Csikszentmihalyi (2011) notes, teachers lack a theoretically underpinned framework for creativity that can be developed in practice; they need support to develop as artistically engaged, research-informed curriculum co-developers. Eisner (2003) asserts that teaching is an art form, an act of improvisation (Sawyer, 2011), and that teachers benefit from viewing themselves as versatile artists in the classroom, drawing on their personal passions and creativity as they teach creatively.

As Joubert (2001: 21) too observes:

> Creative teaching is an art. One cannot teach teachers didactically how to be creative; there is no fail safe recipe or routines. Some strategies may help to promote creative thinking, but teachers need to develop a full repertoire of skills which they can adapt to different situations.

However, creative teaching is only part of the picture, since teaching for creativity also needs to be acknowledged and their mutual dependency recognised. The former focuses more on teachers using imaginative approaches in the classroom (and beyond) in order to make learning more interesting and effective, the latter, more on the development of children's creativity (NACCCE, 1999). Both rely upon an understanding of the notion of creativity and demand that professionals confront the myths and mantras that surround the word. These include the commonly held misconceptions that creativity is the preserve of the arts or arts education, and that it is confined to particularly gifted individuals.

Creativity, an elusive concept, has been multiply defined by educationalists, psychologists and neurologists, as well as by policy-makers in different countries and researchers in different cultural contexts (Glăveanu, Sierra and Tanggaard, 2015). Debates resound about its individual and/or collaborative nature, the degree to which it is generic and/or domain-specific, and the differences between the 'Big C' creativity of genius and the 'little c' creativity of the everyday. Notwithstanding these issues, most scholars in the field believe it involves the capacity to generate, reason and critically evaluate novel ideas and/or imaginary scenarios. As such, it encompasses thinking through and solving problems, making connections, inventing and reinventing, and flexing one's imaginative muscles in all aspects of learning and life.

In the primary classroom, creative teaching and learning have been associated with innovation, originality, ownership and control (Woods and Jeffrey, 1996; Jeffrey, 2006), and creative teachers have been seen, in their planning and teaching, and in the ethos which they create, to afford high value to curiosity and risk-taking, to ownership, autonomy and making connections (Cremin, Barnes and Scoffham, 2009; Craft *et al.*, 2014; Cremin, 2015). Such teachers often work in partnership with others: with children, other teachers and experts from beyond the school gates (Cochrane and Cockett, 2007; Davies *et al.*, 2012; Thomson *et al.*, 2012). These partnerships offer new possibilities, with teachers acquiring some of the repertoire of pedagogic practices – the 'signature pedagogies' that artists use (Thomson and Hall, 2015).

Additionally, in research exploring possibility thinking, which Craft (2000) argues drives creativity in education, an intriguing interplay between teachers and children has been observed. In this body of work, children and teachers have been involved in immersing themselves in playful contexts, posing questions, being imaginative, showing self-determination, taking risks and innovating – together (Burnard, Craft and Cremin, 2006; Cremin, Burnard and Craft, 2006; Chappell et al., 2008; Craft et al., 2012; Cremin, Chappell and Craft, 2013). As McWilliam (2009) argues, teachers can choose not to position themselves as the all-knowing 'sage on the stage', or the facilitator-like 'guide on the side'. They can choose, as creative practitioners do, to take up a role of the 'meddler in the middle', co-creating curricula in innovative and responsive ways that harness their own and foster the children's creativity. A new pedagogy of possibility beckons.

This series, *Learning to Teach in the Primary School*, which accompanies and complements the edited textbook *Learning to Teach in the Primary School* (Cremin and Arthur, 2014), seeks to support teachers in developing as creative practitioners, assisting them in exploring the synergies between and potential for teaching creatively and teaching for creativity. The series does not merely offer practical strategies for use in the classroom, though these abound, but more importantly seeks to widen teachers' and student teachers' knowledge and understanding of the principles underpinning creative approaches, principles based on research. It seeks to mediate the wealth of research evidence and make accessible and engaging the diverse theoretical perspectives and scholarly arguments available, demonstrating their practical relevance and value to the profession. Those who aspire to develop further as creative and curious educators will find much of value to support their own professional learning journeys and markedly enrich their pedagogy and practice right across the curriculum.

TERESA CREMIN

Teresa Cremin (Grainger) is a Professor of Education (Literacy) at the Open University and a past President of UKRA (2001–2002) and UKLA (2007–2009). She is currently Research Director of the Cambridge Primary Review Trust, co-convenor of the BERA Creativity SIG and a Trustee of Booktrust and UKLA. In addition, Teresa is a Fellow of both the English Association and the Academy of Social Sciences.

Her work involves research, publication and consultancy in literacy and creativity. Many of Teresa's current projects seek to explore the nature and characteristics of creative pedagogies, including, for example, examining immersive theatre and related teaching techniques, children's make-believe play in the context of storytelling and story acting, their everyday lives and literacy practices, and the nature of literary discussions in extracurricular reading groups. Additionally, Teresa is researching creative science practice with learners aged 3–8 years and possibility thinking as a driver for creative learning. Teresa is also passionate about (and still researching) teachers' own creative development and their identity positioning in the classroom as readers, writers and creative human beings.

Teresa has written and edited over twenty-five books and numerous papers and professional texts, most recently editing with colleagues *Researching Literacy Lives: Building Home-School Communities* (2015, Routledge), *Teaching English*

Creatively (2nd ed, 2015, Routledge); *Building Communities of Engaged Readers: Reading for Pleasure* (2014, Routledge) and *The International Handbook of Research into Children's Literacy, Learning and Culture* (2013, Blackwell). *Storytelling in Early Childhood: Enriching Language, Literacy and Classroom Culture* is forthcoming (2016, Routledge). In addition, her book publications since 2000 include: *Writing Voices: Creating Communities of Writers* (2012, Routledge); *Learning to Teach in the Primary School* (2014, Routledge); *Teaching Writing Effectively: Reviewing Practice* (2011, UKLA); *Drama, Reading and Writing: Talking Our Way Forwards (2009, UKLA); Jumpstart Drama* (2009, David Fulton); *Creative Teaching for Tomorrow: Fostering a Creative State of Mind* (2009, Future Creative); *Documenting Creative Learning 5–11* (2007, Trentham); *Creativity and Writing: Developing Voice and Verve* (2005, Routledge); *Teaching English in Higher Education* (2007, NATE and UKLA); *Creative Activities for Character, Setting and Plot, 5–7, 7–9, 9–11* (2004, Scholastic); and *Language and Literacy: a Routledge Reader* (2001, Routledge).

REFERENCES

Burnard, P., Craft, A. and Cremin, T. (2006) 'Possibility thinking' *International Journal of Early Years Education*, 14(3), 243–262.

Chappell, K., Craft, A., Burnard, P. and Cremin, T. (2008). 'Question-posing and question-responding: the heart of possibility thinking in the early years', *Early Years*. 283, 267–286.

Cochrane, P. and Cockett, M. (2007) *Building a Creative School: A Dynamic Approach to School Improvement*. Stoke on Trent, Trentham Books.

Craft, A. (2000) *Creativity Across the Primary Curriculum*. London: Routledge.

Craft, A., Cremin, T., Burnard, P., Dragovic, T. and Chappell, K. (2012) 'Possibility thinking: culminative studies of an evidence-based concept driving creativity?: *Education 3–13*. *International Journal of Primary, Elementary and Early Years Education* 41(5), 538–556.

Craft, A., Cremin, T., Hay, P. and Clack, J. (2014) 'Creative primary schools: developing and maintaining pedagogy for creativity'. *Ethnography and Education*, 9(1), 16–34.

Cremin, T. (2015) 'Creative teaching and creative teachers', in Wilson, A. (ed) *Creativity in Primary Education*. London: Sage, 33–44.

Cremin, T. and Arthur, J. (eds) (2014) *Learning to Teach in the Primary School*, 3rd Edn. London: Routledge.

Cremin, T., Barnes, J. and Scoffham, S. (2009) *Creative Teaching for Tomorrow: Fostering a Creative State of Mind*. Deal: Future Creative.

Cremin, T., Burnard, P. and Craft, A. (2006) 'Pedagogy and possibility thinking in the early years'. *International Journal of Thinking Skills and Creativity*, 1(2), 108–119.

Cremin, T., Chappell, K. and Craft, A. (2013) 'Reciprocity between narrative, questioning and imagination in the early and primary years: examining the role of narrative in possibility thinking'. *Thinking Skills and Creativity*, 9, 136–151.

Cremin, T., Glauert, E., Craft, A., Compton, A. and Stylianidou, F. (2015a) 'Creative little scientists: exploring pedagogical synergies between inquiry-based and creative approaches in early years science.' *Education 3–13: International Journal of Primary, Elementary and Early Years Education*. Special issue on creative pedagogies.

Cremin, T., Mottram, M., Powell, S., Collins, R. and Drury, R. (2015b) *Researching Literacy Lives: Building Home School Communities*. London: Routledge.

Csikszentmihalyi, M. (2011) 'A systems perspective on creativity and its implications for measurement', in Schenkel, R. and Quintin, O. (eds) *Measuring Creativity* . The European Commission: Brussels, 407–414.

Davies, D., Jindal-Snape, D., Collier, C., Digby, R., Hay, P. and Howe, A. (2012) 'Creative environments for learning in schools'. *Thinking Skills and Creativity*. http://dx.doi.org/10.1016/j.tsc.2012.07.004.

Department for Culture, Media and Sport (2006) *Government Response to Paul Roberts' Report on Nurturing Creativity in Young People*. London: DCMS

Department for Education and Skills (DfES) (2003) *Excellence and Enjoyment: A Strategy for Primary Schools*. Nottingham: DfES.

Eisner, E. (2003) 'Artistry in education'. *Scandinavian Journal of Educational Research*, 47(3), 373–384.

Galton, M. (2010) 'Going with the flow or back to normal? The impact of creative practitioners in schools and classrooms'. *Research Papers in Education*, 25(4), 355–375.

Glăveanu, V. Sierra, Z. and Tanggaard, L. (2015) 'Widening our understanding of creative pedagogy: A north–south dialogue. *Education 3–13: International Journal of Primary, Elementary and Early Years Education*. Special issue on creative pedagogies.

Jeffrey, B. (ed.) (2006) *Creative Learning Practices: European Experiences*. London: Tufnell Press.

Jeffrey, B. and Woods, P. (2009) *Creative Learning in the Primary School*. London: Routledge.

Joubert, M.M. (2001) 'The art of creative teaching: NACCCE and beyond', in Craft, A., Jeffrey, B. and Liebling, M. (eds) *Creativity in Education*. London: Continuum.

Lance, A. (2006) 'Power to innovate? A Study of how primary practitioners are negotiating the modernisation agenda'. *Ethnography and Education*, 1(3), 333–344.

McWilliams, A. (2009) 'Teaching for creativity: from sage to guide to meddler'. *Asia Pacific Journal of Education*, 29(3), 281–293.

Mottram, M. and Hall, C. (2009) 'Diversions and diversity: does the personalisation agenda offer real opportunities for taking children's home literacies seriously?' *English in Education*, 43(2), 98–112.

National Advisory Committee on Creative and Cultural Education (NACCCE) (1999) *All Our Futures: Creativity, Culture and Education*. London: Department for Education and Employment.

Neelands, J. (2009) 'Acting together: ensemble as a democratic process in art and life'. *Research in Drama Education*, 14(2), 173–189.

Sawyer, K. (ed.) (2011) *Structure and Improvisation in Creative Teaching*. New York: Cambridge University Press.

Thomson, P. and Hall, C. (2015) '"Everyone can imagine their own Gellert": the democratic artist and "inclusion" in primary and nursery classrooms'. *Education 3–13: International Journal of Primary, Elementary and Early Years Education*. Special issue on creative pedagogies.

Thomson, P., Hall, C., Jones, K. and Sefton-Green, J. (2012) *The Signature Pedagogies Project: Final Report*. London: Creativity, Culture and Education. www.creativetallis.com/uploads/2/2/8/7/2287089/signature_pedagogies_report_final_version_11.3.12.pdf (1 June 2012).

Woods, P. and Jeffrey, B. (1996) *Teachable Moments: The Art of Creative Teaching in Primary Schools*. Buckingham: Open University Press.

CHAPTER 1

SETTING THE CONTEXT

Design and technology and creativity

Clare Benson

INTRODUCTION

The birth of design and technology (D&T) education in the primary curriculum

It was during the period 1985–1990 and beyond that the idea for creating the subject D&T was debated not only in England and Wales, but worldwide. Wales joined with England initially, but developed its own curriculum by 1995 (DfE, 1995). D&T is incorporated into Technologies in the Scottish National Curriculum and it is integrated in an area of learning – The World Around Us – in Northern Ireland. Countries such as South Africa, Australia, Bahrain and New Zealand have developed D&T or technology in a similar way to England; France uses the term technology but has included design, while Germany's curriculum – Technic – focuses more on knowledge and skills relating to materials such as wood, plastic and metal. A search engine can be used to find many curricula focusing on primary D&T or technology and related subjects worldwide.

Before 1990 in England, curricula content in secondary schools had been separated into single subjects such as wood work, domestic science and metal work based mainly on skills and knowledge development, and in primary schools there was art that might have included design. The rationale for D&T was that the subject should offer opportunities for pupils to develop skills and knowledge but, as they applied these, they should design and make a product with a user and purpose in mind, think for themselves, make decisions, work in groups and individually, and evaluate their work and that of others. With rapidly changing technologies, it was felt that D&T would be an appropriate subject for the future. Despite the fact that the original panel that drew up the National Curriculum D&T document (DES/WO, 1990) had no primary specialist, it was decided that D&T should be included in the primary curriculum for continuity and to support learning in the changing world of technologies in which primary pupils were growing up. The first document was overwhelming; it contained four attainment targets, and different weightings were given to each one for assessment purposes. For primary teachers facing nine curriculum documents, it presented a challenge, but over 25 years on, D&T is still very much part of the primary curriculum in England. The original curriculum has been modified and developed several times, yet the current document (DfE, 2013) has similar fundamental principles, albeit in a less detailed form than the first one. Access to content might be easier, but the detail did enable teachers who were not confident about the subject to gain a better understanding of D&T. As there are now a variety of schools in England, such as free schools, private schools and academies, that do not have to follow the National Curriculum, it will be interesting to see whether the subject is retained and valued in the years to come.

The nature of D&T

The nature of the subject still needs to be clarified as there can be a focus on making rather than designing and making, and user and purpose can be omitted. Despite the various curriculum reviews over the years, the fundamental nature of D&T has not changed. The first English and Welsh National Curriculum document (DES/WO, 1990) identified three key aspects:

1. It is an activity which spans the curriculum, drawing on and linking a range of subjects . . . improve pupils' understanding of the significance of technology to the economy and everyday life.
2. Pupils will identify a need or respond to an opportunity to make or modify something. They will use their skills and knowledge to devise a solution, realise it practically, and evaluate the processes undertaken and the end product. They will draw on knowledge and skills from other subject areas including science.
3. Pupils' enterprise and ability to work as a team contribute to their success and they will come to realise that technological development rarely ends as evaluation of a product leads on to modifications and further development. Pupils will work to deadlines, keep budgets and reconcile conflicting requirements such as quality, speed and cost.

The current National Curriculum (DfE, 2013) identifies similar aspects:

Using creativity and imagination, pupils design and make products that solve real and relevant problems within a variety of contexts, considering their own and others' needs, wants and values. They acquire a broad range of subject knowledge and draw on disciplines such as mathematics, science, engineering, computing and art. Pupils learn how to take risks, becoming resourceful, innovative, enterprising and capable citizens. Through evaluation of the past and present D&T, they develop a critical understanding of its impact on daily life and the wider world.

Both documents highlight the focus of activity to be the pupils' own needs and those of others, the broad knowledge and skills that are drawn on, and the way in which the subject helps pupils to understand the importance of technology in their everyday lives and the economy. However, the latest document includes creativity and imagination, innovation and risk-taking – all fundamental to successful D&T.

As teachers are thinking about and planning D&T activity in the classroom, what are the key elements that should be included in any D&T project or assignment? One strategy from the Design and Technology Association (www.data.org.uk) was to identify six key elements that should be present:

1. Have the needs of the **user/s** been identified and met appropriately?
2. Does the product have a clear **purpose** that is realistic and meets the needs of the client?
3. Have **design decisions** been made by the pupils, either with support or individually?
4. Does the product **function** (D&T) or is it purely aesthetic or ornamental (probably art)?
5. Is the product **innovative** in some way for the pupil/s who are designing and making? It should not be an exact copy but something that does include a new idea/s for the pupil/s.
6. Is it an **authentic** product? It may be a working prototype but it should not be a model of, for example, a toothbrush made from wood and coloured with pen.

An example of a D&T project, undertaken by 7–11-year-olds, might be linked to the theme of celebrations.

The librarian visits the class to discuss the need for a book to give information about different celebrations around the world to go in the school library for use by the whole school (**clear purpose and user**). The pupils discuss how to make it interesting and appealing to all ages; the use of the computer and mechanisms are two aspects that are identified. Each group chooses a different celebration to focus on. In groups, the pupils discuss design ideas, making some sketches that they think are appropriate and making mock-up/prototypes of a page, practising different mechanisms and page layouts which they can then modify. Some groups choose to make one page; others decide to make several with the same theme (own **design decisions and functionality** of moving book parts). The book proves to be **innovative** as celebrations are portrayed in different ways and the task is **authentic** as the book is needed for the library.

The importance of D&T

The fact that D&T is included in the primary curriculum in so many countries, and more are investigating its possible inclusion, for example, China and Saudi Arabia, emphasises the perception of the importance of the subject. Research has shown (Benson and Lunt, 2007; Lunt, 2009) that pupils do perceive D&T as a subject that is different from others, are extremely positive about the subject, think that it is fun but also hard work, that they have to think really carefully and that they learn to be creative. They do feel that it will be useful in their future lives. Based on Pollard *et al.* (2000) on children's judgements relating to the curriculum, the key reasons for enjoying subjects are given as activity (doing something active), goal orientation (can see where the activity is leading to) and fun/interesting, closely followed by autonomy – all integral to D&T. For pupils to be engaged and on task in school, a subject such as D&T can prove invaluable to motivate and excite pupils – all crucial for learning. D&T can be placed naturally at the heart of the primary curriculum, and pupils can gain and use knowledge and skills in many different areas and apply these through authentic D&T tasks. Possible links include:

mathematics – measurement;
science – materials, electricity and forces;
art – design, colour, texture, shape, form, range of materials;
history – changes in use of materials, see how key events and individuals have helped
    design and make the made world;
computing – creating programs to control products, computer-aided design and
    computer-aided manufacture.

D&T offers opportunities for many different ways of working – group, pair and individual work with adult support, or without. It provides real opportunities for problem-solving, and for pupils to develop their creative, evaluative and critical-thinking skills and investigate issues such as sustainability.

Structuring D&T teaching

When the subject was introduced into the primary curriculum, it was hoped that a pro-gramme of support would be offered to teachers in England and Wales as they were teaching nine subjects – all with new content. The non-statutory guidance for D&T (NCC, 1990) included with the National Curriculum (DES/WO, 1990) was useful; however, it was detailed, all text, and did not include holistic exemplars, including children's work. There can be a tension between providing too much structure and taking a 'laissez faire' approach and it was the Department of Education and Science's (DES/WO, 1990) view at that time that teachers should be free to determine their own ways of teaching the subjects including D&T. There were some excellent examples of D&T projects (Benson and Raat, 1995) where teachers had allowed pupils to be creative and think for themselves, to undertake some designing as well as making, to have time to carry out a complete project, and had acted more as facilitators rather than instructors. However, inspection reports (Ofsted, 2002; 2007) from a wide range of primary schools highlighted the need for pupils to be more involved in making their own decisions, to think about design, not just make, and to evaluate their own work. In a revised English National Curriculum (DfEE, 1999), 'Breadth of Study' was included and it quickly became apparent how useful teachers found this section. Through Ofsted reports (2002) and from feedback on staff development courses, teachers explained that it helped them to understand different parts of a D&T project, the importance of these parts and how they contributed to a holistic experience. Breadth of Study included three parts; investigative and evaluative activity (IEA); focused practical tasks (FPT); and design and make assignments (DMA). Pupils were to be taught know-ledge, skills and understanding through these activities (DfEE, 1999). Over the years, the terms have been modified, such as investigative activity, focused task and design, make and evaluate assignment, but the principles remain the same. Unfortunately, the latest D&T curriculum omits these more detailed terms in an effort to shorten the document, but does include the phrase 'creative and practical activities' (DfE, 2013: 2/3). The following are the types of activity as they were originally named, but still link with creative and practical activities, to provide a valuable framework when planning a project.

Investigative and evaluative activity (IEAs) (also investigative tasks)

This covers activity that might be undertaken throughout the whole design and make project. Generally, pupils will be engaged in investigating and evaluating a range of products associated with the DMA, but in some cases the range of products may be chosen for different reasons. IEA as a stand-alone activity offers opportunities to engage the pupils in interesting writing, speaking and listening tasks. Products could then be chosen so that they excite the pupils. It could be a product that is new and innovative or something newly acquired by the school.

Think about:

- who the products are for and why they are needed
- how they are used
- what criteria the pupils think were given to the designer to create the product
- what materials/mechanisms/structures have been used and why these have been chosen
- what the pupils like/dislike about them
- how the pupils might change them
- whether the pupils can find people who have used them. What are their views?

As the pupils begin to design and make, they need to evaluate their own ideas, designs and products against their own design criteria throughout the whole process. Gradually they need to consider the views of others, including any adult helpers and their peers, and make any changes to their work based on comments from others that they value. The final evaluation of the pupils' finished product might be omitted, often as time runs out, but this is an integral and vital part of any assignment.

Focused practical task (FPT) (also practical task)

This can be a misleading term and maybe 'focused task' gives a clearer message as to the underlying meaning. It includes tasks that develop pupils' techniques and skills as well as knowledge. So, it could include undertaking tasks:

- to develop cutting, joining and finishing skills and techniques
- to gain an understanding about the properties of different materials/ingredients
- to gain knowledge about a range of tools and equipment
- to gain knowledge about mechanisms/structures/electrical and computer control
- to understand how to create questionnaires and undertake surveys
- to develop drawing/sketching skills that may be needed when designing

While these tasks have a specific focus, it is important that they are undertaken within a context that will engage the pupils, ensuring that they can see a reason for the tasks. Examples include:

■ Learning to measure, saw and join wood – make a small photo frame.
■ Create a questionnaire – ask questions about their favourite food and then evaluate if they have all the information they need from the questions posed.
■ Learning to thread a needle, start to sew and simple stitches – create a small embroidery piece that could be inserted into a greetings card.
■ Learning to cut fruit and vegetables – make into a healthy snack for the end of the day.

Design and make assignment (DMA) (also design, make and evaluate assignment)

This brings together the other two types of activity and allows the pupils to undertake a holistic project that involves all elements of D&T. The title 'design, make and evaluate assignment' perhaps better explains the whole process, but teachers are obviously free to choose their own title. There are no set ways as to how an assignment should be carried out, but it is crucial that all the elements of IEAs and FPTs are included to ensure that it is a whole D&T experience. There is evidence, including Ofsted reports (2002), that making has formed a major part in the delivery of D&T with little emphasis on designing. However, designing is an integral part of D&T and pupils need to consider their designs before they launch into making and throughout the whole assignment. Design is not linear but an iterative process, as pupils move backwards and forwards between designing and making; many linear models have been suggested, for example, Johnsey (2000), but an early research model (APU, 1991) exemplifies the iterative nature of design. This is further discussed in Chapter 5.

The issue of how pupils record their design ideas has also been much discussed and debated. Certainly, drawing is one way of expressing design ideas but it is not always appropriate (more in Chapter 6). Talking with, and between, peers and a teacher (or another adult in the classroom) offers an important method of clarifying and modifying ideas (more discussion in Chapters 5, 6, 8 and 12) and modelling ideas in 2D and 3D allows the pupils to see what might be possible as they talk through their ideas. Lunt (2011) provides a valuable critical review of research relating to design from a series of research papers based on primary D&T research conferences. An example of a design and make D&T assignment might be:

DESIGN, MAKE AND EVALUATE A SNACK USING RAW FRUIT AND VEGETABLES

Consider who it might be for; why is it needed?

Pupils can undertake tasks that enable them to taste a variety of fruit and vegetables, ensuring all health and safety considerations have been thought through. Evaluate which ones they think they could include in the snack, thinking about, for example, colour, taste, robustness so the produce lasts some time, and fruit and vegetables that are popular with the user or client.

Pupils could evaluate a range of pre-prepared snacks from, for example, the supermarket. Do they look appetising? What is it that the pupils like/dislike about them?

Pupils could undertake some tasks, in which they learn to cut, grate and chop fruit and vegetables.

Having decided on the user and purpose, the pupils can begin to make design decisions for their product individually, as a class, in groups. They could record their ideas through drawings, labelling, writing and talk.

Keeping their design criteria to hand, the pupils can prepare their snack. Do they want to modify design decisions? How will they record these? Have they chosen appropriate fruit and/or vegetables? They move backwards and forwards through their ideas until the final product is made.

Final evaluation needs to take into account the original user and purpose for the snack. Have any modifications helped with the final product? Have they met the criteria that they chose? What has been the key learning from the assignment?

Creativity and D&T

Having identified the nature of D&T and how teaching might be structured, it is easy to see how links to creativity can be identified and pupils' creativity nurtured and developed if true D&T is experienced. Of course, there is a difference between teaching creatively and practice that nurtures pupils' creativity (more on this in Chapter 2). In addition, links are made between D&T and creativity in the context of each chapter. Many have tried to define creativity but a useful starting point is in *All Our Futures: Creativity, Culture and Education* (DfEE, 1999). The report suggests that we are all, or can be, creative, which supports Craft's idea of Big C, little c in which she states that all of us can be creative with a small 'c' (Craft, 2001).

Creativity is broken down into four characteristics (DfEE, 1999):

- Thinking and behaving imaginatively – opportunities in D&T should arise when pupils are thinking about and designing possible product solutions.
- Purposeful activity – pupils need to consider a user and purpose for the product that they are designing.
- Generation of something original – this refers to something that is original or innovative for the pupil as they solve problems and have ideas that are new to them.
- Value in relation to the purpose.

The teacher supports the pupils to judge the value of their work through asking questions. Does it meet the need and purpose? Is it useful? Is it functional?

The following shows how creativity can be stifled or encouraged.

PROJECT TO DESIGN AND MAKE SLIPPERS

How is creativity encouraged in this scenario?

The teacher leads and says the pupils will be making slippers. They are given the same coloured felt and a template and they are told that the template should be the right size for them. The slippers are cut out by the pupils or if needed with adult support. The pupils are offered a choice of coloured embroidery thread, and are shown how to thread a needle and how to sew blanket stitch to join the slipper pieces together. They are asked what they like/dislike about the slippers and what they would do differently next time. The slippers all look very similar.

How is creativity encouraged in this scenario?

The pupils are involved in a project relating to footwear (links with history and geography). As it is winter, the pupils identify that slippers would be useful to design and make. They choose who they will make them for. The teacher provides several different fabrics and ways of joining the fabrics. The pupils think about their chosen user, what colour and finish they might like. They discuss their ideas with their peers and adult/s in the classroom. They make some sketches and try different styles, creating criteria that they need to meet. They make a template based on their user's foot. They cut out the slippers and join them in different ways, adding a variety of finishes. They give the slippers to their chosen user to see how they like them. Throughout they are making changes to ensure that the slippers meet their criteria.

The second example offers the pupils the chance to make decisions throughout the project, to make their own choices, to think about a user and purpose important to them, to identify their own criteria, to try different designs, to discuss ideas with others and to evaluate in a meaningful way with the real user.

D&T affords pupils many opportunities in different ways to develop their own creativity, something that is so important for life. Employers want young people who not only are literate and numerate, but who can see connections, have innovative ideas, can communicate in different ways, work with others as well as independently, can evaluate a range of possibilities and are able to solve problems – all skills that are needed in real D&T. In each chapter, the authors have identified appropriate links between D&T and creativity that best fit the content focus.

OVERVIEW OF THE CONTENT

When considering the content of this book, decisions had to be made as to what might be considered key areas of D&T and how they linked with creativity and its development. As D&T was a new subject into the primary curriculum in 1990 in England and Wales (and in many countries worldwide), to set the context, it was important that the background to its development was explained and the nature of the subject clarified, drawing links between creativity and D&T (Chapter 1). A more in-depth study of teaching creatively and *for* creativity (Chapter 2) generally and within the context of D&T then allows the reader to gain a greater insight into the links between the two and how these may be developed in the classroom. The early years are the foundation for all children's education and it is vital that these children have D&T experiences that can be built on as they move through their primary education. Chapter 3 provides detailed ideas as to how this can be achieved and provides building blocks for D&T for the next phase of the children's education. A range of starting points are then outlined to help teachers to understand the exciting and engaging ways in which pupils can undertake D&T projects (Chapter 4). Since the introduction of D&T into the curriculum, designing has proved to be an important issue, not only in England but in countries worldwide (Chapters 5 and 6). Often time constraints mean that making becomes the priority in order to have a finished product, meaning that design has played little part in a project. The use of construction kits is then examined as often they are just put out as a choosing or wet play activity and their true value missed (Chapter 7). Talk and conversation should play a vital role in the development of D&T and creativity, and Chapters 8 and 12 discuss this point and provide many useful practical ideas as to how to develop them both. Food is a separate chapter as there can be misunderstandings in relation to how it integrates into D&T; it is an important material and needs to be included in any D&T curriculum (Chapter 9). With the move to link IT across the curriculum, especially in relation to programming, Chapter 10 offers details of a specific case study in addition to further ideas as to how this can be achieved in an effective and practical way. D&T learning should be taken outside the classroom to broaden the experiences of all pupils, and Chapter 11 offers a case study in addition to ideas as to how this can be achieved. The concluding chapter (Chapter 13) looks at past, present and future challenges, provides thought-provoking comments, but always stresses that good D&T links to and supports creative education.

REFERENCES

Assessment of Performance Unit (APU) (1991) *The Assessment of Performance in Design and Technology.* London: SEAC.

Benson, C. and Lunt, J. (2007) 'It puts a smile on your face! What do children actually think of design and technology? Investigating the perceptions of children aged 9–11 years', in Dakers, J., Dow, W.J. and de Vries, M. (eds) *PATT 18 Conference.* Glasgow: University of Glasgow, pp. 297–305.

Benson, C. and Raat, J. (1995) *Technology in Primary Education.* Delft, Netherlands: Technon.

Craft, A. (2001) 'Little c creativity', in Craft, A., Jeffrey, B. and Leibling, M. (eds) *Creativity in Education.* London: Continuum.

Department for Education (DfE) (1995) *Design and Technology in the National Curriculum.* London: Her Majesty's Stationery Office (HMSO).

Department for Education (DfE) (2013) www. gov.uk/national-curriculum-in-england-design-and-technology (accessed 31 May 2016).

Department for Education and Employment (DfEE) (1999) *All Our Futures: Creativity, Culture and Education.* Report by the National Advisory Committee on Creative and Cultural Education (NACCCE) London: DfEE.

Department for Education and Science/Welsh Office (DES/WO) (1990) *Technology in the National Curriculum.* London: Her Majesty's Stationery Office (HMSO).

Johnsey, R. (2000) 'Designing and making skills', in Eggleston, J. (ed.) *Teaching and Learning Design and Technology*. London: Continuum.

Lunt, J. (2009) 'Primary school children's perceptions of D&T', in Jones, A. and de Vries, M. (eds) *International Handbook of Research and Development in Technology Education*. Rotterdam: Sense.

Lunt, J. (2011) 'Research into primary aged children's designing: a review of the CRIPT conference papers 1997–2009', in Benson, C. and Lunt, J. (eds) *International Handbook of Primary Technology Education*. Rotterdam: Sense.

National Curriculum Council (NCC) (1990) *Non Statutory Guidance: Design and Technology*. London: NCC.

Office for Standards in Education (Ofsted) (undated) Design and technology subject survey visits. www.ofsted.gov.uk/inspection-reports/our-expert-knowledge/subject survey-feedback-letters-schools/design-and-technology-subject-survey-visits (accessed 6 March 2015).

Ofsted. (2002) *Report 2000/1*. London: Ofsted.

Ofsted. (2007) *Education for a Technologically Advanced Nation: Design and Technology in Schools 2003–2006*. London: Ofsted.

Pollard, A., Triggs, P., Broadfoot, P., McNess, E. and Osborn, M. (2000) *What Pupils Say: Changing Policy and Practice in Primary Education*. London: Continuum.

Further reading

Alexander, R. (ed) (2010) *Children, Their World, Their Education: Report of the Cambridge Primary Review*. London: Routledge.

Rose, J. (2009) *Independent Review of the Primary Curriculum*. Nottingham: DCFS Publications.

Useful website

The Design and Technology Association www.data.org.uk
It contains a wide range of support materials for implementing primary D&T in school, including Projects on a Page and a large bank of research papers relating to all aspects of D&T.

CHAPTER 2

TEACHING CREATIVELY AND TEACHING *FOR* CREATIVITY

Marion Rutland and Sue Miles-Pearson

INTRODUCTION

The term 'creativity' is explored initially from a psychological viewpoint. Craft (Craft and Hall, 2015) wrote widely on creativity and she saw three waves of creativity in creativity policy. The first was in the 1960s based on the recommendations of the Plowden Report (CACE, 1967) focusing on learning through discovery in the early years of education; a second wave in the late 1990s looked at links between psychology and education; and a third wave in the early years of the twenty-first century where creativity is seen as 'fundamental to twenty-first century learning' (ibid.: 14). A key concept in this chapter is that creativity can be developed in the design and technology (D&T) classroom (Barlex, 2003).

SO WHAT IS CREATIVITY?

As a starting point, creativity can be defined as 'the use of imagination or original ideas to create something; inventiveness' (www.oxforddictionaries.com/search/?multi=1&dict Code=english&q=creativity). At a simple level, it is the ability to produce new knowledge (Dacey and Lennon, 1998). A more complex view of creativity of is of 'a puzzle, a paradox, some say a mystery' and a novel combination of ideas that are new, interesting and of value (Boden: 1994: 75). On the other hand, others see creativity as 'a messy and confusing subject, bringing something to life that was not there before' (de Bono, 1992: 4).

However, of particular relevance to D&T is a conceptual definition for creativity that includes the two essential elements of 'product and process':

> A product or a response will be judged as creative to the extent that a) it is both a novel and appropriate, useful, correct or valuable response to the task at hand, and b) the task is heuristic rather than algorithmic
>
> (Amabile, 1996: 35)

Amabile, as a psychologist, researched creativity in children and adults over many years. She believes that 'all children can be creative, and they can remain creative as adults'

(Amabile, 1989: ix). This view is echoed by Vygotsky who thought that playing at taking on the role of being someone else, or 'pretend' play, is the precursor to creativity, so it can be argued that creativity and imagination are actually formed through play itself (Smidt, 2009).

The expectation for creativity in the classroom was implicit but not clear in the original National Curriculum Technology Orders in England & Wales (DES/WO, 1990), was lacking in the later Design and Technology Orders (DfE, 1995), before being reinforced in the Orders (DfEE and QCA, 1999: 15) as to 'learn to think and intervene creatively . . . become autonomous and creative problem solvers'. It was the Robinson Report (1999) *All Our Futures* that saw creativity as 'imaginative activities fashioned so as to produce outcomes that are original and of value' (ibid.: 29). The key factors were:

- all young pupils have creative capacity in different ways;
- intelligence is multifaceted;
- creativity should not be related to academic ability with a facility for propositional knowledge and linear forms of learning. It is more accurate to think of all children having a profile of abilities across a wide range of intelligences;
- pupils who perform less well in conventional academic tests may be highly able in other areas;
- intelligence is dynamic and involves interaction between various areas of the brain.

The Report defined creative teaching in two ways; first '*teaching creatively*' and second '*teaching for creativity*' (ibid.: 89). *Teaching creatively* is interpreted as when teachers use imaginative approaches to make learning more interesting, exciting and effective (more in Chapter 4). It could be described as merely 'good practice', because the teachers are themselves being creative by taking the initiative to develop materials and approaches to interest and motivate pupils. Whereas, *teaching for creativity* focuses on forms of teaching and learning that are specifically intended to *foster* and *enhance* their pupils' own creative thinking or behaviour in the classroom.

A MODEL FOR EVALUATING CREATIVITY IN THE CLASSROOM

A model, or framework, to evaluate creativity in the classroom (Rutland, 2005) was based on a range of literature. The views of Amabile (1983; 1996) were considered to be the ones most relevant for education. Her conceptual definition for creativity included two essential elements concerning a creative product or a response that is novel and appropriate, useful and of value, within a task that is heuristic rather than algorithmic (Amabile, *op.cit.*).

She highlighted the impact of specific social factors and intrinsic motivation and described creativity as the confluence of intrinsic or self-motivation, domain-relevant knowledge and abilities, and creativity-relevant skills. The creativity-relevant skills relate to strategies that the teacher uses so that the children have tools for being creative. Amabile (1989) argued that it is not enough to train children in skills; it is important to give them opportunities to develop their talents or develop good work habits. Teachers need to help children identify the place where their interests and skills overlap called the 'creativity intersection'. She argued (Figure 2.1) that it is at the 'intersection where pupils' domain skills

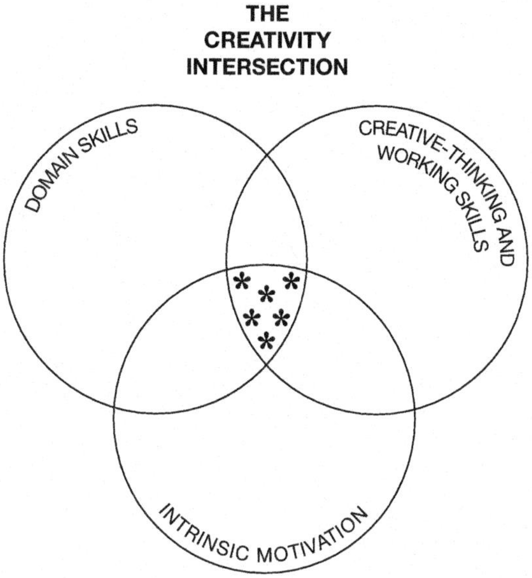

THE
CREATIVITY
INTERSECTION

■ **Figure 2.1** The Creative Intersection (Amabile 1989: 63).

and creative-thinking skills overlap with their intrinsic interests that the pupil is most likely to be creative'.

She saw the supportive social environment or the classroom as a key factor in ensuring that a child's creativity potential is realised. Unlike their individual personal traits, the environment can be influenced by the teacher through the organisation and management of the classroom and the teaching strategies they use.

The framework or theoretical three-feature model (Figure 2.2) is intended to be used to evaluate creativity in the classroom. It emphasises the importance of the environment and that creativity only occurs when the three features converge. The first feature relates to factors in a specific subject domain such as D&T, but the intention is that the other two features are generic and could be used to explore creativity within other domain areas of the school curriculum. The model consists of three essential features:

1. **Domain-relevant features:** a set of practices associated with an area of knowledge, for example, D&T or other subjects such as science and mathematics
2. **Process-relevant features:** influencing, controlling the direction and progress of the creative process
3. **Social, environmental features:** macro/micro environmental, social and cultural issues

The role of the teacher is central in teaching *for* creativity as they are the 'gate keepers' who sanction what should be included in the subject domain (Csikszentmihalyi, 1996; 1999) – for example, making judgements about children's work, their portfolios/sketches and products. However, teaching strategies are of equal importance as they influence the

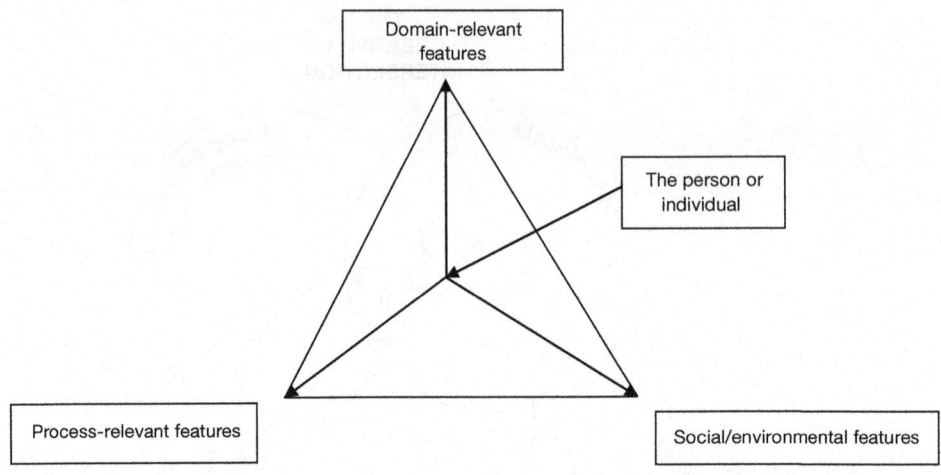

■ **Figure 2.2** Three-feature model of the factors influencing creativity in the classroom
(Rutland 2005: 33)

procedures and processes followed by the children. Teachers should manage and organise their classroom to ensure that the social and cultural environment is conducive to creative activity. Within D&T, the following four criteria for creativity were identified:

■ **The concept or idea** – has the designer proposed a concept that is original, novel, feasible, useful, will function, etc.?
■ **Aesthetic creativity** – has the designer made proposals about those features of the product that will appeal to the senses, for example, sight, hearing, touch, taste and smell? Is there something about these proposals that is particularly novel and attractive?
■ **Technical creativity** – has the designer made proposals about the way the product will work and the nature of the components and materials required to achieve this? Is there something about these proposals that is novel or elegant?
■ **Constructional creativity** – has the designer made proposals about the way the product will be constructed and the tools and processes needed to achieve this? Is there something about these proposals that is novel or original?

FACTORS AFFECTING TEACHING *FOR* CREATIVITY

Prior to the introduction of the National Curriculum in 1990 in England and Wales, excellence in D&T was generally considered to be in 'making skills' or the 'master-apprentice' model (Banks, 2002), where children were shown the skills and techniques of how to 'make' a particular product or item by the teacher. This has been called 'show and copy' or 'recipe technology', where the materials and process are pre-determined and the children are expected to produce a very similar product or item to the one shown to them by their teacher. Any individuality of design or creativity by a pupil is limited, and usually restricted to aesthetic considerations, for example, choosing a picture to stick on the front of a book or a coloured thread to embroider a prepared pattern.

However, the D&T community generally believes in its potential to develop cognitive skills through a variety of teaching methods, including project-based group work (Harris and Wilson, 2003), particularly in the primary sector. It has been suggested (Haffenden, 2004; Archer, 2015) that teachers are often torn between achieving a goal and allowing children time to explore and strengthen their understanding and that they choose the option of compliance rather than being creative. Creativity in D&T requires children to bridge the gap between the cognitive and practical learning and the ability to transform an abstract idea into concrete reality that is very demanding and requires a range of skills and abilities.

Teaching *for* creativity in D&T requires pupils to use a range of knowledge and understanding about materials, concepts and designing-and-making skills not only from the sciences, arts and mathematics but also from other areas of the curriculum. It is important, when working in any one of the material areas of D&T, to remember that pupils will be using the generic skills and processes to generate a range of design ideas, make design decisions as well as use techniques specific to a specialist area.

THE ROLE OF THE TEACHER

The impact of motivation when teaching *for* creativity in D&T is an issue of particular relevance. Extrinsic motivation is defined as working for a reward – for example an examination grade is seen as detrimental to creativity – as compared with intrinsic motivation where pupils do something for its own sake because it is interesting and challenging (Amabile, 1983; 1989; 1996). However, in later writings, Amabile is not so convinced of the damage of extrinsic motivation where she argues that it does not hinder creativity and may actually add incentive. She argues that 'pure' *intrinsic motivation* is crucial in the initial, heuristic stage of ideas generation (op cit. 1996), as can be found in the generation of ideas stage of designing in D&T. In practice, teachers and schools need to consider carefully how, within the constraints of their curriculum and assessment procedures, children's *intrinsic motivation* is taken into account and the impact of extrinsic motivation reduced.

Fortunately for teachers, there are other views. Cropley (2001: 145) considers that it is 'perfectly possible to construct examinations or test factual knowledge in ways that do not block creativity'. Links have been found between pupil achievement and self-confidence, with sources of frustration for children in their level of craft skills and ownership. Issues such as risk-taking and the importance for achievement were noted. It was considered that creativity is fostered when teachers and children share the associated risks. Creative work is likely to bring about novel or different knowledge, which will involve risk-taking. However, exposure to the possibility of 'loss' by the teachers and children, for example poor school and examination grades, a lack of autonomy and intrinsic motivation do not encourage risk-taking, thus highlighting the importance of pupil motivation, self-confidence and risk-taking (Davies, 1999; 2000).

A typical D&T project provides ideal opportunities for pupils to collaborate (Barlex, 2002), with regular progress reviews including teacher and peer critique. Children will benefit from sharing ideas, accommodating other people's responses and listening to and taking note of other people's views and understanding. Increasingly, it has become more common, especially in primary schools, to find D&T pupils collaborating and operating in teams to achieve team goals (Kimbell and Perry, 2001). The D&T primary classroom is unique in that it combines procedural problem-solving activity with 'talk' between peers, physical manipulation, feedback, concrete and mental modelling and graphic com-munication (Hennessy and Murphy, 1999; Harris and Wilson, 2003). More discussion can be found in Chapters 8 and 12.

The curriculum context of D&T projects in schools is a crucial factor when teaching *for* creativity, as it sets the scene for children to be stimulated, use their imagination, generate new ideas and concepts, and make design decisions. Three ways in which teach-ers provide motivational and inspirational starting points include: building on children's interests; identifying real opportunities, and using relevant contexts (Davies and Howe, 2015) – more in Chapter 4. Design briefs with potential creative and original outcomes can be developed in all the areas of D&T. When children follow a recipe out of a book, use a pattern made by a teacher to make a glove puppet or use a 'kit' to make a mechanical toy, they are simply copying other people's designs. This involves little original or individual thinking, and children are engaged in mechanistic learning with little or no under-standing of the concepts and knowledge underpinning the activity. They are not designing, thinking, making decisions and being creative. Further discussion on designing is in Chapters 5 and 6. When teaching *for* creativity in D&T, they should design and make their own products based on a sound knowledge of the working properties of materials and processes. This includes focused practical tasks and product analysis to develop a sound base of knowledge and skills so they can make informed design decisions. Careful curri-culum planning should include open, heuristic 'design and make' activities where creativity is fostered by children being motivated and having opportunities to use what they know and have learnt, to generate new ideas and make design decisions. More examples of food technology projects can be seen in Chapter 9.

The National Curriculum for Technology introduced the concept of information technology (IT) across the curriculum as Attainment Target 5 (DES/WO, 1990). The aim was to enable children to acquire the intellectual and practical skills to use computers as a natural tool for solving a wide variety of practical problems, develop problem-solving skills and enable them to evaluate the impact of the use of computers on their lives (ILECC, 1989). Initially the focus was on the use of computers as a 'tool' to enhance learning, although the term 'increasing creativity' was not explicitly used until later. A main thrust for the use of computers in D&T has been through computer-aided design (CAD) and computer-aided manufacture (CAM), though there are many opportunities for the use of other software, including word processing, desktop publishing (DTP), spreadsheets, painting and drawing packages. In the primary school curriculum, computer control and microprocessor controlled systems play a significant role 'from traffic management to cuddly toys' (Martin and Till 2001: 146). In addition, CAD/CAM has been introduced to design and make, for example, fridge magnets and cardboard boxes (Barlex and Miles-Pearson 2008). Further curriculum examples can be seen in Chapter 10.

Collaborative activities are a strategy for fostering children's creativity, as 'generative ideas emerge from joint thinking, from significant conversations, and from sustained, shared struggles to achieve new insights by partners in thought' (John-Steiner, 2000: 3). She bases her thinking on Vygotsky's cultural-historical views that creative activities are set in a social context and are not confined to one individual thinker. In the world outside school, many professions work as teams, with each person making their individual expert contribution to the final outcome. Teams of designers working on a construction, fashion or electronics product project have specific roles, and it is more effective to allow people to fulfil the roles of their area of expertise. There is the potential for children in D&T to learn from each other by collaborative work, by sharing ideas and stimulating thinking, though it is important to remember that they are 'novice' designers and will not have access to the same level of expertise as adults.

CASE STUDIES

One of the writers, a lecturer teaching primary D&T, has been concerned that there has seemed to be little or no D&T being taught in the primary schools that she has come into contact with over the last 10 years. This has reduced opportunities for children to be creative and she believes that one of the key issues is the lack of confidence that classroom teachers have in being creative with their teaching and fostering creativity in their children.

In this chapter, she shares case studies of modules that are run on a BA Primary Education programme, which she feels show how creativity can be incorporated into the primary school curriculum. The aim is to ensure that trainees understand how to teach *for* creativity and foster creativity in D&T for their children. From these modules, the children would be encouraged by the class teacher to let their creative imagination develop as they envisage how the different products could be generated; not only focusing on the visual impact but also for the children to be creative with the materials that they are going to be using, investigating what resources work well together and are appropriate for the purpose. Each case study will be related to the four criteria for creativity – the concept, aesthetic, technical and constructional creativity identified above (Rutland, 2005).

Case study 1

The first case study focuses on a module for first-year D&T specialists. It is potentially one of the most creative modules for the trainees, as it lends itself for them, as the designer, to be individually novel and imaginative. The scene is set with a stimulating puppet show presentation by a world-renowned puppeteer, who displays a variety of different types and styles of puppets, showing how they were technically constructed. This also helps foster an aesthetic creative interest within the trainees, before they go and research all about puppets and choose a particular type to design and make, whether it be a marionette, hand, rod or shadow puppet. During the design process, the trainees will need to consider technically the range of materials and tools that they will be using to construct the puppet so that their puppet functions as effectively as possible, addressing the purpose, the audience and the user needs.

Group discussion can be used to develop an understanding of the role of puppets within the primary classroom. Many of the trainees are surprised when they begin to realise exactly how much creativity can be achieved just by using a range of technical and constructional strategies in puppet-making such as levers, cams and linkages and making skills. Also, rather than making the larger puppets, younger children could make finger, sock or glove puppets using felt and other fabrics with skills and knowledge appropriate to their age. The puppets can help the children express themselves more easily, which is particularly helpful during circle time for children with special educational needs or English as an additional language, as the puppets support the children's communication skills and the development of their fine motor abilities. The trainees' puppets can be used as a teaching resource or class mascot.

The module helped inspire the trainees with many new ideas, and this creativity was evident in the second part of the module where they were asked to think beyond making a puppet to making a bag/container to hold their puppet. They used different materials such as plastic, card, fabric, recycled materials such as leather and a rage of constructional techniques such as stitching, joining, fastening and decorating that would be functional as well as attractive and useful.

The trainee has used as a stimulus a well-loved children's book family to recreate rod and shadow puppets (Figure 2.3).

■ **Figure 2.3** Trainee's puppets.

■ **Figure 2.4** Trainee's storage containers.

She has experimented technically and in the construction with various materials, including wood, acrylic, wire and paint; she has created her own wire framework to attach her puppets to for ease of storage and she went on to create a clear strong perspex bag to store the puppets safely (Figure 2.4).

The trainees synthesise the concept/idea of their puppet/s and container for a final group presentation, where they reflect and describe the creative journey travelled in constructing their products, which will be used later as a teaching classroom resource. It is acknowledged that the module would not be transferred easily into the primary classroom due to a lack of resources and time limitations, and the trainees are expected to consider how they will transfer and adapt the knowledge and skills that they have learnt and used.

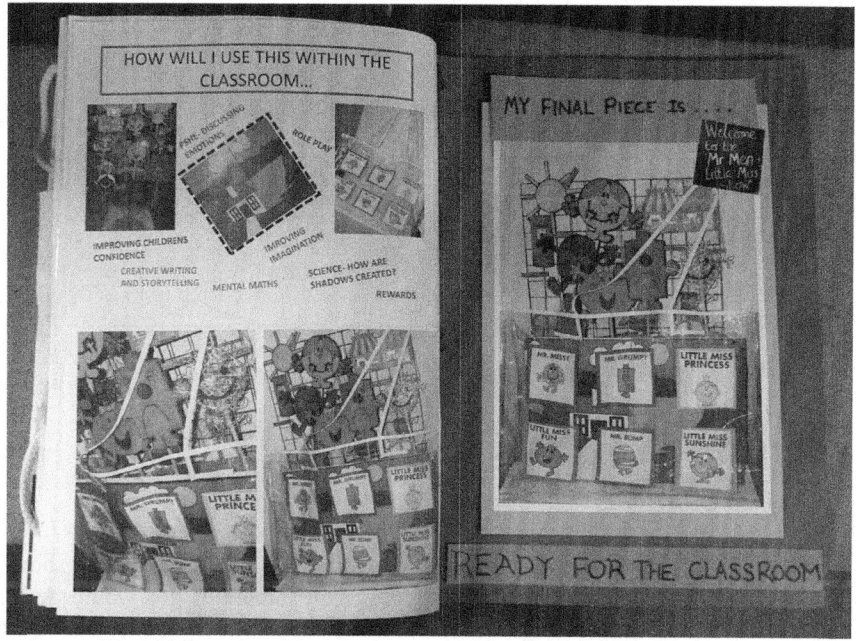

■ **Figure 2.5** Teaching in the classroom.

These reflections (Figure 2.5) show where a trainee has thought about how the puppets might be able to be used in the classroom to foster the children's creativity when they design and make their own attractive, imaginative puppets. Trainee reflection also showed that focusing on puppets can be used to improve confidence in role play, mental maths, and discussions of emotions and in creative writing and storytelling and learning.

Case study 2

The second case study is a cross-curricular module that is run for the BA Primary trainees who are entering their third and final year. The main intention was to get the trainees to use IT as a cross-curricular link to enhance their confidence and creativity. In this particular module, none of the trainees are subject specialists in D&T (although some have gone on to be D&T coordinators in school); it combines IT with the foundation subject D&T and the focus of the module is 'Habitats'.

The trainees began by researching small animals and mini-beasts. They then chose one to research in more detail and design a habitat for. The trainees were encouraged to use the software Google SketchUp (a 3D designing tool), to foster the creative design of their habitats. This was a different approach for many of the trainees who had been used to freehand designing. But they soon found that once they were familiar with the programme they could be very creative, transforming their design ideas into high-quality computer-generated drawings.

The trainees were challenged to consider how they would use this as a cross-curricular project within the classroom. The lecturer has been impressed by the effort and the creativity that the trainees have shown throughout this module – not only making their habitats but including the use of mind-mapping as a technique to develop original ideas and concepts in the medium-term plans (Figure 2.6).

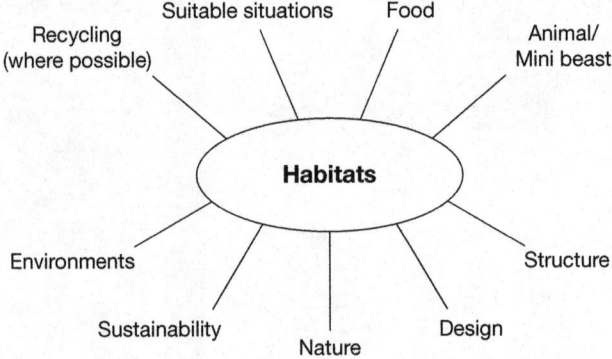

■ **Figure 2.6** Using mind mapping in medium term planning.

There could include cross-curricular link ideas and the trainees showing creativity and originality within their chosen areas. An example of this would be for them to be creative by using recycling materials and focusing on sustainability and the environment. The trainee would think about technical creativity by considering knowledge from their research as to what the animal or mini-beast would be eating. This would then lead to creativity in the positioning of the habitat in a suitable location, for a good food supply and a safe area away from predators.

One of the most positive creative opportunities available for the trainees is being able to design on the computer. This allows them to use the Google SketchUp program to explore a wider range of design ideas as an alternative to hand-drawn 2D designs (Figure 2.7 and 2.8).

This design process was how a trainee created a habitat. The technical versatility of the software and ability to be creative is illustrated through examples of different shape habitats that were created and constructed on screen.

One of the three examples of trainee designs was considered to be creative because of its original and creative concept/idea for constructing a frog habitat (Figure 2.9).

The trainee researched her knowledge of what a frog would need for an ideal habitat and created a novel look. She has used mostly recycled resources from the outdoor environment to construct and create an authentic approach.

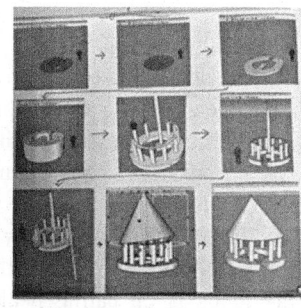

■ **Figures 2.7–2.11**
7: Using Google SketchUp to explore design ideas. **8**: Using Google SketchUp to further explore design ideas. **9**: Trainee's frog habitat. **10**: Trainee's hedgehog habitat. **11**: Trainee's bird house.

Another trainee designed a hedgehog house, but developed an unusual and imaginative idea by converting a familiar-looking house to meet the needs of the identified occupant (Figure 2.10). Some foliage from the outdoor environment has been used to create an aesthetically appealing, attractive and technically appropriate material as camouflage for the habitat. The third trainee has created a small bird house (Figure 2.11).

He/she was constructional and technically creative as recycled tongue and groove wood, left from their parents' decorating, has been used to construct the habitat. A further original and functional idea was that the roof was designed to open on one side to allow access for cleaning if necessary in-between inhabitants. All the habitats were created by the trainees from their own designs. They had minimal help from the lecturer, but they were given health and safety training before they were allowed to use any of the equipment. They found it useful to bounce around creative ideas among each other to see what might be feasible.

The trainees realised that the resources that were available to them might be different from those in schools. This is something that has been taken note of and next year the trainees will be using more everyday resources, such as milk containers and fruit drink cartons, to create their habitats, thus making the project easier to recreate in a school environment. It would also mean that no large machinery for working with wood, such as a sander, power drill and band, as used by the trainees at the university, would be needed, but rather the use of typical school-based resources such as a bench hook and junior hacksaw. Apart from the resources, the rest of the project would be easy to adapt for a classroom environment, especially allowing children to be technically and aesthetically creative with the 3D computer software.

Case study 3

The third case study is based on a module called 'Healthy Living', which also provides related, feasible and novel cross-curricular opportunities. The module links D&T, science and physical education, and runs within an overarching module called 'Connective Worlds' for all BA Primary Education trainees about to complete their final year. In science, the trainees look closely at the heart and how it works by dissecting a heart. In physical education, the trainees look at how the heart reacts to physical exertion and how an individual can monitor and influence the health of the heart through activities and games. In D&T, the focus is on eating healthily and how this can be promoted in the primary classroom. The main intention is to get the trainees to be creative by considering aesthetics, technical and construction ideas as well as encouraging children to eat healthily. The aim was for the trainees to develop a range of resources to support children in the class-room. They spent a day in a school, working in groups, teaching different aged groups of children, and at the end of the day the groups of children presented their work to the whole school.

Most of the trainees had not previously thought about being original, but were still functional when preparing fruits and vegetables for the children to taste. Aesthetic creativity was stimulated by the lecturer's PowerPoint presentation that included strong visual images to inspire ideas. She used colourful examples of fruits and vegetables from the Internet to inspire the trainees to think about how young children can see how fun and interesting eating healthily can be. The trainees thoroughly enjoyed this challenge and were able to transfer their skills and creativity ideas of a range of food products that children could design and make in the classroom, drawing on children's prior knowledge of nursery rhymes and well-known picture books to help inspire them, making very strong links with literacy. Creativity came through the consideration of function and construction, by using a range

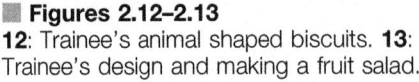

▨ **Figures 2.12–2.13**
12: Trainee's animal shaped biscuits. **13**: Trainee's design and making a fruit salad.

of technical food processes and cooking skills when designing and making a range of nutritionally healthy food products such as smoothies, fruit salads, sandwiches, coleslaw, scone pizza and baked potatoes. All these could be prepared, with careful thought and planning, in a primary classroom, taking into consideration user and purpose.

The trainees designed and made some colourful, animal-shaped biscuits from a basic rubbed-in mix as a stimulus to use with the children in the classroom (Figure 2.12).

They were encouraged to modify the recipe with, for example, wholemeal flour or lemon juice to improve the nutritive value.

The children worked in groups to design and create their own healthy fruit salad from a variety of fruits with a range of different colours, textures and flavours (Figure 2.13). You can find other example of children designing and making with food in Chapter 9.

All the case studies show that problem-solving is important because it is fundamental for designers as they use a combination of aesthetic, technical and constructional techniques and strategies to find a solution for a novel situation (Gagne, 1977). 'Broadly speaking problem-solving involves "actionable knowledge" – interaction between thinking and doing which embodies the intermeshing of thought and action' (Watts 1994: 3). It is the practical use of knowledge that is motivating for children, stimulating enjoyment and interest, developing decision-making and increasing self-confidence and satisfaction. Problem-solving is identified as a key skill in the Robinson Report (1999) as it involves both critical and analytical thinking. Creative thinking generates possible solutions, explores a wide range of ideas and possible solutions, and is called 'divergent' or lateral thinking. Critical thinking, or 'convergent' thinking, looks at the different parts of a problem and selects or identifies a potential solution to explore how it can be completed successfully (Fisher, 1990). Teachers of D&T are very successful in encouraging their pupils to be convergent thinkers and make good quality products. However, encouragement to think creatively is essential when teaching *for* creativity, as it helps pupils think more widely, consider a range of possibilities, look at a situation from different angles, extend their range of options and simply explore ideas 'outside the box'.

CONCLUSION

We have argued in this chapter that teaching *for* creativity is a complex and demanding activity in which the role of the teacher is crucial in creating a calm, supportive environment where children feel motivated, secure and confident enough to take risks. 'Teaching for creativity and fostering creativity is dependent largely on the teacher's professional ability to manage his or her classroom environment to meet these requirements' (Rutland and Spendlove, 2007: 152). It is important to remember that 'the encouragement of attributes like risk taking, independent judgement, commitment, resilience in the face of adversity and motivation will contribute to the development of children's creative potential' (Robinson, 1999: 95).

ACKNOWLEDGEMENTS

We wish to thank the BA Primary Education trainees at the University of Roehampton for allowing us to photograph their work for the case studies.

REFERENCES

Amabile, T. (1983) *The Social Psychology of Creativity*. New York: Springer-Verlag.

Amabile, T. (1989) *Growing Up Creative: Nurturing a Lifetime of Creativity*. Buffalo, NY: CEF Press.

Amabile, T. (1996) *Creativity in Context: Update to the Social Psychology of Creativity*. Colorado: West View Press.

Archer, J. (2015) 'An introduction to design and technology', in Driscoll, P., Lambert, J. and Rodes, J. (eds) *The Primary Curriculum: A Creative Approach*, 2nd Edn. London: Sage Publications.

Banks, F. (2002) 'Teaching strategies for design and technology', in Owen-Jackson, G. (ed.) *Aspects of Teaching Design and Technology: Perspectives on Practice*. London: RoutledgeFalmer.

Barlex, D. (2002) 'Organising project work', in Owen-Jackson, G. (ed.) *Aspects of Teaching Secondary Design and Technology*. London: RoutledgeFalmer.

Barlex, D. (ed.) (2003) *'Creativity in Crisis?' Nuffield Foundation, Design and Technology Association*. Wellesbourne: DATA.

Barlex, D. and Miles-Pearson, S. (2008) 'Introducing CADCAM into primary schools Part 1 of a case study – developing the curriculum', in Norman, E.W. and Spendlove, D. (eds) *Designing the Curriculum – Making it Work: The Design and Technology International Research Conference*, 5–10.

Boden, M. (ed.) (1994) *Dimensions of Creativity*. USA: Bradford Books, MIT Press.

Central Advisory Council for Education in England (CACE) (1967) *Children and their Primary schools, Report of the Central Advisory Council for Education in England (The Plowden Report)*. London: HMSO.

Craft, A. and Hall, E. (2015) 'Changes in the landscape for creativity in education', in Wilson, A. (ed.) *Creativity in Primary Education*, 3rd Edn. London: Sage Publications Learning Matters.

Cropley, A. (2001) *Creativity in Education and Learning: A Guide for Teachers and Educators*. London: Rogan Page.

Csikszentmihalyi, M. (1996) *Creativity: Flow and the Psychology of Discovery and Invention*. USA: HarperPerennial.

Csikszentmihalyi, M. (1999) 'Implications of a systems perspective', in Sternberg, R. (ed.) *Handbook of Creativity*. Cambridge: Cambridge University Press.

Dacey, J. and Lennon, K. (1998) *Understanding Creativity*. San Francisco: Jossey-Bass.

Davies, D. and Howe, A. (2015) 'Creativity in primary design and technology', in Wilson, A. (ed.) *Creativity in Primary Education*, 3rd Edn. London: Sage Publications Learning Matters.

Davies, T. (1999) 'Taking risks as a feature of creativity in the teaching and learning of design and technology'. *The Journal of Design and Technology Education*, 4(2), 101–108.

Davies, T. (2000) 'Confidence! Its role in the creative teaching and learning of design and technology'. *Journal of Technology Education*, 12(1), 18–31.

de Bono, E. (1992) *Seriously Creative*. London: Harper Collins Business.

Department for Education (DfE) (1995) *Design and Technology in the National Curriculum*. London: HMSO.

DES (Department of Education and Science)/WO (Welsh Office) (1990) *Technology in the National Curriculum*. London: HMSO.

DfEE and QCA (1999) *Design and Technology: The National Curriculum for England*. London: HMSO.

Fisher, R. (1990) *Teaching Children to Think*. Oxford: Basil Blackwell.

Gagne, R. (1977) *The Conditions of Learning*, 3rd Edn. USA: Holt, Rinehart and Winston.

Haffenden, D. (2004) 'Compliance and creativity? in *Design and Technology, International Research Conference, Creativity and Innovation.* https://dspace.lboro.ac.uk/dspace-jspui/bitstream/2134/2873/1/dot10.pdf (accessed 25 May 2016).

Harris, M. and Wilson, V. (2003) *Designs on the Curriculum?* Scotland: SCRE Centre, University of Glasgow.

Hennessy, S. and Murphy, P. (1999) 'The potential for collaborative problem solving in design and technology.' *International Journal of Technology and Design Education*, 9(1), 1–36.

ILECC (Inner London Educational Computing Centre) (1989) *Tools of the Mind.* London: Inner London Educational Authority (ILEA).

John-Steiner, V. (2000) *Creative Collaboration.* New York: Oxford University Press.

Kimbell, R. and Perry, D. (2001) *Design and Technology in the Knowledge Economy.* London: Engineering Council.

Martin, M. and Till, W. (2001) 'The place of computer control in the primary school', in Benson, C., Martin, M. and Till, W. (eds) *The Third International Primary Design and Technology Conference.* Birmingham: CRIPT at UCE.

Robinson, K. (1999) *All Our Futures: Creativity, Culture and Education.* London: DfEE.

Rutland, M. (2005) *Fostering Creativity in Design and Technology at Key Stage 3.* Unpublished PhD thesis. University of Surrey: School of Education, Roehampton University.

Rutland. M. and Spendlove, D. (2007) 'Creativity in design and technology', in Barlex, D. (ed.), *Design and Technology: For the Next Generation.* Whitchurch: Cliffeco Communications.

Smidt, S. (2009) *Introducing Vygotsky.* London: Routledge.

Watts, M. (1994) *Problem Solving in Science and Technology.* London: David Fulton Press.

Websites

www.oxforddictionaries.com/search/?multi=1&dictCode=english&q=creativity (accessed 31 March 2015).

Software

Google SketchUp www.sketchup.com

CHAPTER

3

TEACHING DESIGN AND TECHNOLOGY CREATIVELY IN THE EARLY YEARS

Clare Benson

This chapter focuses on children's early years and how design and technology (D&T) is part of their everyday lives, helping to build a foundation on which to develop their understanding of the designed and made world. The importance of including D&T within the early years curriculum is explained, and ideas for planning and teaching approaches that support the development of creativity within D&T are explored. Examples of activities, including a case study, provide practical ideas to support teaching D&T creatively. The definition of early years in relation to educational policy does vary around the world; however, in England, the curriculum for early years is from birth to five, and is detailed in the Early Years/Foundation Stage curriculum (DfE, 2014). The term 'teachers' has been used to refer to all those who are involved in the education of children in an early years setting. The term 'carers' refers to all adults who are responsible for children in their home environment. The term 'setting' has been used to include all places where young children are attending early years education.

A FOCUS ON THE EARLY YEARS

Children's learning from birth is now widely accepted to result from the child's own activity and adaptive behaviour, which is hard-wired into the brain from before birth (Blakemore and Frith, 2005). However, it does require the support of others to develop these behaviours. From birth, children are involved in making choices and decisions. They use all their senses to explore the world around them. One only has to look at the range of toys and comforters that are available to buy for very young children to see that manufacturers are aware that there is no 'one size fits all' for these items. Of course, adults are making the initial choices but are these always based on 'fit for purpose' or on something that attracts them? When the child is given the product, does he/she engage with it? Discarded toys are commonplace and favourites emerge as the child determines his/her preferences.

So very young children are starting to develop designerly thinking skills (Benson, 2003) as they make judgements about the products around them. As the user, they are determining whether it is 'fit for purpose' and if it meets their needs. It is therefore crucial that these skills and knowledge of the designed and made world are built on as the children move through their early years education, so they are equipped to make informed choices in relation to their everyday lives. A recent report highlights the continuing need to build on the early years curriculum to provide continuity of education (OFSTED, 2015), so it is important to create the foundations of D&T at this stage of the children's education. D&T provides so many opportunities for children to engage in authentic tasks through which they can take control of their actions, problem solve and extend their thinking skills – all important in developing their ability to be creative. Examples include:

■ Investigating structures and designing and making a structure to protect someone (teddy) when playing out in the rain.
■ Investigating different types of fruit and designing and making a fruit dish for their end-of-term picnic.
■ Investigating vehicles and designing and making a vehicle for a storybook character for a specific purpose.
■ Investigating capes and fabrics and designing and making a new cape for Little Red Riding Hood.

Curiosity about the designed and made world needs to be fostered as there is evidence that as children move through the early years into more formal schooling, their curiosity is not always encouraged. The curriculum is often narrowed, leading to D&T-related activity that many children are eager to explore being marginalised or even omitted from the curriculum. Early years teachers often lack the knowledge, understanding and confidence to include such activity or to extend D&T opportunities as there has been little professional development in this area (Benson, 2005).

EARLY YEARS CURRICULUM

In England, D&T is named and identified as part of Expressive Arts and Design – one of six specific areas in the Early Years Foundation Curriculum (DfE, 2014). However, aspects of D&T are part of any broad and balanced early years curricula, but teaching subjects separately is not advocated. The idea of a holistic curriculum is promoted not only in England but in the majority of early years curricula worldwide (Bertram and Pascal, 2002). Different approaches such as Montessorri, Rudolf Steiner, Highscope and Reggio Emilia all advocate starting from the children and their interests and developing a curriculum around these. In Miller's review of early years practice (2000) she supported this, taking a child's interest in cars as an example and showing how this focus could be taken in so many different directions. However, to be able to make meaningful links, teachers need to have appropriate knowledge and understanding of all areas of the curriculum, including D&T, otherwise inaccurate messages can be given.

Many early years curricula are theme- or topic-based; planning is then undertaken to try to ensure that the children's experiences are broad and balanced over a specific period of time – a few weeks, a term or a year. Of course, this can vary depending on the children's interests and whatever incidental opportunities arise.

While planning is important for balance, continuity and progression, research has shown (Benson and Lunt, 2011) that consideration needs to be given to breadth, relevance and motivation, space and time, ownership and control, and interaction with others when planning for creativity. Without breadth, opportunities to cover areas of interest that are relevant and motivate may be missed and equity and inclusiveness poorly addressed. Children need to be motivated and see relevance to engage with a task that involves hands-on working. There need to be opportunities for ownership and control of their activities. If the teacher sets the activity in such a way that the child can have little or no input, it is unlikely that he/she will want to think about ways to develop the task, to problem solve, to think critically and to innovate. Many early years settings do have space both inside and outside the setting, and it is important that these environments are set up to offer opportunities for the child to explore, for example, materials, mechanisms, structures and products. Children need time to do this – exploring by themselves, with their peers and with adults. Abbott and Nutbrown (2005) highlight Emilia's principle of the importance of giving children opportunities for discussion with both peers and adults, encouraging children to ask challenging questions – something that underpins creativity. Of course, planning should not be rigid and stifle creativity, but it is important to have a framework within which to plan a curriculum that supports the development of creativity in all children.

TEACHING APPROACHES TO PROMOTE CREATIVITY IN THE EARLY YEARS

There is an argument that children have an innate ability to be creative but teaching needs to foster this; interaction and facilitating in different ways play a large part in this.

Questioning

Young children are curious about the world around them but this needs to be nurtured through a variety of strategies. Recently I was on a train journey, sitting near a young child of about 4 years old. She was looking out of the window and asking a number of 'why' questions. The adult with her answered the first two or three enthusiastically, then returned to her mobile phone. The next few questions were mainly ignored and the child then started to fidget and opened a packet of biscuits that were on the table. No more questions were asked and the child spent the rest of the journey eating and being told to sit still. It can be difficult to always answer a continuous stream of questions both at home and in a setting, but the questions were sparked from the child's curiosity and needed to be encouraged and addressed. Adults need to think carefully about their questions in order that children have role models to follow. The idea that open questions are 'good' and closed questions 'poor' promotes muddled thinking. It depends on the reason for the question. For example, if an adult wants to better understand the child's knowledge of materials, a knowledge question such as 'what material has been used?' would be appropriate. However, if the adult is trying to develop the child's thinking, questions such as 'what would happen if . . .?' 'what can you tell me about . . .?' are more appropriate. Open questions make progressive cognitive demands on children and encourage language development because they require a lengthier response. Bloom's taxonomy (1956) is one way of categorising questions and has proved useful as it offers a framework for planning a range of questions (Benson, 2005). Table 3.1 (Benson, 2005) has been adapted from Blooms' taxonomy and includes suggestions for different types of questions.

It is important that these are not considered to be in a hierarchical order, as young children can tackle all types of questions. If the questions are asked in a supportive way, some children will want to answer, others may think their ideas over, and others may not

■ **Table 3.1** Questioning ideas adapted from Bloom's taxonomy

Knowledge
Designed to build or reinforce core knowledge · What do we call that? Which parts move?

Comprehension
Reinforcing knowledge and understanding · Who do you think would use this? Why do you think the egg cup has wide feet?

Application
Using newly acquired knowledge, ideas and skills in a different situation · Which other products are made of the same material? Which other product can you wear?

Analysis
Drawing conclusions from information · Why do books have pop-ups in them? Why are gloves made from different fabrics?

Synthesis
Extending meaning and pattern from information · What can you tell me about all of these?

Evaluation
Encouraging critical judgements · Which slippers would you want to wear? What do you think about the glasses?

Prediction
Designed to build from a conceptual base and encourage children to extend their thinking · What would happen to the slippers if you wear them out in the rain?

Speculation
Designed to encourage creative and speculative thinking · What would the slippers be like if they were rough on the inside?

Inference
Encourages children to 'see beyond' the given information · Who do you think that this was made for?

understand what is being asked. However, by including a range of questions, it should take all children's thinking – both critical and creative – forward and provide ideas for the children's own questions. This was certainly what the early years' teachers discovered when taking part in the Designerly Thinking project (Benson, 2005). Many expressed surprise at the children's responses and how they then formulated more complex questions themselves. 'Wait time', before asking a child for an answer, was found to be important, and when teachers timed themselves they realised that they often jumped in too soon when a child was still thinking out an answer. The idea of allowing time and space proved to be crucial. While many of the teachers felt that they did think about question distribution among all the children, on closer reflection they found that often this was not the case. Findings indicated that they frequently chose children who appeared to be off task to try to re-engage them, children who were articulate and who could give a clear answer, and children who might prove disruptive if they were not asked. Children who did not attract particular attention for any reason were passed over. Questions that follow on from an initial question are also useful. Echo questions allow children to clarify their own thinking; inviting children to elaborate encourages more complex contributions; and non-verbal invitations to children can encourage some to take part or extend a given answer. Questioning was found to be an effective tool during any D&T activity such as:

■ exploration of products (Table 3.2)
■ use of materials, tools and equipment during practical tasks
■ developing design ideas
■ designing and making products

More recent research has focused on questioning as part of possibility thinking – 'what is?' changed to 'what if?' or 'what might be?' (Chappell *et al.*, 2008). This paper focused on question-posing and question responding – the heart of 'possibility thinking' in the early years – and the study acknowledged how questioning played an important role in creative learning and thinking.

The learning environment

Teachers are aware of the importance of the environment that they create for their children, but from the Designerly Thinking project (Benson, 2005), and further research, findings emerged that indicated that the majority of teachers did not consider how to develop aspects of D&T from their surrounding environment both inside and out. Most did not feel confident about the nature of D&T and therefore how to explore different aspects through, for example, displays, collections of products, investigations relating to joiners, materials, mechanisms and structures. This has been mirrored in primary science (Harlen 2000), which resulted in the overuse of worksheets and kits, rather than hands-on investigation. There were lost opportunities in using the outside environment; structures could have been explored using large building and climbing equipment, mechanisms examined by using wheeled play equipment such as bikes and scooters; and ways of joining investigated through observation of buildings and equipment. However, after suggestions had been made, teachers' feedback from the project included ideas that had been tried successfully.

Exploring things that move up and down/round and round/backwards and forwards; looking around the setting, for example, at windows, doors, containers, and switches; creating a collection of things that move up and down/ round and round/in and out, leaving it on a table and allowing time for children to explore and investigate; looking outside at the play equipment, windows, doors. How do things move? What allows them to move? Why do things stand up? Why do things fall down? Children designed and made products to be used outdoors, including tool bags for gardening implements, and bags for collecting things on a leaf walk. Teachers created wall displays linked to D&T activity. Examples included how different joiners (e.g. paper clips, split pins, masking tape, sellotape) can be used and what glue to choose for different purposes. Large photos of structures and mechanisms around the setting and of different products were displayed alongside a range of questions that could be asked by any of the adults in the setting and to illustrate to parents and other carers the kind of questions that they could be asking. Role-play areas were explored and teachers indicated that they could use these more imaginatively in relation to D&T. Builders' yards, Do It Yourself shops, shops that focused on textile products and cafes were all set up and the children designed and made some of the products to be used in them.

Mechanisms:
How do the wheels turn?
How does the bucket tip?
How do you think the wheels and axles are joined?

Purpose:
Where would you use one of these vehicles? Why would you use it?

User:
Who might like this for a present?

Structures:
Why do you think the wheels are wide? What might happen if they were thin?

Materials:
What materials has the truck been made from?

Example activity – evaluating, user, purpose
Problem-solving suggestions: The adult explains that the truck has been bought for a child's birthday present (age 4). He/she is not sure the child will like it. What do the children think? Pass the truck around. Ask why the child might like it/not like it. What other things in the setting would the child like to play with? Tell the children they have been very helpful and that you will let them know if the child likes it.

Prime areas	Specific areas
Communication and language: listening, understanding and speaking	Understanding the world: similarities and differences in relation to objects
Personal, social, emotional development: self-confidence, making relationships	Expressive arts and design: exploring materials; thinking about users and purposes

Other starting points
Role play: variety of trucks and diggers in the sand tray; vary the contents of the tray – wet sand, dry sand, pebbles, etc. How well do the wheels turn on each vehicle? Why do they think there are differences?
Story: any with wheels as a focus
Planned topic: vehicles, transport, building site

Technical vocabulary

Wheels
Axle
Plastic
Chassis
Bucket
Lever
Pivot
Flexible
Moulded
Turn
Rotate
Wide tyres
Hub
Metal

Teachers felt that, after widening the activities that linked to D&T, children were using some of the ideas in different, creative ways when undertaking their own tasks. Certainly, many teachers reported that the children's questioning skills had developed and not only with those who already had well-developed language skills.

Through all these activities, the children were encouraged to take risks. Teachers were aware of the importance of a supportive environment and encouraged the children to try things out and not to worry if something did not work the first time. They realised that interaction and facilitation were important – but they should not prevent the child from trying things out in different ways and gaining confidence and self-esteem as they found solutions. Young children may not have such fixed ideas about what they can and cannot do and obviously this should be encouraged, so that as they move through primary education they can build on this 'can do' attitude. There is a danger that the idea of a correct solution does become more fixed as children encounter tests and assessments where they are told there is a right and wrong answer, and risk-taking may feel less safe.

One of the most important aspects of undertaking all the activities and changing practice was the teachers' enthusiasm and increased confidence. The majority of teachers had had little if any experience of D&T and having given many of their activities a different focus, they could see how motivating it was.

Authentic tasks and practical experience

Children need to see a purpose for activities that they are given for them to become fully engaged, curious and enthusiastic (Alexander, 2010). The Reggio Emilia approach (Abbott and Nutbrown, 2005) promotes 'Occasions' as a way of providing situations that motivate and are relevant to the children undertaking them and a way of fostering creativity. Often activities can be refocused to provide opportunities to problem-solve, to investigate and to motivate. In one setting, when nursery staff changed their role-play corner every few weeks, they chose the theme and planned in detail the contents and how they would be arranged. They found that children initially were excited when they arrived to find a new area set up but quickly lost interest. By involving the children in the choice of theme, such as a shoe shop to link with the story of Cinderella, and asking for their help in planning, designing and making some products, the children came up with some ideas that the staff said they would not have thought of including. This involved the children in hands-on experiences when they designed and made, for example, a foot measurer. They wanted to make a slider and thus investigated with card how this might be done. Different children wanted different decorations on the final product, depending on their interests, and commented that this would be important in their shop so that all children can use one that attracted them. Hands-on activity made learning relevant and encouraged the children to take ownership of the activities. These child-initiated, teacher-extended activities helped to develop the children's confidence, self-esteem ('I did make it and it worked') and problem-solving skills as well as their practical abilities. However, if children have too much freedom without little structure or support, it can lead to frustration if they cannot see a way forward, and can lead to a sense of failure. Teacher-initiated activities certainly have a part to play in an environment that fosters creativity; it is a balancing act between imposing activities and giving children freedom to develop their own ideas.

Use of other adults in the setting and at home

'Cultivating' creativity (Bruce, 2004) with babies and toddlers highlights the importance of the role that adults play in supporting rather than imposing. She argues that without sensitive engagement with children and their families, 'emergent possibilities for creativity that are in every child do not develop and are quickly extinguished' (Bruce, 2004: 12). Unless the adult helpers understand the nature of D&T and how creativity can be nurtured, there is a danger of adults 'taking over' and making the 'perfect' product. Adults in the setting as well as carers have to understand that children should be given the opportunity to investigate and to follow through with their own designing and making. The finished product may not look 'perfect' but it is the important process that the children have gone through that will develop their thinking and creativity. Offering adults in the home some suggestions on questions they could ask as they talk about the product the child brings home would be helpful; some settings have created booklets to provide information and support relating to the learning outcomes of these types of activities.

Encouraging creativity through D&T activities

While the following activities focus on D&T, all of them involve a range of curriculum areas. For example, language and writing skills are developed through discussion, mark-making and early writing; mathematical skills through measuring; science through observations, knowledge and understanding of materials, mechanisms and force; art and design through form, shape, colour and finishing techniques; and history through investigating products from the past, their users and purposes.

Play is an important part of all the following activities. Different types of play are all considered including active, explorative, manipulative and constructive play (Miller, 2000; Sheridan, 2002; Miller *et al.*, 2008) as are child-initiated, teacher-initiated, structured and unstructured activity. It is the teacher's decision as to how to use them in their settings; providing an appropriate balance can ensure that children's creativity is stimulated and not suppressed.

Investigating designed and made products

Children are well aware of the variety of products around them and while they may start to evaluate them, peer pressure, advertising and a culture of 'I want' may prevent them from making meaningful, considered choices. By involving them in investigative and evaluative activity, opportunities arise for them to continue to develop their critical-thinking skills and use the knowledge and understanding they have gained when creating their own products.

Setting up activities that enable the children to become critical users can be achieved in many different ways. Of course, underlying these activities is a need for the children to see a real purpose for them to engage with the task. The products to be investigated can be chosen for a variety of reasons. These include child-initiated activity based around a product that someone has brought into the setting or teacher-initiated to focus on a particular aspect of D&T.

Activities can be managed in a variety of ways:

■ A display. It may start with one product with new ones added daily or a collection displayed to be freely handled. Discussion including a range of questions should take place as and when appropriate with children thinking about, for example, user, purpose, materials, aesthetics and functionality. Questions can be put around the display to provide support for adults working with the children and to show children how words can be meaningful. They could make value judgements about the products, discuss how their opinions differ and offer some reasons for this. An example might be 'I like that shoe because it is shiny and blue'; 'I don't like the shoe because it will be hard to do the lace up and I like green'.

■ A mystery box/bag. This might start as a teacher-initiated activity and then be extended by the children. A small group of children might choose to take part in the activity or the teacher might choose them. A product is put in the box/bag and the children pass it around using their senses to describe what they find out. Then they can open the container and continue to make more observations. The teacher will listen to all the comments, trying to ensure that all children are involved with the activity and asking questions to take children's thinking further. This might be a weekly activity to link with a current theme; it might be extending the children's knowledge and understanding of a product that a child has brought from home; or it might be that the box/bag is left out for the children to choose to use to develop their own game with different products.

Practical tasks

By involving the children in a variety of practical tasks, they are developing their knowledge and understanding of, for example, joiners, finishing techniques, materials, and the use of different tools and equipment, which they may choose to use when creating their own products. When exploring materials, links with science can certainly be made and it is important that any investigation is put into a real context for the children. Starting points might be:

■ what fabric would be best to use for you/teddy when going home in the dark? The children can be offered a selection of fabrics, to investigate and discuss among themselves and with a teacher. Different items of clothing can be examined to see if they can be seen in the dark.

■ a child wants to make a card for a brother who is not well. What card would be best to use so that it does not bend too much as the brother is a toddler? Different cards could be tested by bending in different ways before the selection is made.

Construction

Having read a story such as 'The Very Hungry Caterpillar', what joiner is best to use when making your caterpillar to put up on a wall display? Depending on the children's experience, they could be given small pieces of card to try different joiners and to see which ones they consider best (do the joints need to move or not?) before completing the caterpillar. The joiners could be different types of glue, treasury tags, paper clips, staples and split pins (Figure 3.1).

A different way is to set up a table of joiners and ask the children to explore what the joiners can do and facilitate the activity with appropriate questions and actions.

■ **Figure 3.1** Using different joiners.

Construction kits are useful for mechanisms as well as structures. To help develop knowledge and understanding, the kits should be used in different ways. Further discussion of this is in Chapter 8. Children need time and space to play with the kits, to explore how the pieces fit together, and what they can make with them. However, intervention is important to take children's creative learning further and maintain their interest. Activities could include choosing pieces such as wheels or hinges and suggesting that the children include them in their model to make something move or open and shut.

Finishing techniques

These activities link with developing ideas about the aesthetic look of a product. It could involve the use of paints, finishes with different papers (tissue, crepe, sticky) and the use of different joiners such as sellotape and masking tape (using scissors not teeth!) The children could work at a 'choosing table' where different materials are put out and the teacher can intervene when appropriate to support their learning as they try different ways of using the materials; alternatively, the teacher can show a group of children how to create a few different finishes, the children could practise these and then choose to create something with one or more of the finishes immediately or later.

Mechanisms

Children find it interesting to see how things move. Set up a table of different mechanisms such as hinges, wheels and sliders. Allow the children time to play with them and investigate how they work. Ask them to find examples of the mechanisms around the setting, both indoors and outside. Take the children on a 'moving walk or a wheel walk'; through discussion, encourage them to think how the mechanisms work.

Structures

Packaging, for example, is seen by children in their daily lives and one of its key features is its structure. Collections of packaging can be explored thinking about purpose and user, and how the strength of the packaging is linked to its use. An egg box is a really good example of a strong package and can be tested in many different ways. Models can be made from construction kits (more discussion in Chapter 8) and given to the children to test and decide how they can be made stronger and more stable. These models could be linked to a story, a visit or something that the children can see around their setting – both indoors and outside – such as a climbing frame, a tent or a seat.

Designing and making

While there is an important place for activities that do not include the whole process of a design and make project in the early years, it is a valuable experience for young children to undertake sustained activity over a period of time, provided that they feel it is authentic to them and they can fully engage with it. The context in which a project is set obviously plays a part in gaining the children's enthusiasm, and they can determine their own user and purpose for the product to be made. Possible contexts include:

■   Stories, rhymes and fantasy. The children can empathise with a character or create an imaginary one – human, animal or make-believe. Examples might be designing and making a vehicle to take Cinderella to the ball, a shelter for some play people or zoo animals, a sandwich for Paddington Bear or an overnight bag for one of the three little pigs.

■   Follow up from a visit. Examples of a designing-and-making activity could include: a container in which to put 'treasures' found at the beach, or on a walk outside; a flap book hiding something for others to guess.

■   A role play area. Examples of a designing-and-making activity could include food items for a café, rulers/measuring sticks for a builders' yard or a textile collage to brighten up the area.

■   Celebrations. Examples of a designing-and-making activity could be food for a celebration, musical instruments to play, hats to wear or puppets to be used to create a play about a special celebration.

A CASE STUDY

A reception class was involved in a project that linked with 'The Three Bears' story. They felt sorry for baby bear and wanted to design and make something for him as a surprise present to make him happy. Different presents were thought about, such as a new bed, a soft toy to take to bed, a new item of clothing and a spoon. Some of the children had had spoons given at their Christening and for baby brothers and sisters. This was the project that the class chose (not the teacher), but at other times some children also designed and made their first-choice present for baby bear.

The children made a huge collection of spoons over a couple of weeks from a variety of sources. Children were given time to observe and handle them, to use them to pick up dried peas and cereal, to discuss the collection among themselves, with the teachers, and with carers who came into the classroom. As children came from a variety of different countries, so did the spoons; some were made from sustainable material such as bamboo; some from metal or plastic; and one was solid silver. Some were very plain and others ornate. Following on from this, the children then made initial designs for spoons using quality, coloured plasticene that could be reshaped easily as thoughts changed during the designing. Having chosen their final design, they then made their spoon using a variety of materials that were available, but were encouraged to ask for anything that they needed that was not on the table. The teachers ensured that the children had quality resources and equipment including different types of paper and card, different glues and joiners, and left- and right-handed scissors. Most chose to make with card, covered with tin foil (the silver spoons were thought to be 'posh' so only the best for baby bear). There were no two products that looked the same and the children evaluated them by trying to pick up dried cereal; they did not want to try the porridge in case it spoilt the spoon! On further investigation of bears led by the teacher, the children noticed that bears do not have thumbs; therefore, baby bear would have difficulty holding his spoon. More discussion followed, a template to go over four fingers was made and the children added their own spoon to the end of the template. They evaluated again and decided that theirs would work. A display was made so that baby bear could see them all and decide which one/s he would like.

Throughout, the children were innovating, were curious, were taking risks, were being imaginative, were asking and answering questions posed by each other and the adults involved, and were totally immersed in the project. Certainly, the children thought that it was an authentic task and were given time and space to play – all key elements of possibility thinking at the heart of creativity (Burnard *et al.*, 2006).

CONCLUSION

This chapter has offered the focus for the important early years that provide the foundation from which every child can grow. It is evident that all adults involved in the planning and teaching of D&T activities need to have a clear understanding of the nature of D&T themselves and how children's creative thinking can be extended. This may well involve more continuing professional development than is currently available or being undertaken. The balance between imposition and freedom needs to be considered carefully to allow children to take their own ideas forward. While the range of teaching approaches could be used with children and pupils of different ages, the examples given are specific to the early years. Play is a vital part of a successful early years experience and provides many opportunities for young children to explore the designed and made world and the examples outlined indicate how this might be carried out.

ACKNOWLEDGEMENTS

Thanks to Sandie Kendall and Chris Cannon for their work on the Designerly Thinking project and to Sue Hancock for her work on the case study.

REFERENCES

Abbott, L. and Nutbrown, C. (eds) (2005) *Experiencing Reggio Emilia: Implications for Pre-school Provision*. Maidenhead: Open University Press.

Alexander, R. (ed.) (2010) *Children, Their World, Their Education: Final Report and Recommendations of the Cambridge Primary Review*. London: Routledge.

Benson, C. (2003) 'Developing designerly thinking in the foundation stage', in Benson, C., Martin, M. and Till, W. (eds) *Fourth International Primary Design and Technology Conference*. Birmingham, UK: CRIPT, 5–7.

Benson, C. (2005) 'Developing designerly thinking in the Foundation Stage – perceived impact upon teachers' practice and children's learning', in Benson, C., Lawson, S. and Till, W. (eds) *Fifth International Primary Design and Technology Conference*. Birmingham, UK: CRIPT, 15–18.

Benson, C. and Lunt, J. (2011) 'We're creative on a Friday afternoon: investigating children's perceptions of their experience of design and technology in relation to creativity'. *Journal of Science Education and Technology*, 20(5), DOI: 10.1007/s10956–011–9304–5. USA: Springer Publisher.

Bertram, T. and Pascal, C. (2002) *Early Years Education: An International Perspective*. London: QCA.

Blakemore, S-J. and Frith, U. (2005) *The Learning Brain*. Oxford: Blackwell Publishing.

Bloom, B.S. (1956) *Taxonomy of Educational Objectives: Vol. 1: The Cognitive Domain*. New York: McKay.

Bruce, T. (2004) *Cultivating Creativity in Babies, Toddlers and Young Children*. London: Hodder and Stoughton Educational.

Burnard, P., Craft, A. and Grainger, T. (2006) 'Possibility thinking'. *International Journal of Early Years Education*, 14(3), 243–262.

Chappell, K., Craft, A., Burnard, P. and Cremin, T. (2008) 'Question posing and question responding: the heart of "possibility thinking" in the early years'. *Early Years: An International Journal of Research and Development,* 28(3), 267–286.

De Boo, M. (ed.) (2007) *The Early Years Handbook*. Sheffield: Geographical Society.

Department for Education (DfE) (2014) *A Statutory Framework for Early Years Foundation Stage*. London: Department for Education.

Evangelou, M., Sylva, K., Kyriacou, M., Wild, M. and Glenny, G. (2009) *Early Years Learning and Development: Literature Review*. Oxford: University of Oxford.

Harlen, W. (2000) *The Teaching of Science in Primary Schools*, 3rd Edn. London: Paul Chapman.

Miller, L. (2000) 'Play as a foundation for learning', in Dury, R., Miller, L. and Campbell, R. (eds) *Looking at Early Years Education and Care*. London: David Fulton Publishers.

Miller, L., Cable, C. and Devereux, J. (2008) *Developing Early Years Practice*, 2nd Edn. Abingdon: Routledge.

Office for Standards in Education (OFSTED) (2015) *Early Years: Report of Her Majesty's Chief Inspector of Education, Children's Services and Skills*. OFSTED.

Sheridan, M.D. (2002) *Play in Early Childhood*. London: Routledge.

Websites useful for resources

www.data.org.uk
www.foodafactoflife.org.uk

CREATIVE DESIGN AND TECHNOLOGY THROUGH STARTING POINTS

James Archer

INTRODUCTION

Creative design and technology (D&T) can be stimulated through the use of *a variety of starting points*. There have been many definitions as to *the nature of creative teaching* and learning with key ideas that often contradict and conflict with each other. Regardless of this, it is believed that a creative approach can enliven and enhance the curriculum, *providing exciting and authentic contexts* in which dynamic D&T teaching and learning can take place.

PRINCIPLES

Creative design often originates from a clear starting point. Design is frequently built on the ideas of others and looks to discover new ways of solving a real problem or design dilemma. Further, it has been suggested that children perform at their highest levels when engaging with a wide range of stimuli (Stables, 2010). In this process, the need for creativity is of paramount importance. Indeed Archer (2015: 87) highlights:

> Creativity should be seen as a golden thread that weaves its way through both the design process and a product. D&T requires of its neophytes a great deal of thought, reflection, possibility thinking as well as the making and changing of materials.

At the outset of this chapter, it is important to acknowledge that the literature highlights the following areas as distinct components of the creative teaching and learning process (Craft, 2001; Haffenden, 2004; Archer, 2015):

- Teaching creatively
- Teaching for creativity
- Learning creatively

However, as Craft (2005) highlights, it is most likely that when a pedagogue seeks to teach creatively, they will also be teaching for creativity and their children will also be empowered to learn creatively (more on this in Chapter 2). This chapter will therefore seek to explore a few key pedagogical approaches that enable the primary practitioner to teach creatively in D&T through starting points. The use of objects, books, environments and special events will all be examined for their role in promoting creativity in primary D&T.

THE ROLE OF OBJECTS

Objects, both natural and made, can be a powerful starting point for creative design. Stables (2010) emphasises that very rarely does design inspiration merely pop into a child's head. It is for this reason that the use of objects as a starting point is of great importance. By observing, playing and manipulating, as well as deconstructing objects, children get to explore how they work. This can also enable them to discover any potential flaws, which can provide the inspiration required for new design.

Natural objects have been inspiring design since the dawn of early man. Everyday products that we take for granted have often found their origins in natural objects. A clear example of this was the development and design of Velcro. Designed by George de Mestral in the 1940s, the product has a legendary design story associated with it. When walking in the Jura mountains, George noticed how parts of the xanthium plant stuck to his trousers and his dog's fur due to hooks that looped round the fabric of his trousers and the fibres of the dog's fur. This observation led to the design and manufacture of the product that we know today.

Buildings have regularly been inspired by nature. An awe-inspiring example is Gaudi's Sagrada Familia Cathedral, which is due to be completed in 2026, over 100 years after work started. The building was based on trees with columns raising skywards and branching out as they hit the ceiling. In and around your locality, you will be able to observe other such examples (Figure 4.1). Below is a photograph of spotlights in Bradford's new Centenary Square. At a quick glance, these could look like any other lights, but on closer inspection it is clear that the lights have large metal leaves and the general appearance of a stalk of grain. Cleverly, the angle and the position of the grains within the stalk inspire the positioning of the individual lights within the lamp.

■ **Figure 4.1** Spotlights in Bradford's Centenary Square inspired by natural objects

Spendlove and Wells (2013) suggest that creativity requires a leap of faith, it has to be risky and returns from it can be low as well as high. When designing from natural objects, children are required to re-imagine structures and borrow elements that best fit their designs. This is a complex process that requires certain levels of design capital. The development of this design capital takes time and is reliant on having opportunites to observe the work of those more advanced and experienced than yourself (Gray, 2013). Designing using natural objects therefore may be most suitable for children in Key Stage 2

CASE STUDY: FLOWER FASHION

Jessica, a second-year undergraduate student, undertook her placement in an inner city three-form-entry school in a Year 3 class (7–8 years old). The learning for the term had been organised within a topic. The theme for the term was 'going green'. A range of environmental topics were being explored across a range of subjects. In science, the children were looking at functions of different parts of flowering plants. The children undertook dissections of flowering plants, breaking them down into their constitute parts and labelling them. As part of Jessica's planning for this topic, she was determined to explore ways of reducing waste with the children. The children quickly became familiar with the 'reduce, reuse and recycle' concept, with the Jack Johnson song being used as the transition and tidy up piece of music for the term. With this in mind, Jessica decided to use the parts of the plants that had been used.

The children looked at the work of Grace Ciao (www.graceciao.com), a young fashion designer, and Elzbieta Wodala (www.elzbietawodala_florotypie.republika.pl/), who uses dried flowers to make designs and impressive artworks. Importantly, Jessica made links with a local florist and supermarket who kindly agreed to provide her with the flowers that they would have thrown away that week. The children were given body templates and were asked to stick the petals of flowers, and any other parts of the flowers that they wanted to, down on the templates to create designs for new garments. Jessica provided the children with A3, A4 and A5 versions of the same templates as she thought the different scales might help the children to reimagine the parts of the plants as segments of garments in a wider range of ways. Once done, the children were encouraged to rework their designs by going back into them using water colour paints or fine tip felt-tip pens with water and fine brushes.

After this, the children looked at trashion – a fashion design form that holds to the principles of reducing, reusing and recycling materials to create new designs and responsible garments. The children worked in small groups to build on the flower design drawings using newspaper and masking tape to create a group design. This then progressed onto using a range of recycled materials to create a final garment. The children hosted a fashion show that parents and carers were invited to attend. This not only provided an opportunity for celebration but also established a rich environment for assessment. In groups the children were asked to present and talk about their design as it was being shown. The children spoke about their process, their choice of materials and the methods used to fix and join materials.

Jessica informed parents and carers of her plans for the D&T sessions. This not only enabled parents to become aware of what was planned, but it meant that materials for the trashion sessions were readily donated. Being mindful that some of her class had allergies to pollen, Jessica was also able to use this communication to ensure that parents could prepare the children by taking any preventative medical treatments that might be required. They could ensure that children could take any necessary preventative medication to enable the entire class to participate in the activities.

CASE STUDY: MAKE TEA NOT WAR

Kobe, a second-year BA (Hons) QTS top-up student, was on a placement in a year 5 (9–10 years old) class in a rural setting in North Yorkshire. As part of his placement, he was responsible for all foundation subject planning. The class teacher had decided that a local history study on a significant part of a local town's history would be the main focus for the term. Wider cross-curricular links were intended to be made to this where possible. Kobe decided to focus on a local tea manufacturer, looking at their history from the late 1800s to the present day. The children explored the physical, social and economic impact of the business upon its locality.

In D&T, the children were going to look at teabags. The teabag has a fascinating history, being first invented by accident by a merchant in 1908 who exported his tea in small sewn bags purely for shipping and packing purposes. When his customers received these packages, rather than taking the tea out of the bag, they simply placed the bag in the water and thus the teabag was born. The idea soon took off and, in World War I, the design was further developed to supply troops with tea in similar cotton bags known as 'tea bombs'.

The children were grouped into small teams of four, adopting names of local towns and villages and creating branding associated with their chosen name and the tea that they hoped to create. After providing the children with the history of the teabag, Kobe provided the children with a range of different teabags to explore, observe and raise questions about. In science, the children then undertook investigations into the impact of the size, shape and material of a teabag. After this, the children looked at fruit teas. The children tasted a range of flavour combinations to identify what composition of flavours they most liked. They selected a few flavours and explored dehydrating the relevant edible flowers, leaves, herbs and fruit, and undertook further science investigations to explore the impact of varying different quantities of ingredients on taste. The children also engaged in focused practical tasks that helped them develop the sewing skills required to make the teabags. When the children had the final results from their investigations, they worked in their groups to design and make their new teabag with their own original recipe inside. These were tested with their peers in a market research format, with their findings from this being presented in tables and links being made with their maths provision. After this, the children made the final tweaks to their designs and then launched their new products to parents and carers at a special after-school event arranged by the class. Finally, the children produced a report on their experience and sent it to the manufacturer suggesting that their products could be a good future line for the company.

(7–11 years old), as they will have had the opportunity to develop their personal design capital. However, Hope and Parkinson (2008) highlight that younger children in Foundation Stage (3–5 years old) and Key Stage 1 (5–7 years old) classes often have greater freedom when designing. As children progress through the primary phase, their designs can often be inhibited by teachers' preconceived schemes and ideas resulting in compromised designs. It is therefore of paramount importance that children are provided opportunties to go wherever the design process takes them.

Made objects can also provide an important stimulus for creative D&T (Table 4.1). Not only can made objects provide an exciting starting point for design but they can provide

Table 4.1 Table of ideas for designing from everyday objects

Item to be deconstructed	Curricular links	What will be discovered	The benefits on future steps in designing
Fabric books	• Design purposeful, functional, appealing products for themselves and other users based on design criteria • Select from and use a wide range of materials including textiles • Explore and evaluate a range of existing products	• Common stitching and joining techniques • Common padding methods • The types of materials that are used in such items • The colour, size and shape of the book at its pages	Without investigating the insides of the product, the children may find it hard to know what materials are needed to be included in their designs. In addition, the apparent complexity of the book, and particularly the joining methods used, may help children consider what materials they could use to make their own fabric books, such as Binca.
Moving cards	• Select from and use a wide range of materials and components, including construction materials • Explore and use mechanisms (for example, levers, sliders, wheels and axles), in their products. • Explore and evaluate a range of existing products	• The types of mechanisms found within moving cards • The parts that are needed for different types of mechanisms • How parts of moving mechanisms are joined • How materials are reinforced to provide durability and rigidity	By deconstructing this item, the children can get templates of successful mechanisms from which they can take numerous observations including measurements. This information, including information relating to materials and joints, will help the children construct their criteria for a successful moving card that can inform the design process.
Stuffed flatbreads	• Use research and develop design criteria to inform the design of innovative, functional, appealing products that are fit for purpose, aimed at particular individuals or groups • Select from and use a wider range of materials and components, including ingredients • Investigate and analyse a range of existing products • Understand and apply the principles of a healthy and varied diet • Prepare and cook a variety of predominantly savoury dishes using a range of cooking techniques	• Ratio of ingredients: often stuffed flatbreads are densely filled • Common combinations of flavours and ingredients • Common methods of stuffing • Children will be able to observe dough seams and joints • Common shapes and sizes	When undertaking food technology tasks, it can be common that there are children to whom the food products are new or unfamiliar. By deconstructing food products, children develop a new repertoire of tastes, techniques and ingredients. They also gain new and valuable vocabulary to describe the new tastes, techniques and ingredients. By deconstructing the product, children raise questions about what they find. This in turn naturally assists new vocabulary acquisition.

the blueprint for future designs as well. Hope (2004) suggests that by deconstructing everyday objects, children become familiar with how these objects are made. In addition, by deconstructing products, children begin to establish the rules of the product, assimilating a criterion of features that make this item successful and unique. This is crucial as often designs are new solutions to problems that others have previously attempted to solve. Problem-solving is a key component of outstanding primary D&T, and deconstructing objects can be an excellent way of doing this (Ofsted, 2011). By understanding how others have created a product, extracting key components and techniques, children can then build their designs. Most everyday products can be used in this way. The table below demonstrates how different objects can stimulate a world of design-and-making opportunities.

Using objects as a starting point opens up the opportunity for cross-curricular learning. Barnes (2015a) suggests that there are a range of models that can be adopted when undertaking cross-curricular teaching and learning. Often D&T is used as a subject to support learning in and across other disciplines. Unfortunately, all too often, this leads to narrow experiences with children making models of historic buildings or of geographical or celestial bodies such as volcanoes and the planets of the Milky Way (Ofsted, 2011). Put simply, this is not D&T. It is imperative when designing that the product user is given consideration. In addition, there must be a clear purpose for the design and attention paid to the products functionality. Although model-making may allow for consolidation of learning discovered in one subject, it does not permit the child to consider how the product will be used and if it meets the needs of the user. Teachers need to be particularly careful therefore when creating cross-curricular schemes involving D&T that this learning involves the key features involved in design. In addition, Barnes (2015a) also stresses that vast links across the curriculum should not be made when seeking to plan a cross-curricular project. He advocates that the most successful cross-curricular learning takes place when no more than four subjects are combined. The case study below highlights how quality D&T experiences can be incorporated within a cross-curricular scheme of work, using an object as a starting point.

THE ROLE OF BOOKS

Wilson and Harris (2004) highlight that there are numerous benefits on literacy and language learning as a direct result of engaging in design activities. It has long been established that good D&T teaching utilises contexts (Martin and Riggs, 1999). It is through this context that children can determine design requirements and evaluate the appropriateness of products. Fiction can be an immensely powerful context from which children can design products. A quality text grabs hold of a child's imagination in a way that makes the fantasy very real. Gripping description of characters, plots and settings make these come alive in a child's mind in a way that can make the lines between real and imagined seem blurred; capitalising on this assists the creative practitioner to success in D&T teaching. Reading a text as a class provides a shared experience that plunges the entire class into a new world with new people. As children get to know characters and come across dilemmas, opportunities for design open up.

Picture storybooks can also help to inspire children to develop crucial designing skills. *Dog Loves Drawing* by Louise Yates is an excellent example. The children can explore how a dog uses drawing to help solve and get him out of real scrapes. Elin Kelsey's *You*

Are Stardust also shows how design and making can influence creating storybooks. The clever illustrations give the impression of stage sets being designed with components of the illustration being suspended. This text could easily move into the children creating set designs for a favourite or chosen text to lead to a whole book being created. Table 4.2 seeks to explore how fiction texts can be used to inspire designing throughout the entire primary phase.

Some of the texts chosen may appear surprising as the intended audience is not directly linked to the age of the children in the identified curricular links. Hewlett (2016), however, highlights that texts intended for a younger age can be used as a successful starting point for children of an older age. Not only can these texts be explored in their entirety at the start of a designing topic with relative ease, but there is also limited impact on learning time and they can help fire imagination. Pages from picture storybooks can highlight design dilemmas for children. Using whole stories can cause children to encounter real-life issues that need design problems. Reading the wonderfully illustrated *Little Elephants* by Graeme Base, children could explore design solutions that would help Jim and his mum bring in the harvest before it is too late. The text here may appear to be relatively simple, but the design challenge that it brings requires a great deal of sophistication.

Non-fiction books can provide a wealth of starting points for creative D&T. There is a fantastic range of non-fiction books that can be drawn upon. The *Horrible Science* series by Tony De Saulles is especially successful at gaining children's interest and entices young children to explore how things work. David Macaulay's *The Way Things Work* is wonderfully illustrated and introduces key vocabulary associated with mechanisms in a way that provides useful information that can influence children's designs. These kinds of texts naturally promote the development of questions that can be explored. Through these experiences, children naturally move into investigating what they have found out through reading the text. For example, a child may read about the types of circuits found within Christmas tree lights; children can then explore by making these circuits and apply this knowledge. This can lead into the making of new products and should be seen as valid as a design process as the formal draw-and-make approach by practitioners.

The Boy Who Harnessed the Wind is an inspiring text by William Kamkwamba and Bryan Mealer. This extremely accessible biography relays William's moving design story. With his village in Malawi facing drought, William, aged 14, took to his local library to gain the knowledge to design and build a functioning windmill. Using scrap materials, he managed to design and build a windmill that harnessed the wind to provide electricity for his entire village. In this account, it is clear that the circumstances that William found himself in provided the scenario for design. Casakin (2016) suggests that presenting young designers' scenarios provides the most powerful design experiences. William's story helps to illustrate this point. Moving from this text, the children could look to design electricity-generating windmills using scrap materials. More importantly, however, using non-fiction texts like this demonstrates to children how young designers can have a real impact on the lives of others. All too often the design activities in the primary setting lack a sense of real-world impact, which can result in undermining the legitimacy of D&T teaching and learning. Texts like this help to bring a seriousness and purpose to the study of D&T that some children and adults may not have fully considered. It is for this reason alone that it is crucial that non-fiction texts are used in D&T teaching.

Table 4.2 Table of ideas for designing from children's storybooks

Book title and author(s)	Context developed	Curriculum links	Possible next steps when using the text
The Smartest Giant in Town by Julia Donaldson and Axel Scheffler	George the giant has given his tie to the giraffe to act as a scarf.	Select from and use a wide range of materials including textiles	The children can design a scarf to help George remain the smartest giant in town.
Pumpkin Soup by Helen Cooper	Where did the pumpkins come from? How could the duck, the cat and the squirrel make the soup?	Understand where food comes from	This book is an excellent starting point to discuss what it means to undertake a collaborative design and make. It is also good at highlighting the importance of getting the recipe right. The children could make their own soup from crops they had grown at school.
The True Story of the Three Little Pigs by Jon Scieszka and Lane Smith	The children are split into two teams – the defence and the prosecution. They need to create structures that help support their legal position either for or against Mr Wolf.	Build structures, exploring how they can be made , stronger stiffer and more stable	The children could be given the task of giving Mr Wolf an alibi or proving him guilty by creating structures out of straw, wood and brick.
Chitty Chitty Bang Bang: The Magical Car by Ian Fleming	Professor Potts needs your help to make alterations to Chitty Chitty Bang Bang to make her the best criminal-catching car she can be.	understand and use mechanical systems in their products (for example, gears, pulleys, cams, levers and linkages)	The children could make Chitty Chitty Bang Bang-inspired vehicles with axles and wheels to also include a trap involving the use of gears, pulleys, cams, levers or linkages.
The Iron Man by Ted Hughes	The Iron Man has been disassembled to be sent to Australia, only to be sent to us instead. Can you reassemble the Iron Man?	Understand and use electrical systems in their products (for example, series circuits incorporating switches, bulbs, buzzers and motors)	The children can design and make their own iron men that include series and parallel circuits with a range of components
The Tiny Seed by Eric Carle	The book starts in autumn. Children explore what seeds are available at what time of the year.	Understand , seasonality and know where and how a variety of ingredients are grown, reared, caught and processed	The children could grow sunflower seeds. The children can then dry out the sunflowers (this takes 3–4 days after harvesting). Once the seeds have been harvested, the children could design and make seed snack bars.

THE ROLE OF ENVIRONMENTS

Hill (1998) suggests that D&T teaching needs to move beyond a closed prescribed design, make and evaluate cycle. She advocates that when learning is placed in real-life contexts and environments, where real problems are explored, a sense of authenticity that inspires creative designing is developed that can motivate even the youngest of designers. Further to this, the programme of study for Key Stages 1 and 2 requires children to work in a range of environments and contexts (DfE, 2013).

Throughout the primary phase, children progress in their ability to design by moving from designing for themselves to designing for others. This takes considerable time and coincides with the child's development. This process is very dependent on children developing attitudes such as sympathy, empathy and curiosity, as well as developing skills such as listening and interpretation. When considering what constitutes a quality environment to be used as a starting point of design, the child's ability, attitudes and broader skills must be well thought-through. An early designer may use environments such as 'myself', 'my family', 'my classroom' and 'my home'. Towards the end of the primary phase, children are considering the needs of others, drawing on environments in the wider community locally, nationally and internationally as appropriate.

It has long been suggested that learning in the outdoor environment brings with it unique possibilities for learning (DfES, 2006). The outdoors can be an exciting environment to stimulate creative D&T. Shirley (2007) notes how children behave differently in the outdoor environment, suggesting that they exhibit characteristics that are much more associated with states of freedom. It could therefore be suggested that when designing in the outdoor environment, children may also be freer in their designing. This is a thrilling prospect for primary teachers that seek to enable creative designing among their class (more on using the outdoor environment in Chapter 11).

Museums and galleries can also inspire investigation. Looking at historic ways in which a design need has been met can stimulate new designs. Design can be inspired by artworks and art forms. When working in environments such as museums and galleries, there is the possibility that children may get overstimulated by the range of starting points that they come in contact with. Barnes (2015b) advocates providing focusing activities for the children when working in such environments. Some examples are:

Magic spot: In this activity, the teacher asks the children to stand in a space and face an object, environment or other stimulus. The teacher slowly takes the children through their five senses, getting the children to note their responses in any way that they feel is appropriate. The teacher discusses with the children what they observed. The teacher asks the children if they think they would have been able to make these observations if they had not engaged in the activity. Finally, the teacher asks the children to consider how these observations could inspire designs.

Take four: In this activity, the teacher asks the children to split an A4 page into four sections. In each section, the teacher gets the children to place the following heading: tone, texture, shapes, joins. Focusing on a single artefact, under each heading the teacher asks the children to make appropriate sketches, possibly with annotations. The teacher asks the children to share what they learnt from their drawings and how this may inform their designs.

Zoom in: With an A3 piece of paper, the children are asked to split it into four sections. In one of each of the sections, the teacher gets the children to place the following heading 0, x10, x20, x50. The teacher asks the children to focus on an object. In each of the boxes, the children can then draw the object or a section of the object at life size and then zoomed in 10, 20 and 50 times. With the children, the teacher explores why zooming in on an object can help when designing. The teacher discusses with the children what they discovered as a result of engaging in the activity.

When using environments such as museums and galleries, there is the opportunity for children to encounter contemporary issues that have ethical and moral dimensions. At the very heart of the making process is the use of materials – from animal skins and furs being used historically in clothing to where our food comes from. Museums and galleries highlight historical and current ethical issues. While it is not the role of a D&T practitioner to evangelically convert their children to a particular way of thinking, developing empathy is a key design attitude that also lies at the centre of what it means to be human. Using museums and galleries in creative D&T enables children to explore ethical issues in design both past and present, which in turn provides an opportunity to discover the views of others. By doing so, and by being sensitive to the needs and beliefs of the children in their class, a creative D&T practitioner can help develop a child's ability to empathise with others, which enriches their ability to design for the needs of others.

THE ROLE OF SPECIAL EVENTS

There is real potential to be capitalised on special events to realise creative D&T opportunities for children within the primary phase. Indeed, Jeffrey and Woods (2003) suggest that the very essence of creative teaching involves engaging learning through cycles, spirals and special events. They suggest that this form of experiential learning promotes a special opportunity for learning where meaning can be made through an interconnected, multi-perspectival and multi-leveled learning. At its very essence, creative D&T teaching that draws on special events helps provide a solid base for designing. Using special events as a starting point, particularly special events that children are, to some extent, familiar with, enables them to make links in designing that can assist creative learning within D&T that can have far-reaching impact on other areas of the curriculum.

When seeking to use festivals and special events, teachers need to ensure that they do not fall into the trap of thinking that undertaking crafts that link to or are inspired by a particular festival counts as quality D&T. Sadly when undertaking supposed D&T related to a festival, children are often made to produce set pieces and identical products. Again, this is not D&T. Although crafting can help children to engage in the sentiments of a season, considering the product user and the product's function as well as designing with a particular purpose is still required here. This said, special events and the legends associated with them can provide a rich starting point for designing. The case study below explores one such example.

CONCLUSION

Creative D&T can be generated through the use of a wide range of interesting and varied starting points. Objects, books, environments or special events can help stimulate curiosity and creativity in children of all ages. Interesting and varied staring points can lead children to design and make *products* that are original and imaginative, yet function as required for the intended user. When given a stimulating starting point, children have a real sense

CASE STUDY: A BASKET FOR BABUSHKA

Samuel, a final-year undergraduate student, undertook his last placement in a lower Key Stage 2 class in the winter months. With his class, he looked at the legendary story of Babushka. This tale that originates from Russian folklore tells of an elderly lady who is visited by the Wise Men on their way to seeing Jesus in Bethlehem. The story goes that the Wise Men invite Babushka to join them on their quest. Being an elderly and poor woman and overawed by the gifts that the Wise Men plan to take, she refuses and sends the Wise Men on their way. After thinking about it for a while, Babushka realises that in a cupboard she has stored up all the items that she needed for the wedding and children that she never had. She thinks that these would make excellent and practical gifts for the baby Jesus. She decides to load up her basket and join the Wise Men. She tries to find the Wise Men but sadly to no avail. Not being able to find the Wise Men, she resolves instead to leave gifts for all the children in their houses. The legend is that since this first Christmas Eve, Babushka has loaded up her basket and places a gift in each house in Russia that either meets a practical need or is of use.

Samuel spoke with the children about what they thought Babushka's basket looked like and how it was made. He decided that the best way to start designing baskets with the children was to undertake some newspaper modelling. He provided the children with newspaper and masking tape and asked them to model their initial first designs for a basket for Babushka.

The children undertook focused practical tasks using art-straws to explore weaving techniques. Looking at their newspaper designs and the skills learned through the focused practical tasks, the children then went on to make an improved basket design out of the straws. Samuel made links with a local secondary school through transition work he had undertaken in his placement, and invited the school's art technician in to work with the class. The technician led the children in a range of focused practical tasks to help develop their abilities in willow-weaving. Using their art-straw designs as a starting point, the children sought to make their design using willow withies. The children really benefitted from the expertise of the art technician. The links to the special event and the character link helped focus the children and gave a real sense of audience for their designing and making. This experience also opened up the opportunity to explore how special occasions are celebrated in different cultures and countries. This in turn gave an opportunity for Samuel to explore the British value of mutual respect for and tolerance of those with different beliefs in spiritual, moral, social and cultural (SMSC) sessions (Ofsted, 2015). When completed with their makes, the class held an assembly showing their designs and sharing the story of Babushka, widening the impact of mutual respect for others.

of purpose that can fire the imagination and transform the experience into a powerful teaching and learning opportunity.

REFERENCES

Archer, J. (2015) 'An introduction to design and technology', in Driscoll, P., Lambirth, A. and Roden, J. (eds) *The Primary Curriculum: A Creative Approach*. London: Sage.
Barnes, J. (2015a) *Cross Curricular Learning* (3–14). London: Sage.

Barnes, J. (2015b) 'An introduction to cross curricular learning', in Driscoll, P., Lambirth, A. and Roden, J. (eds) *The Primary Curriculum: A Creative Approach*. London: Sage.

Casakin, H. (2016) 'Approaches in design technology: the role of patterns and scenarios in the design studio'. *Problems of Education in the 21st Century*, 69, 6–21.

Craft, A. (2001) *An Analysis of Research and Literature on Creativity in Education: A Report*. London: Qualifications and Curriculum Authority.

Craft, A. (2005) *Creativity in Schools: Tensions and Dilemmas*. London: Routledge.

DfE (2013) *Design and Technology Programmes of Study: Key Stages 1 and 2 National Curriculum in England*. London: DFE.

DfES. (2006) *Learning Outside the Classroom Manifesto*. London: DfES.

Gray, C. (2013) 'Factors that Shape Design Thinking'. *Design Teachnology: An International Journal*, 18(3), 9–20.

Haffenden, D. (2004) 'Compliance and creativity? Compliance or creativity', in Norman, E. (ed.) *Creativity and Innovation, DATA International Research Conference* (79–88). DATA Sheffield University.

Hewlett, C. (2016) 'Science from stories', in Roden, J. and Ward, H. (eds) *Teaching Science in the Primary Classroom*. London: Sage.

Hill, A. (1998) 'Problem solving in real life contexts: an alternative for design in technology education'. *International Journal of Technology and Design Education*, 8, 203–220.

Hope, G. (2004) *Teaching Design and Technology 3 – 11: The Essential Guide for Teachers (Reaching the Standard)*. London: Continuum.

Hope, G. and Parkinson, E. (2008) 'Design across the curriculum: expanding opportunities for pupil agency and creativity'. *The British Educational Research Association Annual Conference*. Heriot-Watt University, Edinburgh, United Kingdom.

Jeffrey, B. and Woods, P. (2003) *The Creative School*. London: Routledge.

Martin, M. and Riggs, A. (1999) *Lost Contexts and the Tyranny of Products, IDATER 1999 Conference*. Loughborough: Loughborough University. Available at https://dspace.lboro. ac.uk/dspace-jspui/handle/2134/1400 (accessed 27 July 2016).

Ofsted (2011) *Meeting Technological Challenges?* London: Ofsted.

Ofsted (2015) *School Inspection Handbook from September 2015*. London: Ofsted.

Shirley, I. (2007) 'Exploring the great outdoors', in Austin, R. (ed.) *Letting the Outside In: Developing Teaching and Learning Beyond the Early Years Classroom*. London: Trentham Books.

Spendlove, D. and Stables, K. (ed.) (2010). *Ideas Worth Sharing: The Design and Technology Association Education and International Research Conference*. Keele University, United Kingdom.

Spendlove, D. and Wells, A. (2013) 'Creativity for a new generation' in Owen-Jackson, G. (ed.) *Debates in Design and Technology Education*. London: Routledge.

Stables, K. (2010) 'The inspiration pitch: where do design ideas come from?' *D&T – Ideas Worth Sharing: The Design and Technology Association Education and International Research Conference*. Keele University, United Kingdom.

Wilson, V. and Harris, M. (2004) 'Creating change? A review of the impact of design and technology in schools in england'. *Journal of Technology Education*, 15(2), 46–65.

CREATIVITY IN DESIGN

Remke Klapwijk

INTRODUCTION

This chapter is based on research and practice in Dutch schools and mirrors best practices that teachers in England are developing and undertaking. Designerly thinking is an excellent vehicle to develop creativity in classrooms and can be applied to any topic – from designing a digital game to learning mathematics, developing an accommodation for polar bears to organising an Easter party for parents.

However, creativity does not always come naturally. The good news is that skills for creativity in design can be developed at an early age and throughout our lives. As a teacher, you can create an environment in your classroom that will stimulate the development of creative design skills. Even a few changes in the design assignment and process guidance given will lead to enhanced creativity and skill development.

Based on various design and technology (D&T) projects conducted in Dutch schools, this chapter will present and discuss five key strategies to enhance creative thinking in design for pupils in the primary age phase (4–12 years).

WHAT IS CREATIVITY IN DESIGN?

The following quotation, often attributed to Albert Einstein, emphasises the creative and generative nature of design:

> Scientists investigate what already is, engineers create that which has never been.
>
> Albert Einstein

Creativity is always about something that is not yet there; it is about the future. Creativity is the ability to produce work that is both novel (original, unexpected) and appropriate (useful, relevant) (Sternberg and Lubart, 1999: 3). Through creative D&T projects, pupils learn to develop new or original solutions. For pupils in primary schools, the design outcomes do not have to be original in the sense that they have never been thought of before. Most important is that pupils create outcomes and solutions that are new for them.

The result is not copied, but a result of the pupils' imagination and therefore authentic. Cremin calls this type of creativity 'Little c, or personal, or everyday creativity, i.e. purposive imaginative activity generating outcomes that are original and valuable in relation to the learner' (Craft 2001; Cremin *et al* 2012: 77).

Creativity is characterised by Robinson (2001) as being at the heart of what it is to be human. Robinson also emphasises the need for finding and developing one's own passion. When pupils are allowed to use their imagination and to make their ideas in real life, they start to understand their own importance. They will discover their own uniqueness in projects that have no preconceived answers, because nobody else has exactly the same idea and prototype. The pupils learn to express themselves and will discover that their contributions are needed to feed the classroom community and also that they need contributions of other pupils to learn and develop a final solution. (There is more on creativity in Chapter 2.)

Although outcomes of pupils do not have to contribute to society at large, they frequently do. Quite a number of products exist only due to the creativity of young children.

■ **Figure 5.1** Maths game developed by primary school children

Both LEGO and IKEA produced toys that were designed by children. In one of the Delft University of Technology projects, Shannon's class developed an educational game that was brought onto the market. She proudly told the newspaper reporter: 'It is a strange idea that something that we have designed will be played by other people' (see Figure 5.1).

THE SOCIAL VALUE OF D&T

What is technology? Technology has a dual nature. On the one hand, technology is about materials, pins and nuts, hardware and tangible products. On the other hand, technology is about serving people and making life better. This makes designing a meaningful activity for pupils, especially when design problems are related to their own lives. Through D&T, pupils can become socially involved and participate. In it, they go beyond analysing problems as they develop ideas to solve the problems and bring hope and change.

AERODYNAMIC UMBRELLA

Umbrellas have been around for centuries but until very recently their design had hardly changed at all. As a result, the old-fashioned umbrella retained various design flaws – turning itself inside-out in strong winds and breaking easily.

The SENZ umbrella (see Figure 5.2) addresses these design flaws. Its aerodynamic form means that the umbrella always finds the best position in the wind, making it more comfortable to use. The umbrella's design means that it can withstand winds of up to force 10.

The idea to use an asymmetrical design came from a student of Industrial Design Engineering.

The rear of the SENZ is longer than the front. When a conventional round umbrella is caught by the wind, it will immediately tip so that the wind turns it inside-out. With the SENZ, the shorter side always turns to face the wind, meaning that it will actually catch less wind.

■ **Figure 5.2** The SENZ umbrella

Usually, lay people think that engineers focus mainly on high-tech innovations such as robotics or space science. However, there are a great many everyday life problems that are not yet solved. The new SENZ umbrella developed recently shows the value of designers for daily life and the value of the ability to 'find problems'. To develop creativity, it is important that pupils become aware of problems that are part of their living environment and are allowed to work on them.

EDUCATIONAL MODELS OF THE DESIGN PROCESS

Each design process is unique. All designers as well as pupils need to develop their own style and approach. For educational purposes, a number of cyclic models of design processes with primary school pupils have been developed. These models help to guide progression from a fuzzy problem situation to a concrete, tested solution. These can be useful, but it is important to remember that the process is neither linear nor cyclical in real life. It is iterative and pupils as well as designers move backwards and forwards throughout the process, changing their ideas and evaluating as they go along. This has been clarified in the latest National Curriculum for D&T in England (DfE, 2013).

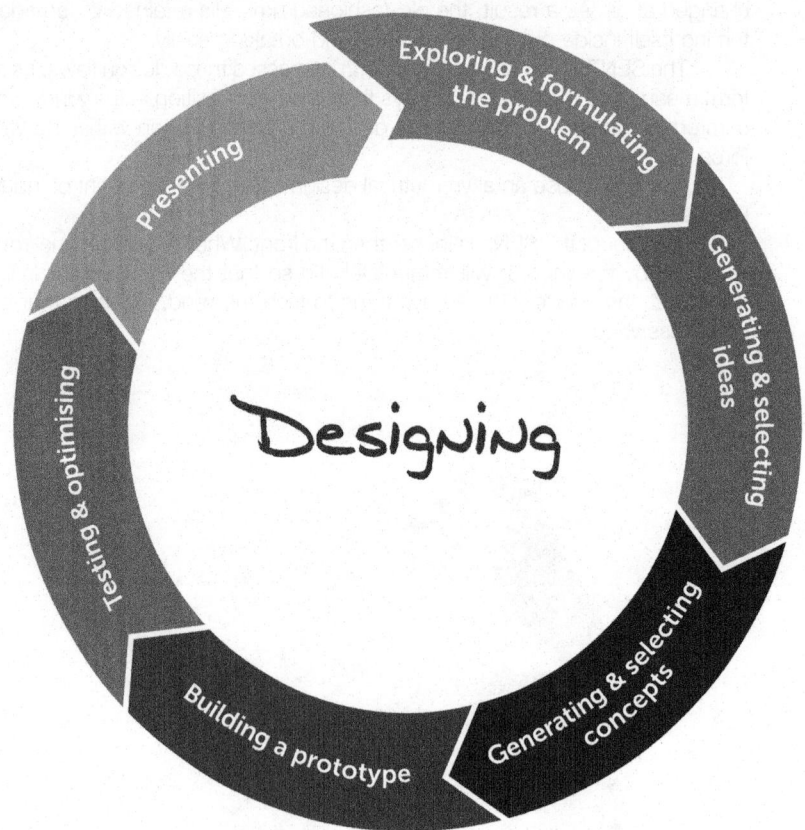

■ **Figure 5.3** Model of a design cycle

Source: Wetenschapsknooppunt TU Delft.

Six activities in a design process (see Figure 5.3) are illustrated using a biomedical design project. Pupils (8–12-year-olds) were asked to develop solutions for everyday routines for people with a limitation in their locomotor apparatus, for example, Dylan in a wheelchair or bus driver John who has only one arm.

EXPLORING AND FORMULATING

A design process can start with a problem or a wish, thinking about user and purpose. In this case, bus driver John loves to cook food but it is not easy to do the cooking with one arm. Through simulations, pupils experience the problem (see Figure 5.4). In addition, they conduct interviews with the user target group or use personas. Then a description of the problem and a design brief can be created.

■ **Figure 5.4** Simulations

GENERATING AND SELECTING IDEAS

Creative people spend a lot of time on the early front stage of a process (De Bono, 1973). Therefore, a generative session to think of as many solutions as possible is often organised in the creative design process. Various divergent techniques are applied to develop varied and original ideas. Figure 5.5 shows ideas to enable Dylan, who needs a wheelchair, to play marbles: for example, lowering the wheelchair or playing marbles at a table.

Next, the pupils' design team can select one or two ideas. As they discuss the qualities of the ideas from the brainstorm and converge towards a few ideas, they apply evaluative and critical thinking. What is special about the idea? How does it solve the problem?

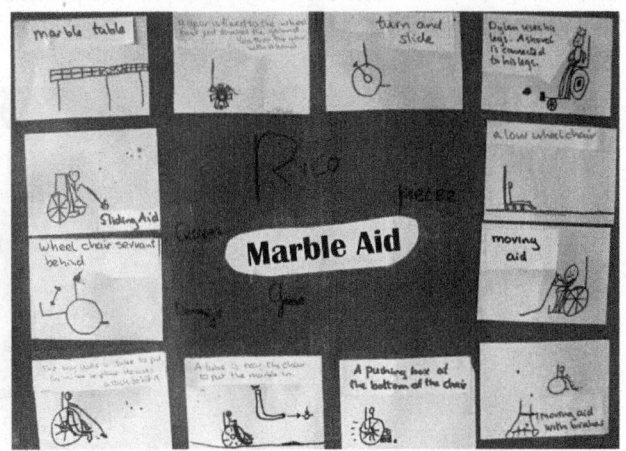

■ **Figure 5.5** Generating ideas

ELABORATING AND SELECTING CONCEPTS

In this activity, a coherent picture of the solution and its elements emerges. The drawing in Figure 5.6 shows how equipment to play marbles is attached to a regular wheelchair.

BUILDING A PROTOTYPE

Building a prototype takes place. Usually, building and testing are done in an iterative way. Iteration is 'doing the same activity again but in a different way'. Small variations are tried and tested. During the testing of the chair, the pupils found out that the marble got stuck at the bend. They solved it by realising that a test with the marble was not proper and did it again with a small glass bead. When the prototype does not work as intended, pupils may even develop a new concept (elaborating the idea) or redefine the problem.

TESTING

Here we show another example from the biomedical design project. A milk opener for Uncle John, who has only one arm, is tested (see Figure 5.7). Although, the milk was spilt when

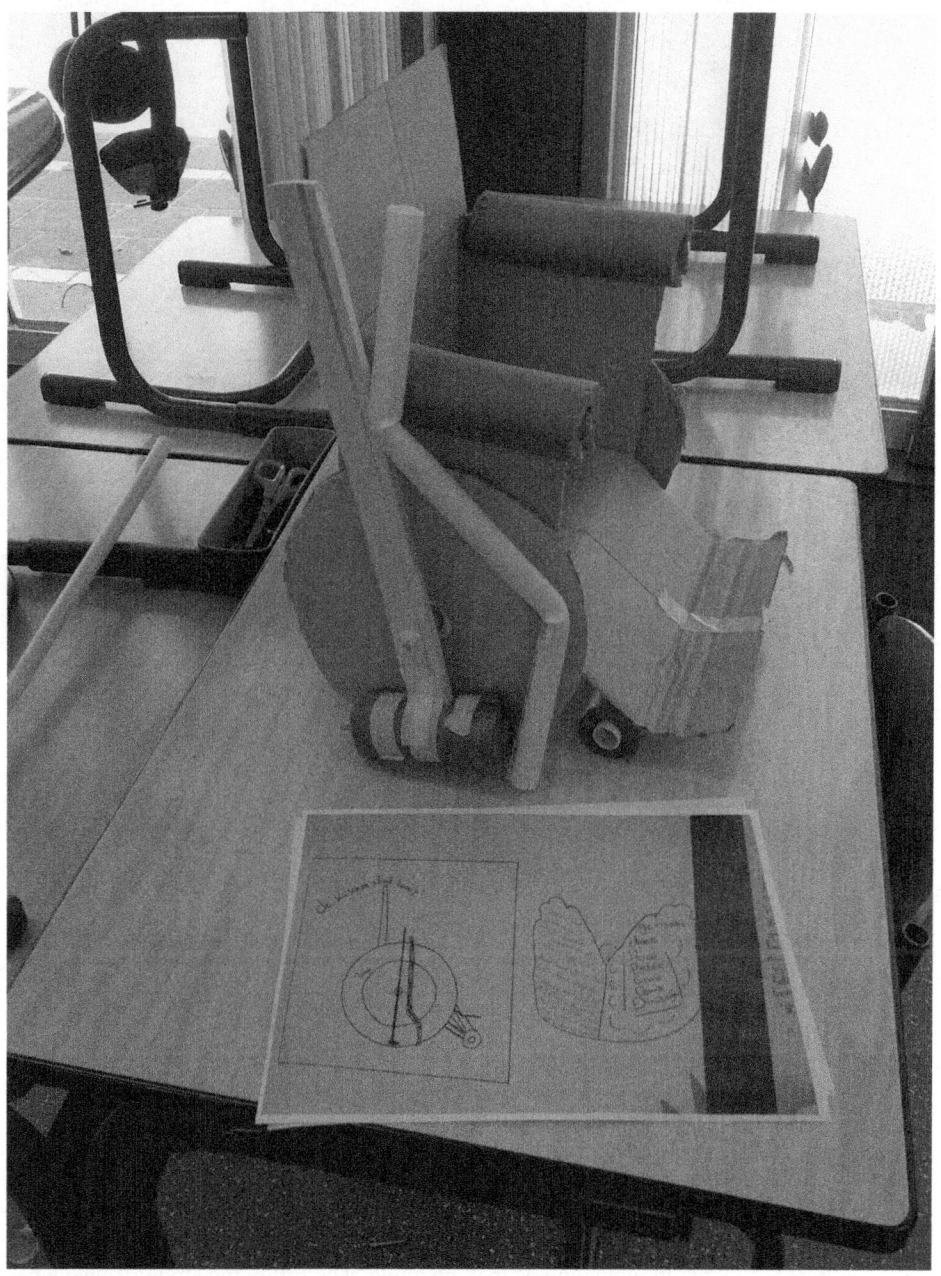

Figure 5.6 Elaborating the concept

▧ **Figure 5.7** Testing a solution to open a milk bag

the bag of milk was thrown on the nails, it is evaluated as a promising solution. The dominant principle used – throwing – is original as most children develop solutions based on 'turning'.

PRESENTING

Communication and sharing ideas takes places during the whole process. Pupils may present their final solution to a variety of stakeholders.

A design cycle is well known and there are many variations. The model supports teachers, developing and scaffolding problem-oriented working and creativity, but just following the model is not enough to develop creativity. In practice, the design process is iterative (see Figure 5.8) inspired by the Delft Design Guide.

Rigid application of the design cycle model can hamper creativity (Atkinson, 2000). Use the idea of iterative design to overcome this. Encourage pupils to move backwards and forwards throughout their designing and making, evaluating what they have done and making any changes they think appropriate, rather than following a rigid step-by-step approach, without evaluating as they go along. The following strategies have been trialled and have proved useful in planning for creativity in D&T projects.

STRATEGIES TO STIMULATE CREATIVITY

During our research, we developed the following five strategies that can help plan for creativity.

Figure 5.8 The iterative nature of a design process

(inspired by a picture in Van Boeijen *et al.*, 2014)

The first strategy is about getting the pupils started:

■   Open problem formulation and time to experience it with all the senses

The next three strategies help to stimulate the flow of imagination during the design process but also the purposeful elaboration and testing of their ideas:

■   Shifting between divergent thinking and convergent thinking
■   Using energisers and divergent-thinking techniques
■   Embracing 'failure' through iteration

Finally assessment for learning can be applied. Through it, a class develops ideas about quality in design and will develop creative design skills in a conscious way:

■   Integrating formative assessment

STRATEGY 1 OPEN PROBLEM FORMULATION

To enable creativity, it is crucial to use an open problem formulation. This is a formulation that allows many solutions in different directions. Compare, for example, the approach of these two teachers.

> Anna reads a story about a bridge that has been blown away. She asks her children to build a new, strong bridge.
> Mary reads the same story. The children feel sorry for the villagers who cannot meet anymore nor bring relief supplies to the other side of the river. Mary places a big blue paper in the front of the classroom and asks: how can people and supplies move from one side to another.
> Both Mary and Anna provide each design team of three pupils with a bag containing different construction materials.

Open problem formulations do not usually contain nouns because nouns point to existing objects. Instead a verb is used because verbs focus on the function that will be provided, for example, crossing the river. A function can be fulfilled by different objects, for example, a bridge or a cableway.

How-Tos are problem formulations written in the form of questions that stimulate children to think of ideas in many directions. For example, 'how can people and relief supplies cross the river in a fast way?'

You can make your own How-To formulation in the following way:

1   Start with a How-To, How can? or How should I?
2   Use a verb that describes the service that needs to be provided.
3   This is often followed by a specific challenge – something that needs to be improved.
4   You may add a specification of the situation or target group.

Examples of How-To (H2) formulations

■ How to carry luggage in an airport?
■ How can knights and ladies living in the Middle Ages protect themselves effectively against enemies?
■ How can a boy in a wheelchair play marbles?

When you hesitate about your formulation, check the level of openness of your problem formulation by asking yourself why you want to achieve the goal mentioned. For example, you are planning to ask your pupils to design a garbage can (Holla *et al*., 2016). Starting from there, you ask yourself: why is a garbage can needed? Your answer is: because we want a clean schoolyard. Your next question is: why do we need a clean schoolyard? When answering becomes difficult – for example, a clean schoolyard is just nice – you have probably arrived at an open question that is still focused. The final design question evolves: how can we keep the schoolyard clean and pretty? The right level of abstractness is important in How-To questions (Van Boeijen *et al*., 2014).

Csikszentmihalyi (1996) interviewed about 100 successful creative artists and scientists and noticed that their passion about a problem led to creative flow. Therefore, children should not only understand design problems in a cognitive way, but also empathise with the problem and the intended users before they start idea generation.

During the problem exploration, a link needs to be established between the pupil and the problem situation. For most pupils, it is helpful to experience the problem with all their senses. The following techniques stimulate empathy:

1   Demonstrating the problem in a scale-model
2   Reading a story book
3   Using simulations
4   Having an interview with users
5   Using personas

Teacher Mary in the example demonstrated the problem by using blue paper for the river. This can be done on a small scale, but it is also possible to use chalk to make a huge river on the schoolyard or to go to a real stream.

Stories are meant to connect to its characters and their problems. Many storybooks or movies contain problems that are suitable for D&T projects. For example, in the storybook 'Rabbit and Mole' (De Beer, 2014), the rabbit was wounded when he crossed a busy motorway. He wants to get back to his friends, but cannot cross it by walking. Can you help him?

Interviews with real people were used in the biomedical project. For example, one girl noticed that her uncle was not able to clean his own glasses and started working on a solution together with her classmates.

It is not always possible to provide pupils with direct contact with users. A persona can help to develop empathy as well. Personas are archetypical representations of intended users for whom the children will design. The wishes, needs and behaviour of a fictitious person are described in an interesting way.

DYLAN

During break time, Dylan (10 years old) races with his wheelchair in the playground. His friends find it cool to hold on to the wheelchair and roller-skate. Dylan has the nickname 'Bumper' because he pushes objects away with his wheelchair. He loves to participate in other games in the playground. Playing marbles looks great to him or playing hockey. But how can you play marbles when you are in a wheelchair?

In the biomedical design project, personas such as Dylan were presented. The pupils became strongly connected to Dylan. For example, Ben had spent a great deal of time thinking – mainly when he was playing himself – about how Dylan wanted to play. He then added many additional ideas about Dylan's wishes to the original assignment.

Teachers and pupils can also make their own personas. A possible procedure is given below (Van Boeijen *et al.*, 2014: 95; Klapwijk and Van Doorn, 2015).

▨ Collect a rich amount of information and insights on intended users.
▨ Select characteristics that are most representative of your target group and most relevant to your design project.
▨ Create three to five personas.
   – Give each persona a name;
   – Use text and a picture to describe the persona;
   – Add some demographics such as age, job;
   – Include the major responsibility and goal/wish of the persona.

When you present design problems, allow problem exploration through one or more of the above presented techniques.

STRATEGY 2 SHIFTING BETWEEN DIVERGENT AND CONVERGENT THINKING

Many researchers in both the field of design and the field of creativity have emphasised the two different kinds of thinking modes in creativity (De Bono, 1973; Lubart, 2000–2001; Isaksen, *et al.*, 2011):

▨ Divergent thinking
▨ Convergent thinking

(More on divergent and convergent thinking in Chapter 12.)

Divergent thinking is the process to create many, varied and original ideas in a fluent way. According to scientists in the creative cognition tradition, one should start with generating as many ideas as possible using all kinds of media. Through a process of association and recombination, new ideas pop up.

Convergent thinking is a process that goes in the other direction and is about making sense of the many ideas. This process ends with a single, very concrete outcome.

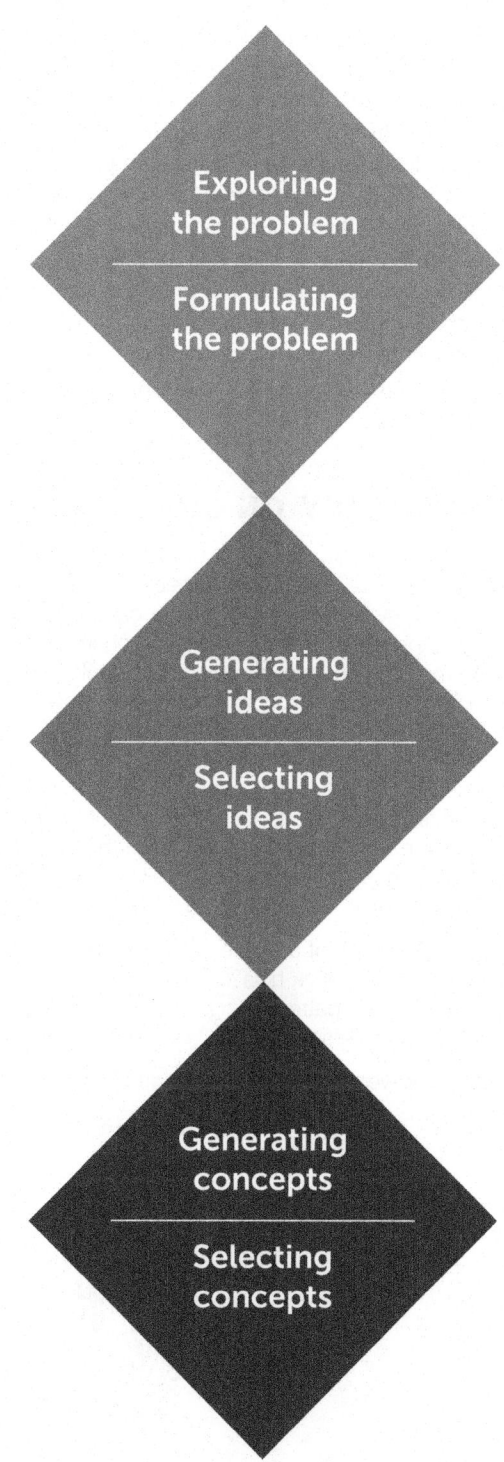

Figure 5.9 The design process as a series of diamonds

Source: Wetenschapsknooppunt TU Delft.

Both thinking modes need to be developed, starting at primary schools, and should get their proper place in designing. Atkinson (2000) discovered that especially creative children are hampered by the rigid way schools apply a design cycle model.

Knowing about this problem, we applied the Creative Problem Solving (CPS) Approach (Tassoul, 2009; Isaksen *et al.*, 2011) in primary schools. In the CPS Approach, the divergent- and convergent-thinking modes are explicitly separated (see Figure 5.9).

The CPS or Diamond Approach is especially valuable in the first three stages: problem formulation, idea generation and idea elaboration. Later on, during making and testing, both thinking modes are also present, but much more intertwined.

Divergent thinking on the problem will result in finding an interesting problem to work on or an interesting perspective on the problem. The various techniques to explore problems described in the previous section all stimulate divergent thinking. Pupils develop

GUIDED FANTASY ON SPACE EXPLORATION

In this project, pupils designed new exhibitions about outer space for a science centre. (See Chapter 11 for more on activities outside the classroom.)

The pupils went outside to the school garden and guided fantasy and collage techniques were applied. The change of atmosphere and these techniques stimulated the children's emotional connection with space exploration.

Pupils first listened to a story in which they travelled in space, usually with closed eyes and sitting and laying on the grass. They developed images and authentic questions on space. Next, we led the pupils directly to a table full of colourful pictures, most not about space at all, and asked the pupils to express their curiosity about space in a collage. They were not allowed to talk at all about their experience, because analytical thinking would harm the stories that arose from their hearts.

Using the collages, for example the one in Figure 5.10 they shared their questions about space. Beautiful and fascinating questions arose:

▨ How does the inside of a space shuttle work?
▨ What is behind the black hole?
▨ Does space have a pattern?
▨ How does the universe smell?

The questions were used to generate ideas for new exhibits in the science centre.

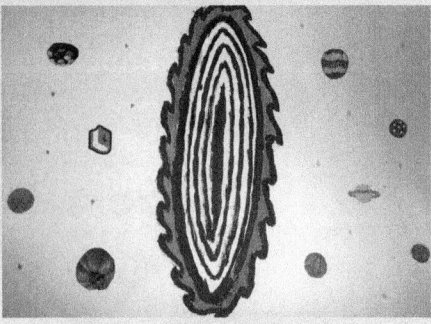

▨ **Figure 5.10** What is behind the black hole?

a deeper understanding of the various aspects of the problem and became passionate about specific problems and users. In the subsequent convergent-thinking stage, pupils will determine for whom to design and for which daily situation and formulate How-To questions.

The two different thinking modes each require their own classroom conditions. Based on Howard-Jones (2002), I will discuss the favourable conditions of divergent thinking because these are less known than the conditions for convergent thinking.

■ Relaxation: Relaxation is helpful to develop associations and new combinations of existing elements. In a controlled experiment, Forgays and Forgays (1992) showed that adults scored higher in an alternate-uses test after a relaxing session in a floating tank.

■ No competition: Various studies show that divergent thinking is not served by competition, probably because it encourages a goal-oriented mentality that hampers divergent thinking (Amabile, 1996).

■ Change of climate: This also stimulates associative thinking (Howard-Jones, 2002).

The guided fantasy project on a new space science centre exhibit is a practical example of these conditions.

STRATEGY 3 USING ENERGISERS AND VARIOUS DIVERGENT-THINKING TECHNIQUES

Teachers usually have experience with convergent-thinking strategies. Divergent and especially generative thinking are relatively new in schools. Therefore, we describe a number of techniques that are helpful for this thinking mode. Below, we present a number of the favourite techniques of Dutch teachers and in-service teachers. These are part of a toolbox available in Dutch and are translated from professional design practice to the primary school situation (Holla *et al.*, 2016).

In design, it is quite common to organise idea-generation sessions once the problem has been defined. These idea-generation sessions start usually with an energiser and are followed by a brainstorm session based on generative or divergent techniques.

A well-known energiser is the human knot. In a circle, people put their arms in and hold someone else's hand, then try to unravel the knot without letting go of hands. This activity involves getting physically close to others, stretching, laughing and problem-solving.

Another energiser is related to materials for rapid prototyping. The pupils are asked to think of other uses for these materials. For example, I can drink with a straw, but also use it as a spoon or make a small mouse slide from it when I cut it in half.

These energisers are used before the actual brainstorm. Pupils get connected, have fun and it helps them during the brainstorm to freely express all the ideas they have.

Brainstorming is usually done in teams of three to five pupils. In brainwriting, each pupil writes his or her ideas on a post-it and sticks them on the shared group paper. While doing this, the pupil says the idea out loud, which may inspire others to associate further on the idea, while staying in their own flow. In 20 minutes, a class may have developed over 200 ideas (Klapwijk and Sjoer, 2011).

A similar technique is the hand-over drawing. Each pupil draws on a paper with twelve boxes a few ideas and passes the drawing over to the next. Additional inspiration may arise when the teacher asks the children to think about a figure from a fairy tale and use this to develop more ideas. A similar strategy is described by Howard-Jones (2002) where children were asked to travel on a 'brain-train' – an imaginary train that stopped at different parts of their minds (their last holiday, their favourite TV show) during idea generation (more on drawing in Chapter 6).

Finally, for young children we use the idea-starter (see Figure 5.11). The little boy in the boat wants to go to the island. How can he cross the rocks sticking out of the water? Each child gets a picture of the situation and draws his or her ideas. The techniques allow introvert children to think about an idea before they share it.

Mednick (1962) relates creativity to the ability to draw connections between previously unconnected ideas. Pupils who have access to remotely associated ideas have more ideas available for combination into original concepts. Sharing ideas is one way to bring in different perspectives and ideas. Research shows that pupils using divergent-thinking techniques generate considerably more original ideas than when simply asked for all the ideas they could think of (Howard-Jones, 2002).

Brainstorming with materials is also possible. In the mystery bag approach (Holla *et al.*, 2016), each team gets the same problem but different building materials to solve it and build rapid prototypes.

During brainstorming, pupils need to learn to postpone judgement and to value any idea at this stage. Use brainstorm rules to develop an open atmosphere.

To prepare for divergent thinking, small exercises can be used, such as the alternate-uses exercise developed by creativity researcher Torrance (1966). In this exercise, pupils think of many other ways to use a product. For example, the teacher shows a compact disc (CD) and asks: what are other uses for a CD? Think of as many as you can. There is no good or bad; all answers are good! A CD is also a pizza cutter, a frisbee, a hat . . .

▨ **Figure 5.11** Idea-starter

BRAINSTORM RULES

▨ Everything is allowed
▨ Postpone your judgement
▨ Create as many ideas as possible
▨ Ideas are owned by everyone!
▨ 1+1=3
▨ Draw
▨ Give each other compliments

Holla *et al.*, 2016

STRATEGY 4 ITERATION, RAPID PROTOTYPING AND EMBRACING FAILURE

In reality, design processes are not linear. The recent literature clarifies the value of iteration as an essential part of the design process (Martinez and Stager, 2013). The makers-education stream expresses this by the word tinkering. The emphasis is on learning through making and testing, and things that do not work directly are greatly valued. Bamberger and Cahill (2013), who describe the practice of teaching engineering design, include a stage of redesigning and rebuilding. Design concepts become complete through iteration of analysis, synthesis and evaluation (Chusilp and Jin, 2006).

Question: Watch the movie 'Designing for knights and ladies'. What do the children discover when they test their swords?

www.ontwerpenindeklas.nl

In D&T, it is important to allow for tinkering, iteration and playful experimenting by pupils. In the spontaneous playing behaviour of pupils, there is a lot of iteration to observe (Looijenga *et al.*, 2015). Playing includes experimenting with the same thing, with small variations, over and over again (Gopnik, 2012).

How is it possible to organise these iterations in your classroom? We can learn from Looijenga, a kindergarten teacher at a Dutch Montessori school, who conducted research on the effect of iteration on playfulness, creativity and learning (Looijenga *et al.*, 2015). She gave a class of 8-year-olds the following design challenge: How can you use and fold a sheet of aluminium foil, with a fixed size, to let as many marbles as possible float on it?

In her approach, three phases of 45 minutes were organised. Each time, the same design assignment was given.

▨ During the first phase, each pupil had to make its first carrier, while cooperating and deliberating with another child, chosen by itself. After this, the pupils were free to continue and build more carriers or select another assignment.

- In the second phase, they had to make a carrier together with another pupil, chosen by the teacher.
- The third phase offered the pupils a lot of freedom. They were allowed to make a carrier on their own or in pairs with a self-selected partner. They could also choose to do an alternative handicraft activity.

The pupils had ample room for testing their carriers in a number of small washtubs and in a big tub in front of the (research) camera. When testing was done in the big tub, they had to tell 'the camera' how they made it and why they had made it that way, before filling the carrier with marbles. After the explanation, they put the marbles on, until the carrier sank.

By trial and error, the pupils made a lot of different designs in the first stage. Most pupils were at first not aware of the importance of having a big surface to put the marbles on.

At the end of the first phase, the pupils gathered for an evaluation. All carriers were shown from those that had the least to those that contained the most marbles, and the teacher asked the pupils if they could see reasons why a certain carrier was better than another in bearing marbles. Some thought a high edge was important, but soon understood that a large base was of greater importance.

In the second phase – approximately a week later – the teacher gave the design assignment again, but now she made the pairs of two pupils with a difference in approach. The pupils did not show much motivation at the start; they showed shyness and were careful in making contact with their partner, but soon became enthusiastic. The average number of marbles increased from 40 to 116 and building techniques changed.

In the third phase, about half of the children selected the carrier assignment, noting 'we want to improve the carrier more to get a new record' or 'we like it very much'. At the end of the project, all pupils in the class understood why their carriers became better and a great many of them could tell this verbally, for example, 'this is my third boat (today), it is entirely flat with a small edge'.

The largest variety of designs was detected in the second phase, whereas children optimised the best working carrier in the third phase. They followed an iterative process of divergent and convergent working. Testing leads to one or more new ideas that are made and tested again.

The repetition of the assignment, as well as the many testing facilities and different partners to work with, gave them the necessary experience to design high-quality solutions. Through iteration, their knowledge and insights and explanation in words have grown. This is in accordance with Maria Montessori's observation (1912) that children first have to experience, before they are able to explain and identify in words. There is even evidence that in some cases, young children are much better problem-solvers than average grown-ups because they are very playful, and explore and iterate more than adults usually do. They succeed, for example, better in the Marshmallow challenge than average grown-ups (Wujec, 2016).

In summary, providing room for iteration is beneficial for creativity and learning. As a teacher, you support iteration by creating the following conditions (Looijenga *et al.*, 2015):

- Use an open problem formulation that has a tangible goal that allows for self-correction.

■ Allow freedom of choice in the way pupils conduct the experimenting.

■ Organise testing facilities; make the pupils independent in their experimenting and let hands and minds interact.

■ Stimulate explanation in the convergent-thinking stages and help pupils to generate ideas for further explorations.

■ Give sufficient time for various iterations.

Be careful to limit initially the amount of analytical questions (such as, is it strong enough?) during the divergent-thinking stages, and to encourage exploration and extension of the first ideas, for example, what other forms are possible? What other features could be added? Are there different ways to mould the aluminium?

Failure of the design during testing is a natural way of learning and supports the detection of scientific misconceptions. Failure should not be seen as a problem, but as a source of pleasure. For example, a team at a school for special educational needs designed and built a place for the teacher's dog. The pupils carefully measured the dog and built a dog kennel with exact measurements. When it was finished, the dog was brought in, and the children discovered that by using exact measurements the dog was cramped in his new kennel. I assume that they will never forget this experience and will use it in subsequent building projects.

STRATEGY 5 ASSESSMENT OF CREATIVE THINKING

A final strategy to increase creativity is formative assessment of skills related to the creative process, product and personality. Quite often, teachers and children are not aware of what they can learn through a design process and may even think that learning new scientific concepts is the only learning goal. Sharing learning intentions in combination with eliciting and interpreting the pupils' achievement is an effective strategy in developing creativity.

What do children learn exactly when they learn to be creative? Based on a literature search for design education and creativity, the following skills are considered the most relevant for primary school pupils (see Figure 5.12) (Klapwijk *et al.*, 2016):

1   Think in all directions (divergent thinking)
2   Develop empathy
3   Make productive mistakes (early and frequent iteration)
4   Make ideas tangible (convergent thinking)
5   Share ideas (communication)
6   Define your direction
7   Make use of the process and develop your own style (meta-cognitive skills)

Summative assessment of these skills is difficult, however, because fixed standards and rules are absent. Each context, design assignment and child may ask for a different creative approach. In formative assessment, the focus is different. Wiliam (2011: 43) writes:

An assessment functions formatively to the extent that evidence about student achievement is elicited, interpreted, and used by teachers, learners or their peers to make decisions about the next steps in instruction that are likely to be better, or better founded, than the decisions that would have made in absence of that evidence.

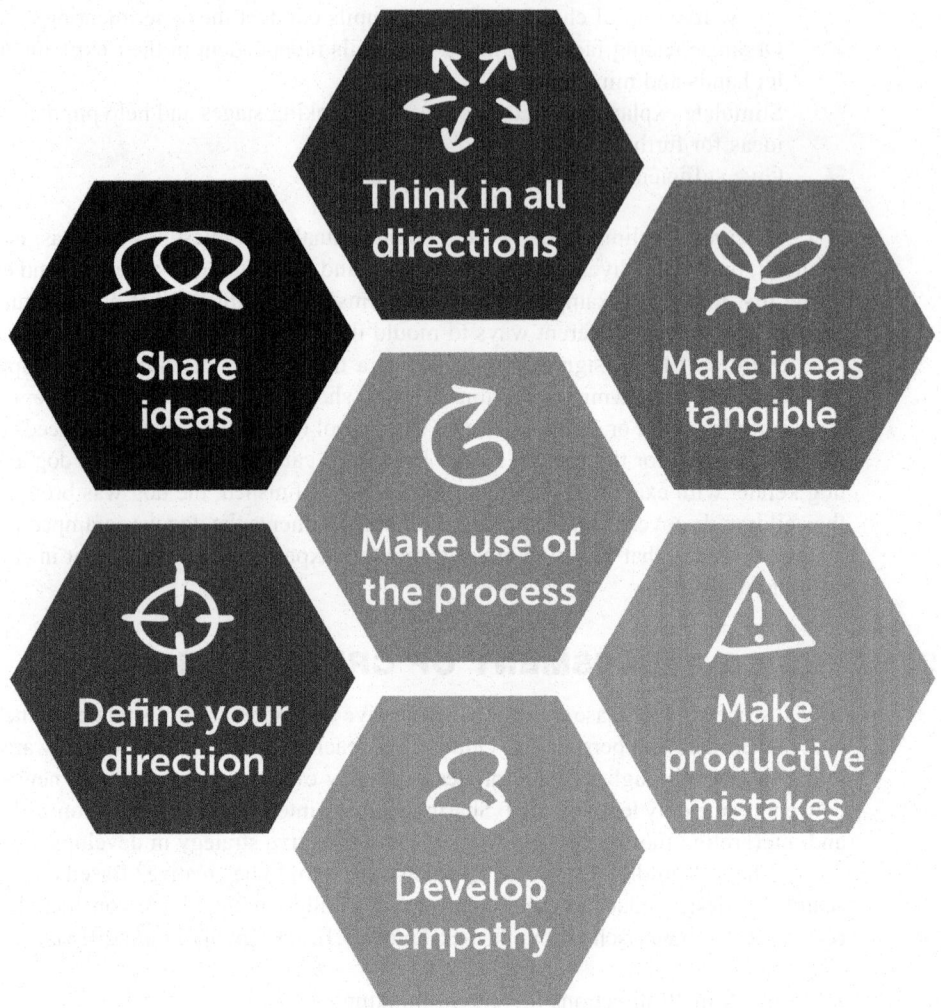

■ **Figure 5.12** Design skills (Klapwijk and Van Doorn, 2015; Klapwijk *et al.*, 2016)

Formative assessment of divergent thinking has been more beneficial for the development of creativity than summative assessment. Research from Butler (1988) shows that pupils who get specific feedback from their teacher on the ideas they generated during the Torrance alternate-uses exercise demonstrate progress of 30 per cent in the next exercise. Pupils whose teachers gave only scores for their results or gave both scores and specific comments did not improve at all in the next test.

Another way to elicit evidence of learning is to organise first a short classroom discussion on one or more skills. Next, during the design process, pupils are asked to give each other tip-offs on this skill by sticking memos on a board. Other pupils can use these to reflect on their own design strategy and, if necessary, apply a new strategy. Literature shows that when research skills are discussed and peer-reviewed in secondary science education, great results are booked, and especially low performers perform a lot better (White and Frederiksen, 1998).

It is important, however, that formative evaluation does not interfere with divergent-thinking activities. Feedback – even self-feedback – is considered to undermine intrinsic motivation (Deci and Ryan, 1985; Howard-Jones, 2002). According to Wiliam (2011), feedback should be specific and contain a message of hope – showing how one has done well in the past and can improve through practice.

CONCLUSION

Teachers make a difference when designing. They can greatly enhance the development of pupils' ideas by applying key strategies such as using open but tangible identified problems, giving pupils the opportunity to experience the problem, looking at solutions from different perspectives and sharing ideas or solutions when planning for creativity. A teacher might think about the balance between divergent and convergent thinking or how ideas are generated and supported using brainstorming rules and the classroom environment. Not all strategies in this chapter need to be applied at the same time but considering one or two during a design lesson could develop the right conditions for creativity in design.

REFERENCES

Amabile, T. (1996) *The Social Psychology of Creativity*. New York: Springer-Verlag.
Atkinson, S. (2000) 'Does the need for high levels of performance curtail the development of creativity in design and technology project work?' *International Journal of Technology and Design Education*, 10(3), 255–281.
Bamberger, Y. and Cahill, C. (2013) 'Teaching design in middle-school: instructors' concerns and scaffolding strategies'. *Journal of Science Education and Technology*, 22(2), 171–185.
Butler, R. (1988) 'Enhancing and undermining intrinsic motivation: the effects of task-involving and ego-involving evaluation on interest and performance'. *British Journal of Educational Psychology*, 58(1), 1–14.
Chusilp, P. and Jin, Y. (2006) 'Impact of mental iteration on concept generation'. *Transactions of the ASME*, 128, 14–25.
Craft, A. (2001) 'Little c creativity', in Craft, A., Jeffrey, B. and Liebling, M. (eds) *Creativity in Education*. London: Continuum.
Cremin, T., Craft, A. and Clack, J. (2012) Creative little scientists: enabling creativity through science and mathematics in preschool and first years of primary education, D2.2. Conceptual Framework, Addendum 2 of 4. *Literature Review of Creativity in Education*, www.creative-little-scientists.eu (accessed 14 July 2016).
Csikszentmihalyi, M. (1996) *Flow and the Psychology of Discovery and Invention*. New York: Harper Collins.
De Beer, H. (2014) *Haas en Mol zoeken een uitweg*. Rijswijk: De Vier Windstreken.
De Bono, E. (1973) *Lateral Thinking: Creativity Step by Step*. New York: Harper & Row.
Deci, E. and Ryan, R. (1985) *Intrinsic Motivation and Self-determination in Human Behavior*. New York: Plenum.
Department for Education (DfE) (2013) www. gov.uk/national-curriculum-in-england-design-and-technology (accessed 25 June 2016).
Forgays, D. and Forgays, D. (1992) 'Creativity enhancement through flotation isolation'. *Journal of Environmental Psychology*, 12, 329–335.

Gopnik, A. (2012) 'Scientific thinking in young children: theoretical advances, empirical research, and policy implications'. *Science*, 337, 1623–1627.

Holla, E., Kok, E., Visschedijk, J. and Klapwijk, R. (2016) www.ontwerpenindeklas.nl, (accessed 15 May 2016).

Howard-Jones, P. (2002) 'A dual-state model of creative cognition for supporting strategies that foster creativity in the classroom'. *International Journal of Technology and Design Education*, 12(3), 215–226.

Isaksen, S., Dorval, K. and Treffinger, D. (2011) *Creative Approaches to Problem Solving: A Framework for Innovation and Change*. Los Angeles: Sage.

Klapwijk, R. and Sjoer, E. (2011) 'Ontwikkelen en begeleiden van creatief technisch ontwerpen in de middenbouw'. *Kennisconferentie Talentontwikkeling en Wetenschap & Techniek*, 27 mei. Platform Bèta/Techniek, Oegstgeest.

Klapwijk, R. and Van Doorn, F. (2015) 'Context mapping in primary design and technology education: a fruitful method to develop empathy for and insight in user needs'. *International Journal of Technology and Design Education*, 25(2), 151–167.

Klapwijk, R., Kok, E., Visschedijk, J. and Robbertsen, R. (2006) 'Toolbox for formative evaluation'. on www.ontwerpenindeklas.nl (in Dutch: Ontwerpen in Beeld).

Looijenga, A., Klapwijk, R. and de Vries, M. (2015) 'The effect of iteration on the design performance of primary school children'. *International Journal of Technology and Design Education*, 25(1), 1–23.

Lubart, T. (2000–2001) 'Models of the creative process; past, present and future'. *Creative Research Journal*, 13, 295–398.

Martinez, S. and Stager, G. (2013) *Invent to Learn: Making, Tinkering, and Engineering in the Classroom*. Torrance. CA: Constructing Modern Knowledge Press.

Mednick, S. (1962) 'The associative basis of the creative process'. *Psychological Review*, 69, 220–232.

Montessori, M. (1912) *The Montessori Method*. New York: Fredrick A. Stokes Company.

Robinson, K. (2001) *Out of Our Minds: Learning to Be Creative*. Chichester: Capstone.

Sternberg, R. and Lubart, T. (1999) 'The concept of creativity: prospects and paradigms'. *Handbook of Creativity*, 1, 3–15.

Tassoul, M. (2009) *Creative Facilitation*. Delft: VSSD.

Torrance, E. (1966) *Torrance Tests of Creativity*. Princeton, NJ: Personnel Press.

Van Boeijen, A., Daalhuizen, J., Zijlstra, J. and Van der Schoor, R. (eds) (2014) *Delft Design Guide: Design Methods*. Amsterdam: BIS Publishers.

Wiliam, D. (2011) *Embedded Formative Assessment*. Bloomington: Solution Tree Press.

Wujec, T. (2016) 'Build a tower, build a team'. www.ted.com (accessed 14 July 2016).

White, B. and Frederiksen, J. (1998) 'Inquiry, modelling, and metacognition: making science accessible to all students'. *Cognition and Instruction*, 16(1), 3–118.

CHAPTER 6

DRAWING AS A TOOL FOR THOUGHT

How children can use drawing to develop their creative design ideas

Gill Hope

INTRODUCTION

Creativity is a valued aspect of 'product success' and the research discussed in this chapter therefore involved making judgements about the novelty of each child's design ideas. This in turn led to a consideration of what it means to be creative within the context of design and technology (D&T) rather than, say, art, science or literature. If design and technology involves answering a need-based problem, then any response that does not answer that specific problem is not, by definition, a creative solution to it. But is this too harsh? Is the response still creative? Is it creative in some other sphere, closer to a narrative or artistic response, perhaps, but not as a design solution to a specified technological problem?

BACKGROUND TO RESEARCH

These thoughts prompted my questioning of the nature of creativity within technological design and its relationship to identifying constraints while exploring possibilities, which I came to view as being somewhat like understanding and accepting the rules of a game. This questioning led in turn to considering not just how situationally specific creativity might be, but also the relationship between the product and the process and whether being more creative in terms of *process* inevitably leads to a more innovative *product*. The process that I was examining was the way in which young children could use drawing as a means of developing their design ideas.

DRAWING AS A TOOL FOR THOUGHT

I must first make clear my position on drawing for design. My research was entitled 'Drawing as a Tool for Thought' and this still encapsulates my belief about the role of drawing for designing. The aim of using drawing for designing is to enable children to develop their creative ideas about something that is to be made. The purpose of design drawing is to develop ideas for making a product, not to produce a pleasing drawing (Hope, 2011). Therefore, design drawings do not need to look pretty. They can have crossings-out, erasures, fresh starts – and even require several sheets of paper. A drawing of the final product may not actually appear on the paper at all. Drawing is a tool within the design process, not a by-product. Many teachers seem not to fully understand the ephemeral and procedural nature of a design drawing and this seems to be one reason why children do not develop the ability to use drawing as a tool for thought in a meaningful way.

The transfer of models of industrial design practice to school D&T lessons has not been helpful to the primary school child. Danos' (2014) taxonomy of graphicacy usefully catalogues drawings of all kinds. Under 'drawing', she includes drafts and sketching of which she says:

■ Products finished to an appropriate level of accuracy to closely mirror an idea/observation;
■ This is often a means to achieve/get to the next stage

To be decoded the observer needs to identify the idea/observation.

(Danos, 2014: 214)

Under 'diagrams', she includes engineering/technical drawings, of which she says: 'To be decoded, the observer has to have developed the relevant spatial abilities and understanding of the techniques' (Danos, 2014: 214).

This last is equally true of the producer of the diagram. The design work of young children will almost always fall into Danos' (2014) 'drawing' category, with some features of 'diagrams' developing as they reach the last years of primary school. Therefore, children of this age should not be required to produce clearly labelled working diagrams of what they want to make before they are allowed to make their product. For a start, they often do not have sufficient experience of handling the materials to know what they can successfully make with them. Or if familiar materials, such as paper and card, are to be used, then what they are being asked to make may not be a working product but a *model* of a working product.

Sometimes, the form of the product is pre-decided by the teacher and the children's design decisions are limited to the decoration. For younger children, this may be appropriate. For instance, a class of 5-year-olds in a primary school in South East England were making a simple bag as a present for Mother's Day. Their teacher had supplied a range of different handbags to the dressing-up box and encouraged the children to discuss the kinds of bags their mum used on different occasions (or indeed any other female that was important to them in their everyday lives). They were going to use sections of trouser legs for their bags to minimise the amount of cutting and sewing. A whole lesson was spent experimenting with fabric paint, applying ribbons and beads, and doing some stitching on scrap fabric. The children combined this practical knowledge with their analysis of their mum's bag preferences to design the customised detailing for their bag using annotated drawing to develop and record their ideas.

For such young children, focusing on using drawing to decide on the decorative features is an appropriate introduction to design drawing. Before age 6–7 years, most children cannot really understand the nature and purpose of drawing for designing (Hope, 2010). Even when designing something fairly simple like a hand puppet made from card, they regard doing a drawing as a completed activity unrelated to the 'second' activity of making the product (*'Miss, why are we doing this twice?'*). Some children may even draw in a narrative style, that is, a true picture of the user holding or standing next to the product, maybe even with sun and clouds at the top of the paper.

I found it was far more effective to ask such young children to explain their design ideas to each other once they had chosen their materials rather than using drawing. If they are working in a small group, they can tell an audio recorder what they intend to make (*'Dear tape recorder, what I'm going to do is . . .'*) More on using talk and conversation in Chapters 8 and 12.

Children of this age also find it far easier to produce a design drawing if they have already chosen their materials. On one occasion, I was working with a class of 6-year-olds who had been learning about the sea. I wanted them to make boats but to go beyond the conventional toy-tugboat shape. I divided the resources into three large tubs: Tub A contained cuboids of various sizes and proportions; Tub B had cylinders and truncated cones (e.g. yogurt pots); Tub C was a miscellaneous selection of other three-dimensional forms. They were told to choose one item from each tub and then return to their seat to draw a boat made from what they had chosen. Once everyone had chosen, they could go back and choose more materials if they wanted. The children produced good drawings of viable model boats with correct proportions according to their chosen materials and made them accordingly. Each boat was different in size, form and imagined function.

This anecdote underlines another important principle of using drawing for designing: the drawing does not need to be the first activity in a lesson or series of lessons, preceding the choice and handling of materials. However, if the teacher simply puts a box of materials in the centre of the table ready for use once they finish drawing, the children will simply rush the drawing stage in order to 'get started' as they see it and the real designing will take place once they have those materials in their hands.

If the purpose of the drawing is 'blue sky thinking', then beginning the design process with drawing may well produce wonderful ideas that cannot be made by the child from the materials available. This is not a problem if the final outcome is a *model* rather than a *product*. For instance, I asked a class of 7-year-olds to design a method for Frosty the Snowman to cross a melted lake to reach the shop on the other side (no boats allowed on the lake!) This task produced a range of creative ideas for bridges, tunnels, aerial ropeways, cable cars and rocket launchers, which were then modelled in paper and card, often using rolled newspaper to create structural features.

However, if a real working product is to be made from specific materials, then children are hardly likely to produce a realistic design for something that will *work* and can be made if they have not handled or previously worked with the materials. If children are going to work with unfamiliar techniques or materials, they need a guided task to teach them the technique or how the material handles before they can have their own creative design ideas.

In the 1995 National Curriculum for England, a three-stage process was specified:

▨ Investigating and disassembling existing artefacts
▨ Focused practical tasks
▨ Design and make activities

(Additional discussion in Chapter 1).

The wisdom of this approach is still to be recommended and drawing can be used (or not) as part of each phase of the project. I once taught a sandal-making project to a class of 7-year-old children in which the first lesson involved investigating and discussing the merits of various styles and types of the sandals piled on the tables. The children were then asked to record their preferences and design a sandal they thought they could make, using either writing or drawing as they wished. Interestingly, all the children chose to write a list of features they liked and they all drew one single idea for potential making.

TYPES OF DESIGN DRAWING THAT CHILDREN USE

After analysing about 400 drawings produced in design and technology lessons by children aged 5–9 years old, I conducted a 15-month longitudinal study of two parallel classes of 6–7-year-olds (they were, of course, 7–8-year-olds by the end of the study). I taught D&T one afternoon a week to my Focus Class, and the Comparison Class were taught by their class teacher. At the end of each school term, I conducted the same single lesson activity with both classes and these became my assessment tasks. With the exception of Zara and Nikki, the examples of children's drawings shown here come from the Focus Class; however, the categorisation of the drawings come from the initial wider survey.

In my research, I called recordings of one idea 'Single-draw' if there was just one item on the page or 'Multi-draw' if there was more than one item, but these were so similar as to be essentially the same idea drawn twice (for instance, if a child was dissatisfied with their first attempt and redrew it more neatly). These single-idea drawings can occur as:

▨ Canonical image: the child only has one way of drawing the object to be made. This is most commonly seen among younger children when asked to design something which they frequently draw (see Figure 6.1, taken from Hope (2005), a boy's plan for a simple puppet – his finished product is an almost identical copy of this drawing onto card).
▨ Clarifying what they have been asked to make: children are not using drawing to design their product; they are simply establishing that they understand the task; for example, if teddy needs a travel bag for his holidays, they will produce one drawing of their idea for his bag. This is typical of younger children, those who have little experience or have not been taught how to use drawing to develop design ideas.
▨ Recording a final idea for a product when designing has been carried out in another medium. This could be through extended discussion, modelling in scrap materials (e.g. newspaper, scrap fabric, modelling material) or through extensive hands-on development of their ideas. This is a more informed use of a single-draw than the two previous ones, as it is recording well-developed design ideas.

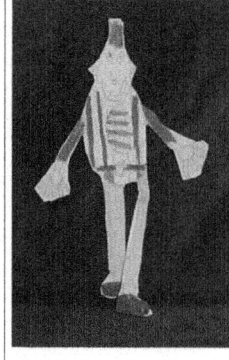

■ **Figure 6.1** Single-draw

At first sight, this is what 7-year-old Hayley's clear plan for an Easter Egg Holder and her final product appears to be (Figure 6.2). However, she has clearly thought about the parts to be attached as she has drawn these separately. It is possible to almost 'look over her shoulder' and see her mind working and thinking about those wings and tail. She has had a good idea and uses the drawing to work out how to make it. The written note indicates a decision made about what she will make while she was doing the drawing. The drawing has done more than clarify to Hayley what her teacher wants her to make; she has used the drawing to support her design thinking. These kinds of drawings I called 'Progressive', because although frequently simple, they show the development of design ideas through the use of drawing.

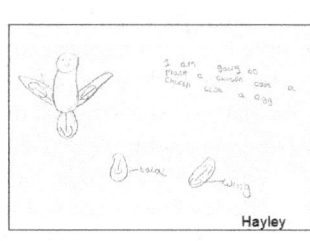

Hayley

■ **Figure 6.2** Progressive drawing 1

This is also shown in Craig's work (Figure 6.3) on the same Easter Egg Holder task. At the end of the lesson, Mrs. J discussed his work with him:

Craig: I decided to cut the tube because it's too wide . . . That's that bit there . . . Then sellotaped it to make it thinner . . . That's it bended round. That's the top – that circle. That's me decorating it *[pencil drawn on design sheet]*. I did the handle but it was too thin, the card was too thin. It went *ugh*, all floppy.

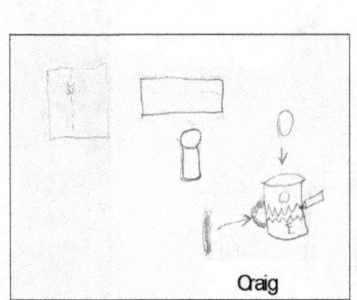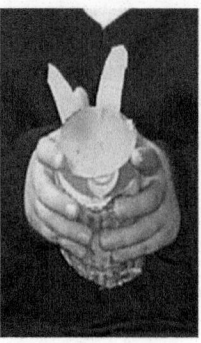

■ **Figure 6.3** Progressive drawing 2

Mrs. J: Are these rabbit's ears? *[on product]* That's different to your drawing. Why did you do those?

Craig: Someone else had done that and I thought 'That's a good idea' so I stuck them on my top.

The striped suit that he then gave his rabbit holder can be glimpsed between his hands. Using drawing to work out an effective solution to the practical problem left Craig's mind free to decide on the decorative scheme later. He had drawn a handle on the side, but when the card was not suitable he looked for inspiration elsewhere. This small hitch did not deter him from making a successful completed product as he already had a working holder based on his carefully thought-through construction technique.

Progressive drawings occur when a child immediately has one good strong idea and just needs to work out the detail. Another way in which young designers use drawing is what I called 'Multi-design', which occurs when they have a whole rush of ideas and produce a stream of quick sketches, none of them particularly developed. For instance, Richard, aged 7, produced several rows of little figures in response to a puppet-making task (Hope, 2005). Although he had used the same basic body shape, each of these little drawings turned out to be different characters: 'I did that one, and then that one . . . that is a Superman one . . . then Karl said that one looked like a crocodile . . . so I did that one . . .'

Neither Progressive nor Multi-design is 'better' than the other. Nor are they associated with different kinds of children or different kinds of design tasks. The choice of approach is purely dependent on whether or not the child sees one strong idea in their mind's eye or a stream of possibilities. Both are equally valid; both are experienced by adult designers. The important feature is that the child's design ideas are developing across the drawing(s).

Where evaluation and redesign can be seen as an integrated part of the drawing, the process can be seen as more fully interactive. At this point the child begins to have a conversation with the drawing, seeing the drawing as a means to work out what will be made and how to make it. This can sometimes be seen as a combination of Multi-design and Progressive. More than one design idea or more than one way to make the product may be recorded, and these are evaluated and developed through more drawings, perhaps combining and discarding elements of several drawings. Several related ideas, styles or construction methods might be considered and combined to develop a firm idea of a final product. Further ideas about previously drawn solutions may be recorded after other solutions have been developed as the child begins to combine ideas.

Michael's puppet-making designing (Figure 6.4, from Hope, 2005) shows signs of being interactive. It can be seen immediately that Michael has also focused on the mechanics of the task and that his product is something he could immediately play with, rather than being particularly aesthetically pleasing. However, his work is beginning to show a more sophisticated use of the drawing-to-record the thinking-process. He has produced two views of his idea – an x-ray diagram to show how the puppet is attached to a stick that passes through the base of the envelope, and a drawing of the outside view of the product. He then finalised his ideas in the quick sketch that he labelled 'made'. This did not need to be well drawn or detailed; the drawing process had served its purpose and he knew what he was going to do.

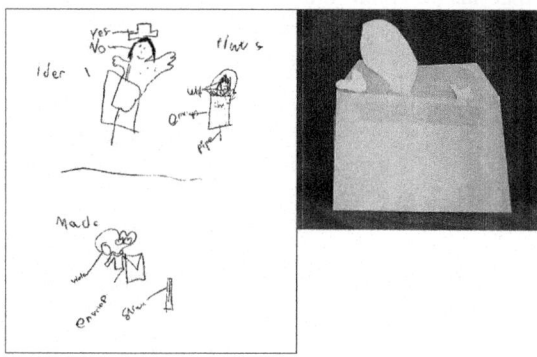

■ **Figure 6.4** Interactive drawing 1

Nine-year-old Nikki's drawing (Figure 6.5, from Hope, 2005) shows more clearly this interactive use of drawing in which a conversation appears to be going on between the drawing and the mind's eye. The task was to create a Surprise Box toy in which the contents played on the idea on the outside but contained a joke or surprise based on the

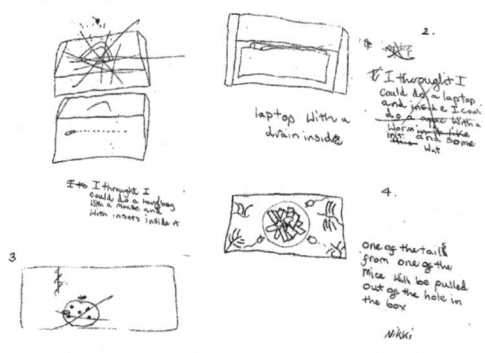

■ **Figure 6.5** Interactive drawing 2

theme. The children were shown a box that looked like a little doll's house, which contained a heart hanging on a string; the theme was 'the Heart of the Home'. In her first two drawings, Nikki had some ideas around a laptop case but then looked back over them and was not satisfied (see her crossed-out comment on the right). Drawing number 3 shows an apple inside the box – she is beginning to think of words with two meanings related to computers. Her final design represents a leap of imagination into a successfully original idea: the outside is a laptop and inside are chips, a mouse and some bugs.

There appears to be a plateau of realisation of the use of drawing for designing (see Figure 6.6, from Hope, 2005) that is evidenced by the Multi-design/Progressive phase. Once children are using these as tools to support and develop their design thinking, they have then reached an important milestone. Up to this point, they are seeing drawing as static, containing ideas of what might be made, but not realising that the drawing can move their ideas forward and help to create a range of possibilities or develop a good idea into something that has potential to actually work. If older pupils are going to be expected to use drawing interactively, they cannot do so unless they have reached this plateau of realisation.

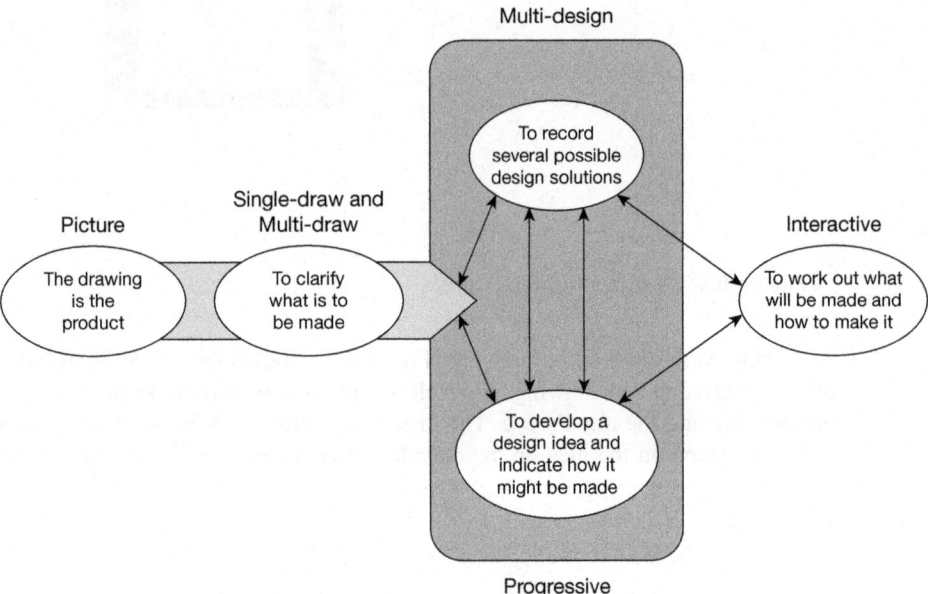

■ **Figure 6.6** Plateau of understanding purpose of drawing for designing

IDEAS ON A JOURNEY

So, how were such young children able to use drawing as an effective design medium? Did I use a special design drawing programme and teach the Focus Class what to do and how to do it?

No. The answer was much simpler but, in a way, much less obvious: they were taught the *purpose* of using drawing for designing. This was achieved through the use of a dual metaphor: drawing as both a container and a journey (Figure 6.7, from Hope, 2008). The drawing contains the designer's ideas but these are not static; they travel across and/or around the page. A genuine design drawing shows some evidence of the development of ideas.

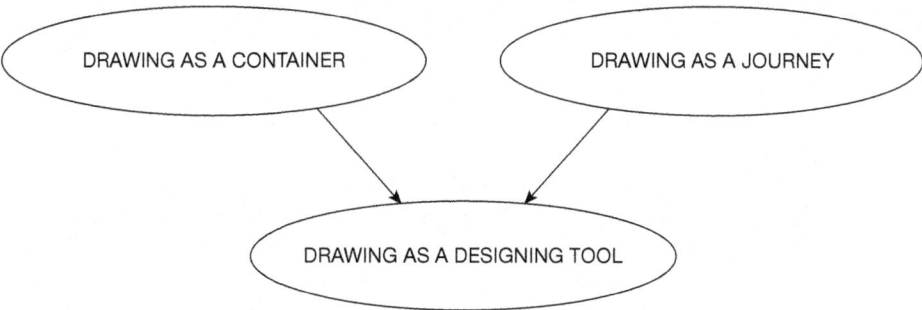

■ **Figure 6.7** Container/journey metaphor

The Focus Class of 6–7-year-olds in my research were shown some design drawings done by older children that clearly demonstrated ideas being developed on paper (including Nikki's drawing; see Figure 6.7) and also some ordinary pictures these children had drawn, the design drawings displayed together on one side and the pictures on the other. I asked the Focus Class children if they could see any differences between the two groups of drawings. 'Those are pictures', they said. 'What would you call the others?' I asked – and one little girl said, 'planning drawings?' We put the pictures aside and I explained how the planning drawings contained the children's ideas for what they wanted to make but we could see that these ideas had developed across the paper and would have continued to develop off the paper and into making the real thing. The ideas had gone on a kind of journey across the page.

I expressed my wonder to them whether they could use drawing to develop their ideas to design a puppet. They looked sceptical, but they did.

The children in this class were not told to do specific kinds of drawings, what they were to include in them, how many drawings to do or how to label them. They were never told such things as 'This is a Multi-design and if you have lots of instant ideas this is what you do' or 'I want to see some Progressive features in your drawings' or anything like that. In fact, the children never knew that I was categorising drawings in this way at all.

My aim was to impart a holistic understanding of the role of drawing within designing, not to teach particular techniques or process order. The design drawing is not a product; it is a staging post along the way towards a product made in real materials. The ideas recorded in it are place-holders; they contain the developing ideas so that these can be remembered, examined, discussed, appraised and developed. This cannot be done effectively within the mind's eye alone. Externalisation of good ideas is essential for moving them forward in an effective manner. How children used drawing as a design tool was up to them; its *purpose* is to aid their creative thinking, not to produce a particular type of drawing.

The first indication that the child is beginning to use the drawing to plan a product is the recording of the colours *in writing*. A child who simply colours the design sheet is not necessarily planning the colours to be used in the product, whereas a child who spontaneously labels the drawing with colour words more frequently is. Once children understand a planning drawing, they begin to annotate them because they are seriously considering them as plans for making something. They also become less concerned about their ability to draw a realistically accurate image of what they have in mind. They will simply annotate it and then say 'that is meant to be a so-and-so', because they know the drawing is only an aide-memoire/development tool.

Once children understand the purpose of the drawing as a *working drawing*, conveying sufficient information to guide the making of the product, they can begin to use labels, annotations, expanded drawings to show small or separate details, diagrams that attempt to show different viewpoints or results of movement. With older pupils, who are adept at using drawing for designing and are already using it interactively, the teaching of specific techniques may enhance their efficiency. Likewise, if children are going to be sharing their drawings with others, perhaps in peer evaluation, then deciding together beforehand how key features would be shown would enable others to read the drawings more easily. By the time my Focus Class were 8 years old, some of them were importing drawing techniques they had used in other contexts. Some of them were using legends to indicate key features (a dotted line means a fold, for instance). Kelly and Sung (2016) found that the children in their study were exporting the lessons they had learnt about design drawing into a language arts context.

Older pupils with little experience of design drawing will learn to do so relatively quickly once the role of drawing for designing as 'ideas on a journey' is explained to them, and this is what Kelly and Sung (2016) discovered working with 8–9-year-olds in New York State. The pupils with whom they worked had little previous experience of designing, and yet many of them soon exhibited elements of the plateau stages once they had received basic instruction about sketching to enable them to understand the purpose of drawing for design drawing. Referring to the diagram shown as Figure 6.7, Kelly and Sung emphasised:

> the line of distinction (Border line of Plateau of Realization) between the category of Container for Ideas and Plateau of Realization, it is the 'crossing over' from sketching as a method to contain the designers' ideas to design sketching as a way of communicating and design cognition.
>
> (Kelly and Sung, 2016: 2)

Certainly, this is the essential border point which, once crossed, means that the child understands that drawing can be used as a means to take design ideas forward – the 'drawing as a journey' of Figure 6.7.

IS AN IMAGINATIVE RESPONSE SUFFICIENT?

In response to the Easter Egg Holder task, one of the girls in the Comparison Class (Zara, Figure 6.8, from Hope, 2004) designed a shoulder bag with the egg sitting in a hole in the top. It is innovative (she was the only child in either class to consider turning the tube on its side) and the drawing certainly shows a progression of ideas, worked out in some detail. I would class this as Interactive. However, as the photo shows, there were serious problems with the viable functionality of the idea. The holder does not stand up. It rolls over and the egg falls out. The structures at the top of the drawing are strings to enable the holder to be worn over the shoulder like a bag (a string can be seen in the photo), but this still does not prevent the egg from falling out, balanced precariously as it is in a little cup. So, although her ideas are innovative, she has not really addressed the technological task that was set: to design an Easter Egg Holder from the wide card tube so that the egg is held securely.

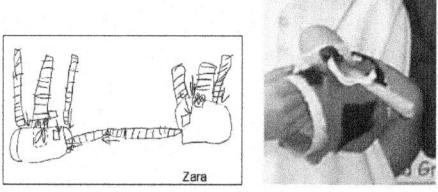

■ **Figure 6.8** Zara 1

A similarly unique response occurred when asked to design and make a model of the Maze to help Theseus escape from the Minotaur (Figure 6.9). After exploring some interesting ideas, her third drawing shows that her mind had moved onto something else. Zara made a simple box 'maze' and then made a river outside the castle walls with a crocodile in it and a boat to help Theseus escape from the crocodile.

Zara: This is for the crocodile to come in *(blue).*
Lee: It's a Minotaur.
Zara: No, a crocodile is in the garden; I'm doing a boat, walls and a door.
Later: Playing with it – walking a cut-out Minotaur about – she said to me: When Theseus has escaped from the Minotaur there's a crocodile in the river and he needs a boat to escape from the crocodile.

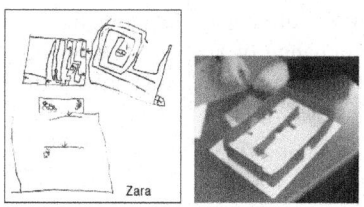

■ **Figure 6.9** Zara 2

Was this creative, divergent or just plain off-task? If the creativity she was displaying was (perhaps) inappropriate to D&T, would it have been relished by her art teacher or applauded as a new take on the tale in creative writing? What about addressing the design criteria? In designing a working product, it is not enough to have interesting ideas. Creating a product that satisfies a pre-determined set of criteria (how to hold a small egg securely inside a wide tube) requires the ability to think through how to make it. Craig's original ideas were far less imaginative (the rabbit idea was borrowed from someone else; I think it was Nikki's younger sister Natalie), but his product worked.

Another child (Maria) also set me thinking through her inappropriate response to a science question: '*How could we help the seeds in the dark cupboard grow better?*'

Maria: 'Draw a picture of the sun and rain and pin it up inside the cupboard for the seeds to look at.

It may not be science but surely this is the stuff of children's literature of metaphor and poetry and jumping from reality to fantasy and creating a new world order in which such things are possible. I want to create a story in which the bad teacher had put some poor seeds in a dark cupboard but then a child came along and drew a picture of the sun and rain for them to look at and overnight the seeds grew and grew . . .

Wittgenstein (1969) referred to the construction of meanings within separate domains of human endeavour as 'language games', each with their own rules and internal logic from which phenomena are 'seen as'. Croft (2012) used the term 'thinking *in*', which also conveys the sense of reasoning within a problem frame to perceive its constraints and possibilities to find a creative solution. Successful problem-solving depends on the ability to set up, reason and imagine within a clearly defined mind-space. It is the ability to image fantasy onto reality, what *might be* onto what *is*, and to accept and reason within the fantasy/reality interface inherent in the design task. It has a family resemblance to a game of football in which players with flair can exploit the game potential while remaining within the constraints of the game's rules. Zara was not playing my game; she was using my ball to play her own.

HOW CAN USING DRAWING FOR DESIGNING HELP?

This became clear with the Theseus' Maze task (the pupils were now aged 7–8 years). The Focus Class talked as they drew; the Comparison Class elected to draw in silence and then began sharing ideas once they were engaged in making the maze. However, at this point they lost the plot. Instead of making a model maze to help Theseus escape, they were now designing snake pits and trap doors for him to fall into or, in Zara's case, creating Episode 2.

In her discussion of 'exploratory creativity', Boden (1994) remarked that mental spaces are easier to change or adapt than physical ones. It would appear that the Focus Class had learnt to use drawing as a means of scaffolding their thinking. Statements such as 'What I'm going to do is . . .' 'What you could do is . . .' could be heard, including, crucially 'What it needs to do is . . .' This enabled a greater level of product success and a far wider range of viable ideas.

I became convinced, therefore, that part of understanding the purpose of the drawing was to see it as a *discussion document* through which ideas could be modelled in order to become visible to themselves and others, and thus available for review and discussion. Ariff *et al.*, (2012) found this also to be true of adults. For older primary pupils, a powerful use of drawing, therefore, could be to allow 30 minutes of sketching and discussion, followed by a time of quiet in which to think and draw a final annotated design proposal, which represents an intent to make. If the making is not going to occur immediately (and this is frequently the case) then before they begin making, it is sensible to allow children time to evaluate and review their proposal and to supply them with stick-on notes for quickly drawing or writing down any changes they wish to make. This enables them to re-engage with their ideas, remember what they were thinking and add new insights as they see fit.

CONCLUSION

This chapter has drawn heavily on my own research into young children using drawing for designing. However, the final words must come from Kelly and Sung (2016) who have replicated my findings in New York State. For me, the most significant of their findings is:

> Teachers' understanding of the role of sketching as a way of design thinking is critical to students' success and how the teacher talks with the students about the design sketch is important for students to be motivated to improve sketching.
>
> (Kelly and Sung, 2016: 4)

When teachers and pupils understand the purpose of design drawing – that it can both contain their ideas and move them forward ('ideas on a journey') – then they will begin to see drawing as a powerful means of generating and developing creative design ideas that can be made into successful, creative, innovative and functional products.

REFERENCES

Ariff, N.S.N.A., Badke-Shaub, P. and Eris, O. (2012) 'Conversations around design sketches: use of communication channels for sharing mental models during concept generation'. *Design and Technology Education: An International Journal*, 17(3), 27–36.

Boden, M. (1994) 'What is creativity?', in Boden, M.A. (ed.) *Dimensions in Creativity*. Cambridge, MA: MIT Press.

Croft, M. (2012) 'A speculative approach to drawing as visualising thinking'. *Design and Technology Education: An International Journal*, 17(3), 61–69.

Danos, X. (2014) *Graphicacy and Culture: Refocussing on Visual Learning*. Loughborough: Loughborough Design Press.

Hope, G. (2004) '"Little c" creativity and "Big I" innovation within the context of design & technology education'. *Proceedings of DATA International Research Conference*.

Hope, G. (2005) 'The types of drawings that young children produce in response to design tasks'. *The Journal of Design and Technology Education*, 10(1), 43–53.

Hope, G. (2008) *Thinking and Learning through Drawing*. London: Sage.

Hope, G. (2010) 'Beyond knowing how to make it work: the conceptual foundations of designing'. *Design and Technology Education: An International Journal*, 14(1), 49–55.

Hope, G. (2011) 'Taking ideas on a journey: designing in a Kent primary school', in Benson, C. and Lunt, J. (eds) *International Handbook of Primary Technology Education*. Rotterdam, The Netherlands: Sense Publications.

Kelly, T.R. and Sung, E. (2016) 'Sketching by Design: Teaching Sketching to Young Learners'. *International Journal of Technology and Design Education*. Available at: http://link.springer.com/search?sortOrder=newestFirst&facet-content-type=Article&facet-journal-id=10798#page-2 (accessed 5 July 2016).

Wittgenstein, L. (1969) *Philosophical Investigations: The Blue Book; The Brown Book*. Oxford: Basil Blackford.

The 1995 National Curriculum for Design and Technology for England is available at: www.gov.uk/government/publications/national-curriculum-in-england-design-and-technology-programmes-of-study (accessed 5 July 2016).

Note: It has been superseded by the 2014 National Curriculum for England.

CREATIVE LEARNING AND TEACHING WITH CONSTRUCTION KITS

Eric Parkinson

INTRODUCTION

The idea of making things in primary classrooms predates the emergence of a National Curriculum that has been introduced in many countries worldwide including England and Wales (DES/WO, 1990). Children have worked in what might be termed 'free building' situations with recycled and reclaimed materials such as card, lolly sticks, cardboard rolls and PVA glue. This mode of construction has enabled children to encounter a range of materials by cutting, shaping and fixing. Parallel to this, and providing a complementary experience without cutting, shaping and fixing with glue, is the process of making things with construction kits.

Construction kits are available in most primary schools; they have become part of the essential fabric of the early years classroom and beyond. These resources are most likely to be seen in action during episodes of 'free play' or self-directed learning and they often involve young learners (Figure 7.1). Usually, the kits in these early years classrooms comprise collections of brightly coloured plastic pieces that are manipulated to fit together in various ways, facilitated by the particular shapes of the pieces themselves. Thus, even timber bricks and blocks can also be considered as part of the construction kit repertoire. Timber bricks are of course less secure in their attachment to each other than most modern construction kits, relying only on gravity and frictional forces to keep parts in their desired places. Kits become less common in classrooms as children progress through the primary years of schooling, arguably limiting modelling opportunities in the upper primary years. They are often provided for a specific, teacher-directed activity to support understanding of a concept such as forces or mechanical control. The important play element is often absent due to time constraints and lack of understanding of its value. Opportunities are therefore missed to explore how the parts of the kit fit together, what they can create with different arrangements, and consequently the children may not gain a broader knowledge and understanding of construction.

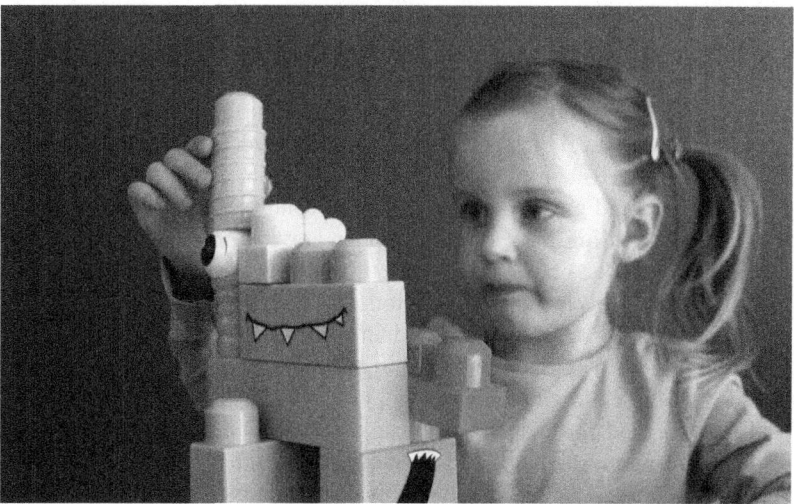

■ **Figure 7.1** Free play with construction kits can promote imaginative outcomes

DEVELOPMENT OF CONSTRUCTION KITS

Educational construction kits have their beginnings in the move towards formal schooling in the Germanic heartland of Europe. Friedrich Fröbel is widely seen as the father of construction kits. This great educator and originator of the term 'kindergarten' likened the early years setting to a place for the nurturing of children's minds (Hill, 1908). Fröbel was pivotal in curriculum innovation. He devised sets of practical activities for children. Central to these activities was the idea that learning should not be seen in isolation, but be part of a sequence. This idea of sequencing is recognised in modern curricula under such terms as 'progression' and 'continuity'. Fröbel believed in a linear sequence of experiences, and devised not only activities to support these, but also particular resources. These included timber blocks that could be assembled in various ways. This early expression of a construction kit was a product of the creative mind of Fröbel and, in its time, would have been seen as an imaginative approach to teaching. It was less so for learners, where the presumption for a linear sequence of learning was founded simply on hunches developed from experiences within the kindergarten (Fröbel, 1887).

Perhaps as an accompaniment to a long tradition of German engineering and innovative architectural practice, there has been, since the days of Fröbel, a similar evolution of construction kits in the heartland of Europe. Kits were produced to emulate engineering practice with nuts and bolts and miniature girder-like steel structures. In Britain, this approach was notably captured by Frank Hornby with his iconic steel construction kit. His seminal kit 'Mechanics Made Easy' dates from the early 1900s and enabled children to model structures and mechanisms. As a contrast to what was essentially child-sized mechanical engineering, a parallel strand of architectural 'building' developed as a range of bricks and blocks.

The intended purposes of these activities concerned replicating the adult world whereby children would assemble pieces in a particular order to produce a specific outcome. With instructions, the child could follow a sequence to produce a particular mechanism and be assured of success. Similarly, a sequence of block-by-block building steps would enable the child to emulate adult building practice.

The growth and development of construction kits has extended beyond the early ideas of Fröbel and Hornby. Today there is a diversity of forms of kit, characterised by two particular attributes. First is the way they fill space. Some kits, such as bricks and blocks, fill space in well-defined faceted units. Other kits occupy space in more complex ways such as rods and girder-like pieces. The second factor concerns connectivity, with some kits simply settling piece-on-piece under gravitational and frictional influences as with bricks and blocks, or via a multitude of twisting, turning and push-fit manipulations.

These two characteristic factors of space-filling and connectivity impact on the creative learning responses of children. They produce challenge in terms of the various representations that kits offer. An intriguing interaction occurs between the constructional aspirations of children and the spatial possibilities offered by kits. This is a complex area of learning and the outcome is an extending of the minds of children as they wrestle with their initial intentions and reconcile these with the limitations and fresh possibilities offered by kits to fill space in new, interesting and, crucially, stimulating ways. A similar learning opportunity is offered by the ways that kit components fit together. Children will wish to develop their constructions to achieve various functional purposes such as the appearance of their products. Functional outcomes may also embrace some anticipated aspects concerning the transmission of forces and motion. Broadly, we can refer to this latter idea as concerning 'mechanism'.

For the child who wishes to construct a home for the purpose of accommodating a doll or model animal, the structure will need to have walls or containment bars of appropriate height or spacing. The child will have, in all probability, unwittingly defined a set of conditions for keeping their doll or animal secure. These self-imposed specifications for the performance of the modelled outcome will stretch the thinking of the child as they problem-solve, looking at the options offered by the kit, with their own ideas. Within all of this, it is the kit itself that may offer fresh possibilities. This is a fundamental creative attribute of the construction kit whereby first-hand interactions with tangible pieces, manipulated in various ways, produce new prospects. Kits therefore have the capacity to generate and maintain curiosity, and each avenue of spatial problem-solving advances the ways that the child is able to design and develop their idea.

CONSTRUCTION KITS AND CREATIVITY IN PRIMARY EDUCATION

As part of a brief introduction to the use and purposes of construction kits in classrooms, we need to understand how, both historically and functionally, they have been used to develop designs and thinking. Two powerful ideas have driven the development of construction kits.

The first of these powerful ideas concerns the making of simple components that can be assembled one to another to produce a larger and often more complex outcome. We can refer to this as 'pre-construction'. Assembling pre-made parts to produce a more complex whole accelerates construction.

The second powerful idea underpinning the role of the construction kit is the notion of the serial manufacture of consistent, replicated units. Much of our built world is essentially made from pre-fabricated parts based on serial manufacture. Bricks, for example, made from fired clay, or mud and straw, are individual units of known, consistent dimensions that enable rapid, quality-controlled building to proceed. Pre-construction and serial manufacturing actions are purposeful technological behaviours that underpin civilisation itself. They simplify the ultimate building experience and give greater certainty of outcome. Using these ideas, considerable thoughtfulness has been applied to the design of construction kits with their range of pre-formed components. Children can build quickly and reliably with usefully shaped components that have the means of making secure connections between them. In addition, mechanical and electrical control parts can be integrated easily into a structure so that different movements can be tested and adjusted.

TECHNOLOGICAL BEHAVIOURS AND CONSTRUCTION KITS

Pre-construction and the serial manufacture of parts are products of our technological society in which we make things, and change and control our world to suit our purposes. As we have seen, construction kits for children embody both of these technological markers. In an educational context, kits enable children to rapidly create artefacts to change and control their world for their own purposes. The term 'technological actions' can be understood through five key characteristics: Making, Manipulating, Modifying, Mending and Modelling. All these characteristics can be recognised in the ways that children utilise construction kits for creative purposes.

Making

A feature of our technological age is our ability to change and control aspects of the world. To do this, we make things. In a broad sense, the idea of making things is a cultural human trait. As adults, we erect structures for shelter and protection and thus modify our surroundings to suit the circumstances in which we wish to live. There are of course organisms other than humans that organise resources to control their environment, but the outcomes are predictable and consistent. Beavers, for example, make the same sort of dams each time they control the flowing of watercourses. Hornets and ants construct communities with consistent spatial characteristics to accommodate specialist functions. However, these sorts of structures are not progressive. Our species has a characteristic restlessness that urges us onward in search of new ways of sourcing and arranging materials. Making is a recognisable outcome of children working with construction kits. The outcomes carry significance for teachers, since they indicate the ways that children are thinking creatively as well as acting.

Manipulating

When we make things, we often require special tools. These are employed with skills to shape, cut and then decorate outcomes. Construction kits provide an alternative pathway to tool-reliant making since they require no tools or special skills. Children benefit from this key attribute of construction kits. Manipulation of the pieces of kits is achieved by actions such as pushing and twisting parts together and pulling them apart. Children are thus able to construct quickly and, within the limits of the kits, to make outcomes of far greater complexity than can be gained from the free-building resources of card, lolly sticks and glue. This promotes creative responses by children. There is also a tactile dimension concerning children in their interactions with construction kit components. As children push, pull and twist pieces, they are exposed to a range of stimulating shapes that they may not have encountered before, such as tubes, clips, rods and blocks. Stimulation leads to curiosity and further exploration.

Modifying

Making is never straightforward. As we construct, we can often see new options and possibilities to the course of construction we have initially chosen. We modify things as we problem-solve. Through construction kits, modifications are possible due to the ease with which children can manipulate parts. Children are able to modify their constructions speedily and with certainty, and this enhances prospects for technological explorations with creative outcomes.

Mending

We all make mistakes. Indeed, it may be argued that we learn more from things that do not go according to plan than those that do. As children build, then elements of their constructions will not produce the desired results. You can see this when children push pieces of their intended construction together and the whole thing falls apart. As they build, then trial and error, or trying things out, becomes a fundamental way of learning. Successful ventures are repeated and unsuccessful ones filtered out of experience. The value of mending is that it requires us to go back one stage in construction and analyse why the anticipated outcomes have not occurred. Potentially better, more considered building is an outcome. Mending develops attitudes of patience, commitment and endurance. Mending requires thoughtful reflection and pushes learners to seek new ways of building, thus promoting creativity.

Modelling

When children build, they produce products. Sometimes children simply reproduce some object they have seen previously and in a scaled-down format. Or they may thoughtfully construct objects that they have within their minds, or more likely, as a hybrid part-conceived, but with contributions from things seen in the world around them. These objects are generally referred to as models. Models act as representations and are a key feature of construction kits. In these activities, it must be remembered, however, that the children are not engaged in a whole design and make project. They are engaged in practical tasks that will support the development of their knowledge and understanding, together with expanding the possibilities of their design skills.

When we make things, there are two measures that may constrain or enable us. The first is the limitations of the materials that are available. The second constraint is the power of our imagination. The articulation of these imaginings can be seen in the ways that we model ideas. For children, modelling – and indeed modelling through the medium of the construction kit – is a key way of making concrete representations.

There is an intimate and profound interaction between the mind and the hand (Kimbell *et al.*, 1991) that results in the release of design ideas by making an outcome suit some purpose. Should the maker be using a construction kit, with all of its prefabricated pieces, then the release of an idea from the mind into the made world is rapidly achieved. Speed is important. Young children tend to be impatient and will quickly tire of activities that do not bring an immediate, satisfying yield. This view of the interaction of mind and hand is perhaps insufficient when applied to young learners. Mind, hand *and* speech all contribute to the development of a new and creative idea.

PROMOTING SPEAKING AND LISTENING SKILLS

Modelled ideas – our imaginings – need to be articulated in order to share them with others. We need to express these ideas as concrete representations for reflection and development to produce new ideas as part of an iterative process. The most direct and immediate way to do this is by talking (further discussion of this in Chapters 8 and 12). Verbal modelling explains possibilities. It is also social. Children will use both verbal and visual signalling to show others what they are thinking. Signalling with twisting and turning hand gestures and the waving of arms may accompany speaking as children attempt to communicate height, size and motion.

Through talk, the purposes of design become evident. Children may suggest who the outcome is for (often themselves), where it will go and what it will do. This generation of ideas is an iterative process and through this, further development of the product may occur. As an example, take the idea of a child who has made a model spaceship. Held aloft, the vehicle is taken on a 'space journey' around the classroom. A story accompanies this journey. The ship hovers over some alien landscape and a ladder is needed for astronauts to disembark. The ladder is added to the artefact due to the quick snap-fit capability of the particular kit that has been used. The story continues. The now folded-away ladder under the spacecraft is seen to project out in front. This stimulates the thinking of the child and a fresh chapter of the story evolves. The projecting ladder may be useful for the next encounter the spaceship makes with an alien planet, as it can now become a battering ram with which to chip away rocks to uncover a secret door to a planetary interior. This kind of co-development of both story and artefact is a distinctive aspect of the creative learning that is enabled due to the rapid building associated with construction kits.

DRAWING

Drawing should be mentioned at this point. Drawings can communicate ideas quickly and vividly. In forms such as doodles and sketches, drawings clarify meanings and offer graphic feedback to generate ideas to be shared. Often, the idea of drawing first is referred to as a design task, or design process. We need to make sure that drawing is not counter-productive and performed for the sake of it. This may defeat creativity (see Chapter 6). There may be a mismatch between what can be drawn and what it is possible to make. Children's drawings may be seen as a replication of the acts of the adult designer who commits ideas to paper prior to final construction of an artefact. There are, however, fundamental differences between the adult designer, who understands a range of materials and their characteristics, and the child. For the child, it may be frustrating to generate a drawing with the purpose of then producing a concrete outcome – only to discover that it is not possible to make within the capabilities of construction kits. This all too common idea of 'draw-me-one-then-make-it' (Constable, 1994: 9) may become a disincentive to learning and creativity.

EVALUATING

Design-as-you-make is readily accommodated by the construction kit. Research evidence (Welch, 1997) suggests that children like to design as they make things. This mode of activity is an iterative process whereby each change to an artefact by mending, modification and testing in trial and error circumstances assists in gaining a better-functioning final outcome. Iterative micro-loops of designing, making and evaluating continually improve and develop outcomes.

CONSTRUCTION KITS AND MECHANISM

Beyond static constructions such as buildings, representational options become more complex when the child enters the world of mechanism. Mechanism concerns the transfer of the kinetic energy of motion from one place to another through the application of forces. Moreover, this motion is controlled and replicable. In addition, all mechanisms must be accommodated in some non-moving, stable structure. For children, journeys into mechanism may be initiated with the simple addition of wheels to vehicles or hinging lever pieces on a stable frame. Opening a door or turning on a tap are simple everyday expressions of the way we rely on mechanisms to control our world. Beyond simple levers and wheels, and through the use of advanced technically dedicated construction kits, the range of mechanical outcomes becomes wide-ranging. Mechanisms include levers, wheel and belt or gear-to-gear modes for transferring force and motion (Figure 7.2).

Besides the sheer fun of adding wheels to models, there are other situations that can enable children to engage with mechanism. For example, nursery rhymes such as 'Ding Dong Bell, Pussy's in the Well', can enable children to experiment with the idea of a windlass – a winding mechanism – to raise and lower the bucket for the well. In the classroom, having a range of construction kits available to children promotes new ways

■ **Figure 7.2** Young children explore a mechanism with large, safe gears

of acting and thinking. What one kit can offer in terms of space-filling and the attachment of different parts will be a contrast to other kits.

THE MANAGEMENT OF FREE PLAY

Construction kits are often utilised in classrooms as part of free play (undirected) or self-directed activity. This allows the child to make choices and to fulfil their own self-set purposes about what they interact with, and to construct their own solutions as they do so. Eavesdropping on children in free play tells us about the worlds they seek to create, and the outcomes they produce often change and transform rapidly. These outcomes are a significant part of the creative realm that children are able to inhabit, courtesy of construction kits. For the child, this is the land of discovery that reveals fresh possibilities and these reside at the creative heart of construction.

The organisation of construction resources and consideration of access to these in the classroom can influence modelled outcomes. We have seen that free-play situations provide opportunities for children to make discoveries about the designed and made world and that in doing so, they also set and overcome their own design challenges. Discoveries, quite inadvertently, are often shared. Children may put part-made, or more likely part-dismantled, models back into classroom storage areas at the end of their making journey. These outcomes may thus be abandoned by one child, and then taken up by another. Discarded part-built outcomes, as curiosities, are in themselves fresh stimuli to initiate new journeys of discovery. As teachers, we need to be aware that encouraging children to undertake the total dismantling of models after making sessions may actually be counter-productive.

PART-DIRECTED CONSTRUCTION

Teacher-directed opportunities for learning will be part of the range of activities that children experience. For example, as part of a learning theme on wheels and motion, the children may have visited water mills, the surface headframe of a mine or a dockyard crane (links here to Chapter 11). A teacher might envisage a making task based on the representation of some part of the mechanism and structure of these complex features as part of a focused practical task. Or, perhaps as part of a learning theme in which children explore aspects of plants or animals linked to a book, children could be set the task of representing an insect or land mammal with articulating joints. Children would need, for example, to observe closely the places in which legs have bends in them, and which way they actually bend. Articulating pieces of modelled animal legs serves as a reminder that mechanism is not something just concerned with a sterile world of machines. We too, as animals, rely on the highly efficient mechanisms of our joints to maintain mobility. Of course, these activities are not whole design and make projects but practical tasks that support the development of knowledge and understanding.

GENDER ISSUES

It is easy to assume that by putting out kits for free play, both boys and girls will interact with them, albeit in different ways; however, providing children with a variety of activities is not enough. The teacher needs to observe play and to interact with all the children to try to ensure that all are exposed to a range of kits, offering opportunities to explore mechanisms and structures. Even when teachers intervene, girls can tend to sidestep the activity or become support for the boys' activity. One strategy to encourage girls to use kits was trialled by Sherwin (1990). She detailed a project that she carried out in school where girls were introduced to new kits individually, then in pairs and groups, before working in mixed-gender groups. The girls gained confidence working in this way and were able to create complex models including mechanisms alongside the boys. Adults in the home do not necessarily provide support for gender equity. Francis (2010) undertook research with parents and found that the majority felt that boys should be making things, using their hands and problem-solving, while girls should be caring and nurturing. This could lead to boys focusing on movement involving mechanisms and girls favouring static outcomes such as houses, and making greater use of play people. Gerhardt (2004) suggests that the brain differences associated between male and female are a result of their different experiences. Boys are more likely to develop parts of the brain associated with spatial awareness as they play with cars and construction kits. With these things in mind, as teachers we need to be aware that we can provide stimulation and challenge to tasks that provide both girls and boys with opportunities to use construction kits in a variety of ways in order that creative responses can be made to fresh, challenging situations.

THEMES AND IDEAS FOR USING CONSTRUCTION KITS IN THE PRIMARY CLASSROOM

A sky and space-based learning theme could embrace representations of lunar rovers and rocket-launching apparatus. Moving vehicles are popular with children of all ages in any theme involving transportation. Some of the most common themes for learning that can involve construction kits concern the pieces of apparatus to be found in the playground and fairground. These can embrace simple structures such as slides and climbing frames, or more complex areas with moving parts such as swings, roundabouts and Ferris wheels. Links to literacy may provide a context and purpose for the child. For example, David Almond's *The Boy Who Swam with Piranhas* (2012) is set in a fairground. It is a funny, freewheeling, fishy fable about a boy's journey to fulfil his destiny. This could provide a context for the creative use of construction kits in the primary classroom.

With young children, there are opportunities for extending the creative experience of modelled concrete ideas by encouraging children to 'show and tell' to peers and staff where a sense of focus and collaborative learning can be fostered. This is an excellent way of enabling children to increase their speaking and listening skills. These whole-class activities have further significance for the teacher since they provide opportunities to assess the performance of individual children.

EXAMPLE ACTIVITIES

A class is engaged in a learning theme revolving around ideas from a Christmas pantomime. The story involves the fairy tale of Cinderella. One of the central themes of the story concerns Cinderella and her mode of travel in a coach that has been magically created from a pumpkin. The coach can become a focus for designing-and-making tasks using construction kits. Initially, the children may decide to design and make a coach and through discussion identify that the coach should have four shiny wheels. Children will find inspiration and guidance through looking at pictures, and the chosen construction kit will suggest possibilities for action. But there is more. This concerns the key idea of differentiation as children make more of their own decisions and have certain criteria given to them as part of a specification. This, of course, is a key part of designing activity and it can apply to the designer of civil engineering projects imagining future bridges or buildings or to children in classrooms. Bridges, for example, have to meet the performance criteria set for safe usage. A bridge will be built to span a certain distance, to carry a maximum load and to be constructed from materials that provide a certain lifespan within a given budget for a particular purpose. Both the designer in a civil engineering partnership and the child in a classroom building to a specification exercise creativity to meet their intended ends as they build.

Teachers can set criteria in a graduated way by varying the degrees of challenge for individuals and groups, but it should be the intention to involve the pupils and eventually they will set their own criteria. For example, beyond the basic set task of making a coach for Cinderella, the differentiated design demand could include a roof covering so that Cinderella could keep out of the rain or snow. The addition of dolls or figures can make a significant contribution to aid the problem-solving activity. The coach could have a roof and a seat so that a seated doll could be accommodated. The coach could have a roof, seat and an opening door so that Cinderella could gain an elegant and safe entry and exit to the vehicle. Thus, additional layers of challenge and complexity are added – just as they would be for designers in commercial, industrial or civil engineering situations. Adding a roof is a structural task, and so is adding a seat. Adding an opening door elevates the demand of the task as the construction kit is required to go beyond structures and things that do not move into elements of mechanism, whereby things are required to move in a replicable and controlled way. Specifying elements of performance underlines the purposes behind construction and enables children to understand when objectives have been met.

A further example may be the construction of a bridge. Having discussed the need and the users of the bridge, the criteria will obviously relate to the span of the bridge, modelled in the classroom as a specified gap between two tables. The criteria might also add layers of demand, such that a toy vehicle can traverse the structure. It therefore has to be sufficiently wide and free of obstructions to ensure unrestrained passage.

For such an activity, the teacher can add challenges relating to the type of construction kit to be employed. For the child, the limited numbers of parts that are available to combine may be a source of challenge – the same as any designer would face. Teachers need to be aware of the learning prospects that are offered by limiting children's access to construction materials. Teachers need to develop awareness of how construction parts fit one to another and how they fill space so that they may have sufficient awareness of kit capabilities to specify particular components for particular tasks. To take small pieces and produce large, stable structures leads to challenging design decisions. The girder bridge of the structural engineer is in reality simply small girder pieces attached to each other in a pattern of triangles. We can translate discoveries and challenges like this into problem-based classroom settings.

Construction kits permit the development of mechanisms of far greater complexity than it would be possible to achieve with free-building measures. At the later stages of Key Stage 2, the addition of electric motors may permit an element of remote control over components that can be made to turn or twist. A system of gears, or belts and pulleys, can produce the property of 'mechanical advantage'. An electric motor may have a rapidly rotating shaft that is able to wield a relatively weak twisting force directly to other components. If these turning forces are directed through a system whereby small gears drive larger gears – otherwise known as reduction gearing – then a slow-moving, strong force may result. Add computer control to all this and the automatic switching on and off of electrical devices becomes possible. If computer sensing is added, then further creative situations can be devised. Examples of projects where computer-controlled mechanism can be found include modelled fairground rides, lifts and automatic barriers. Computer sensing and control programs offer opportunities since they make links between information and communication technologies and the concrete world.

MANAGING CONSTRUCTION KITS

Ensuring that the construction kits in school are well cared for and ready for use is vital if the children are going to use them creatively. Broken and missing pieces can lead to frustration and lack of enthusiasm for the task in hand and can certainly hinder creativity.

Points to consider:

▪ Who will have overall care of the kits?
▪ Who will audit the kits to check on the range available in school?
▪ Where will all the kits be kept in order that teachers can access them easily?
▪ How will they be sorted and ready for use?
▪ How will the use of the kits be timetabled to avoid double booking?
▪ Who will support staff, identifying which kits would be useful for particular aspects of D&T, for example, mechanisms, structures?

Auditing the kits will provide the information needed to check on the provision in school and to ascertain if there is a range of kits that could be used in different ways, for structures and mechanical, electrical and computer control, and would link to all the themes being undertaken across the school.

▪ **Table 7.1** Analyse school kits

Name of kit	Useful for . . .	Links to school themes
Reoclick	Frame and shell structures	Houses; Playgrounds; Out and about
Mobilo	Wheels; frame structures	Transport; Playgrounds; Moving around

CONCLUSION

Construction kits provide first-hand, concrete learning activities, enabling children to enjoy the pleasure of manipulating and adapting solutions for themselves, rather than watching a screen or the teacher. Kits provide a stimulating, tactile experience, generating curiosity and questions as solutions are explored and tested. By 'making', children model ideas, often through trial and error, as they mend and adjust the kits to find a solution. This interconnection of experiences can provide novel and creative solutions that work, thus demonstrating the value of construction kits to promote creativity.

REFERENCES

Almond, D. (2012) *The Boy Who Swam with Piranhas*. London: Walker Books Ltd.

Constable, H. (1994) 'A study of aspects of design and technology capability at Key Stage 1 and 2'. *IDATER 1994 Conference*: 9–14, Loughborough: Loughborough University.

Department of Education and Science and the Welsh Office (DES/WO) (1990) *Technology in the National Curriculum*, London: HMSO.

Francis, B. (2010) 'Gender, toys and learning', in *Oxford Review of Education* 36(3), 325–344.

Fröbel, F. (1887) *The Education of Man* (translated by Hailman, W.N.) New York and London: D. Appleton and Company.

Gerhardt, S. (2004) *Why Love Matters: How Affection Shapes a Baby's Brain*. London: Routledge.

Hill, P.S. (1908) 'The value and limitations of fröbel's gifts as educative materials, part 1 and 2'. *The Elementary School Teacher*, 9(3), 129–137, www.jstor.org/stable/992761 (accessed 17 June 2016).

Kimbell, R., Staples, K., Wheeler, T., Wosniak, A. and Kelly, V. (1991) *The Assessment of Performance in Design and Technology*, Schools Examinations and Assessment Council. London: HMSO.

Sherwin, J. (1990) 'The use of construction kits to foster equal opportunity, CDT and collaborative learning', in Tutchell, E. (ed.) *Dolls and Dungarees*. Buckingham: Open University Press.

Welch, M. (1997) 'Year 7 students use of three-dimensional modelling while designing and making'. *IDATER 1997 Conference*: 61–67. Loughborough: Loughborough University.

CHAPTER 8

EXPLORATORY AND DIALOGIC TALK AND CREATIVE LEARNING

Caroline Colfer

INTRODUCTION

Many design and technology (D&T) activities are conducted as collaborative group tasks, giving rise to necessary dialogue in order to create a solution to a problem, the success of which often relies on talk between individuals. Such problem-solving talk, typifying the nature of collaborative designing and making, is the focus of this chapter.

We start by illuminating how the key theories of constructivism and social constructivism can help us understand how children learn and offer insights into the specific role that talk plays. A consideration of compelling research on exploratory talk led by Mercer *et al.*, (1999) and Alexander's (2006) passion for dialogic talk gives us concrete evidence for how these two specific types of talk drive learning and are, therefore, so relevant for our teaching. The second half of the chapter offers practical suggestions for how we might encourage and facilitate exploratory and dialogic talk in D&T activities to fully exploit children's learning potential.

EXPLORATORY AND DIALOGIC TALK

Although research identifies different types of talk (Barnes and Todd, 1977; Mercer *et al.*, 1999; Alexander, 2006), it is exploratory and dialogic talk that have the greatest potential to drive learning. The following discussion focuses on highlighting research that convincingly argues that when children use specific types of talk to reason, it positively impacts on their ability to think and problem-solve both in groups and alone, thereby driving cognition. Since getting children to think is so fundamental to our pedagogy, this research is deemed of most significance. The discussion looks, in particular, at the work of Barnes and Todd (1977), Mercer *et al.* (1999) and Alexander (2006) in an attempt to elicit, specifically, what constitutes the types of talk that drive cognition, advance children's thinking and result in successful and creative learning.

HOW CHILDREN LEARN AND THE ROLE OF TALK AS EXPLAINED BY CONSTRUCTIVIST THEORY

Constructivist theory sees talk as *a result of* thinking and learning. It argues that we construct our own understanding individually through concrete experiences. Piaget's research led him to conclude that children's cognitive thinking developed in phases. For Piaget, learning took place as children interacted with their world, through active experiences, making links between known and new ideas. To explain this theory Piaget used the notion of schema: a network of nodes and linkages representing ideas, images, smells and insights about something. As we encounter new experiences, new information is continually added to our schema (Piaget, 1977). In D&T teaching, the curriculum is planned so children continually add to existing schemas; for example, for a schema related to wheels and movement, a reception child (aged 4–5 years) will use a jar top stuck to the side of a box, which does not move but which they still call a wheel. In Key Stage 1 (5–7 years), this child's schema is challenged by having to create wheels that move when attached to a box, so they learn that wheels need to be attached to axles. In Key Stage 2 (7–11 years), the child's schema develops further by learning that wheels can be different shapes, called cams, and these create different types of movement. More nodes and links are added to their schema when they learn that wheels can be attached to motors and controlled by electricity. A concept map could be considered a visual representation of a child's schema.

When ideas are added relatively easily to existing schema, Piaget described this as 'assimilation'. However, when it is difficult to link new information with existing schema or prior learning, Piaget named the challenging process by which we make sense of this cognitive conflict as 'accommodation'. For Piaget, only once we have assimilated and accommodated new learning are we then able to talk about it. Implications for our teaching in D&T are that we plan and teach, building on prior knowledge or existing schema. Bruner (1983) advocates learning in this way and suggests we organise a 'spiral curriculum' in which children revisit and build on prior concepts. As such, activating prior knowledge, often through talk that recaps learning, and assessing what children know and can do is so significant if children are to make progress.

While Piaget acknowledged that interactions with others could prompt children to adjust their schema leading to cognitive learning, for him, children were intrinsically motivated by their own 'agency' to learn. Further, he warned us that adult intervention can interfere with this process. Hence, his ultimate stance is that learning is an individual, problem-solving process, prompting the image of children as 'lone scientists'. Importantly, there are times when children discover learning for themselves in D&T.

HOW CHILDREN LEARN AND THE ROLE THAT TALK PLAYS, AS EXPLAINED BY SOCIAL CONSTRUCTIVIST THEORY

Vygotsky (1978) and Bruner (1983), although working independently of each other in Russia and America, agreed with many aspects of Piaget's constructivist view of learning. However, they both disputed his suggestion that learning happened in the mind of an individual, who could then talk about it with others. For them, learning happened *as a result of talking* with others; hence the label 'social' constructivism. An understanding of social constructivism helps us realise the key role that talk plays in learning.

Social constructivism is rooted in the notion that learners have the potential to achieve more. Like Piaget, Vygotsky recognised that children go through phases of development and can learn alone. However, Vygotsky's theories suggested that more could be achieved by children when working with more knowledgeable others. He proposed the idea that learners have a 'Zone of Proximal Development' (ZPD) described as 'the distance between the actual development level, as determined by individual problem-solving alone, and the level of potential development, as determined through problem-solving under adult guidance or with more capable peers' (Vygotsky, 1978: 86). For learners to cross their ZPD, the task must be carefully structured so the teacher encourages the child to bring prior knowledge and skills to the challenge, which then can be built on. For example, knowing children had prior experience of cutting and shaping play dough with a plastic knife, a teacher might ask her class to remind her how they held the knife and show her how they can already cut safely. To start them off, she might demonstrate the 'fork secure' cutting technique with soft fruits. Moving them on, she might model the 'bridge' technique with a metal paring knife and a harder fruit. In this teaching scenario, she talks through her thinking and actions, reminding the children to find the flattest side of the fruit, explaining how to tuck away forefinger and thumb and to press down with the knife. When the children can do this, she might go on to model the 'claw' technique, asking which fingers need to be tucked away. Having assessed that children have achieved this, she might challenge them to try with a harder, smaller, juicier fruit. As a result of working with a more knowledgeable other, modelling, talk in the form of explanation, questions and answers together with practice, social constructivists would argue that the child has crossed the theoretical space, described as their ZPD, and fulfilled their greater potential, thus making progress in learning. Mercer and Littleton (2007) query the emphasis on one-way dissemination between a more knowledgeable other and learner. Instead, they prefer to describe learning, in scenarios such as this, as learning in the Inter Developmental Zone. Here, learners and more knowledgeable others co-construct understanding in a more fluid theoretical space by 'inter-thinking' and staying attentive and carefully attuned to each other's developing understanding through their talk.

Inherent in a social constructivist view of learning is the notion that knowledge is co-constructed together as a result of talk. Bruner's (1983) work emphasises the cultural aspect of learning. He saw adults as 'vicars of culture', communicating what was important about living in a culture, through talk, to their children. Accepting this view allows us to see knowledge not just as constructed through talk, but something that changes throughout time and is bespoke to individual cultures.

Implications for our teaching are that when problem-solving and talking in pairs or groups, children should be encouraged to co-construct their own understanding. For the teacher, an acceptance that understanding evolves as a result of what each group deems important – and therefore outcomes will be different – is key. Accepting that there is no right answer but a number of possible solutions can be a comfort to children, facilitate further thinking and lead to more creative responses.

WHAT IS EXPLORATORY TALK?

In the seminal work of Barnes and Todd (1977), investigating pupils' talk in small groups, the researchers described talk of an 'exploratory' nature:

It is ... a collective relationship that we observed in our small group discussions. Members were free to shift the topic, to try out new formulations and to explore alternatives, since none of the questions asked concealed positional claims to impose a frame on the discussion to guide its direction or to judge the relevance of answers. The members of our groups cast their bread upon the waters. They were each others' (sic) resources and most of their utterances were contributions to thinking.

(Barnes and Todd, 1977: 126–127)

Subsumed in this quote is the belief that knowledge is not fixed but can be treated as a negotiable commodity. Barnes and Todd observed that pupils were most likely to engage in such dialogic exchanges when they were among peers and beyond the control of a teacher. In such a context, they saw pupils take more active and independent ownership of their learning. This finding has particular resonance with the theories of Piaget who felt children would be unlikely to take issue with the opposing views of an adult because of the differences in power and status. However, disagreement with peers served to highlight alternatives to the child's point of view and necessitate resolution; thereby prompting children to intellectual progress. For Piaget (cited in Mercer and Littleton, 2007: 10), 'criticism is born of discussion and discussion is only possible among equals'. Such an argument has significant implications for pedagogy since it suggests that, to truly foster children's talk and thinking, the teacher should only facilitate the discussion, not be a part of it.

Building on the work of Barnes and Todd (1977), Mercer *et al.* (1999) found most classroom talk could be categorised into the following typology: disputational, cumulative or exploratory. The typology is evaluative and hierarchical in terms of educational value. It provides a framework to analyse talk in terms of its effectiveness for joint reasoning and knowledge construction. Exploratory talk, representing the pursuit of rational consensus through dialogue, is deemed the type of talk that encourages collaborative reasoning and drives cognition – that which we should be striving to foster in D&T lessons.

The extract of talk is from a group of Y6 children and exemplifies what exploratory talk looks like in a design and technology scenario. They are designing and making controllable vehicles and have been asked to find the best way to join wheels to axles and axles to chassis: an evaluative and investigative activity.

Exploratory talk is:

... talk, in which partners engage critically but constructively with each other's ideas. Statements and suggestions are offered for joint consideration. These may be challenged and counter-challenged, but challenges are justified and alternative hypotheses are offered. Partners all actively participate, and opinions are sought and considered before decisions are jointly made ... in exploratory talk knowledge is made more publically accountable and reasoning is more visible in the talk.

(Mercer and Littleton, 2007: 59)

Design Process/ Behaviour	Dialogue	Type of Talk
Modelling Jo reaches for elastic and dowel to model as she explains	**Jo**: You know when we get a piece of doweling then, can you pull it off please?, thank you, and then erm, you got the wheel on, and then this is quite, have we got any thick ones, oh I don't think we have got any thick ones, you could wrap it round it like that.	Sharing idea
Evaluating weaknesses	**Annie**: The only problem with that is that the wheel'll slide off the other end	Critical but constructive engagement
	Tim: And if, and if the elastic band	Active engagement
	Annie: (interrupts) Breaks, see, that's holding the wheel from going down the axle that way, the only problem with that is the wheel might slide off the other way	Critical but constructive engagement
Generating idea	**Edmund**: But then you put an elastic band both sides	Alternative hypothesis presented
	Tim: That's, yeah	
	Annie: Yeah, so	Joint agreement
	Edmund: So	
	Annie: Yeah so that's your idea	
Modelling Ed uses wheels and axles to demonstrate his understanding	**Edmund**: So your wheels are like that, yeah, and you put elastic band there to block it (Jo hums) elastic band, yeah but the thing is	Elaborating on Jo's idea/active engagement
Generating idea	**Annie**: (interrupts) You're going to have to do one wheel at a time	Critical but constructive engagement
Evaluating	**Edmund**: No the elastic band might slip off	Justified challenge
Evaluating	**Annie**: True	Critical but constructive engagement
	Tim: And, and really	
	Jo: No, cos its really tight	Counter challenge
Generating idea	**Annie**: You could tape it	Alternative hypothesis offered
Evaluating	**Tim**: There's another thing, there's another thing, the elastic band might snap	Reasoning
Generating idea	**Jo**: Yeah, you put an elastic band then tape around it	Elaboration
Evaluating	**Annie**: It, it strengthens the elastic band doesn't it?	Reasoning
	Edmund: Yes, yes that's a good idea.	Confirmation/joint agreement

Talk among this group (Table 8.1) was almost wholly exploratory and exhibited all the features of that defined by Mercer *et al.* (1999). All children shared ideas and were listened to. Ground rules were adhered to throughout. The value of exploratory talk is clearly illustrated.

Jo's initial suggestion was to wrap elastic bands around an axle, at the outer edge of the wheels, to secure them to the axle. All peers actively engaged with her idea and contributed collaboratively in proposing a securer and stronger fixing. Children voiced their concerns – 'the wheel might slide off' – the other way', 'the elastic band might slip off', and 'the elastic band might snap'; expressing constructive criticality. Speech acts, generating ideas and evaluating them, were chained together to achieve a more sophisticated understanding as possible solutions were 'put through the evaluation mill'. The dialogue was generative and discursive in that as soon as an idea was shared, a possible problem was highlighted and an alternative idea speculated. When challenged, Jo counter-asserted her position by reasoning that the elastic bands would be tightly secured. However, she did accept that adding tape to the elastics, either side of each wheel, would be an improved design. Here, knowledge, in the creation of a more secure fixing, was co-constructed by exploratory talk, taking participants, and most specifically Jo, beyond what they already knew.

Implications for D&T suggest:

1. Evaluation activities have powerful potential to promote true exploratory talk.
2. Cognitive gains can be achieved in D&T when children negotiate meaning and achieve a shared understanding beyond what each child knows individually.
3. Creative outcomes, that are more functional and sophisticated solutions, can be realised when children work collaboratively in groups and reach agreement through exploratory talk.

The exciting thing about getting children to use exploratory talk is that they learn from each other. They are each other's resources and activate each other's cognitive processes, so learning may go well beyond the limits of a teacher's planning.

Mercer *et al.* (1999) argue the case for exploratory talk, which they perceive as epitomising language that embodies accountability, clarity, constructive criticism and receptiveness to well-argued proposals – all qualities that are necessary for participation in 'educated' communities of discourse such as law, science, technology, the arts, business and politics. Consequently, children need to learn and use such exploratory language to not only participate in educational activities but because of the potential impact it may have on their individual cognitive development, their peers' learning and their creative output.

WHAT IS DIALOGIC TALK AND HOW DOES IT DIFFER FROM EXPLORATORY TALK?

Alexander (2006) argues convincingly for the significance of classroom talk that is based on dialogue, understood as a genuine reciprocal discussion that builds shared understanding. Nearly 30 years after the insights of Barnes and Todd (1977), Alexander still sees the need to 'harness the power of talk to engage children, stimulate and extend their thinking and advance their learning and understanding' (Alexander, 2006: 37). In clarifying exactly what kind of talk he sees as productive, Alexander argues for talk that is collective, reciprocal, supportive, cumulative and purposeful. This is explained as talk in which learning tasks are addressed together, ideas are articulated freely, shared, listened to and alternative viewpoints considered, participants help each other to reach common understanding, ideas are built on and chained into coherent lines of enquiry and talk is steered towards meeting specific educational goals. Although such talk may be between pupils as well as pupils and teachers, a teacher hoping to encourage deeper engagement and more creative solutions through dialogic talk will need to explicitly model this with her children.

While this talk might seem very similar to exploratory talk, Alexander (2006) and Mercer *et al.* (1999) differ in the need for participants to reach agreement. For Mercer *et al.*, this is a necessary feature that drives debate. However, Alexander, who argues that when a question fails to give rise to another question it falls out of the conversation, sees agreement as the feature that paralyses the dialogue, bringing it to an end. Comparing classroom talk in five countries, Alexander (2006) concluded that talk in British classrooms remains stubbornly restricted to predominately initiation, response and feedback (IRF) exchanges (see Table 8.2) between teachers and children, explained as:

Initiation: a question from the teacher which is usually one to which she already knows the answer.

Response: an answer from the child, usually in very few words.

Feedback: a response from the teacher, usually 'good', 'yes' or 'no', 'not quite'.

▨ **Table 8.2** IRF example

Design Process	Dialogue	Type of Talk
Investigating/ Evaluating	**Teacher:** Which sandwich snack do you think is the most appealing?	Initiation
	Ben: The duck and hoisin wrap	Response
	Teacher: Good	Feedback

In dialogic talk, the IRF exchange is replaced by a more questioning and elaborating approach which seeks to reciprocate and extend what a speaker offers, thus balancing the conversation and probing for deeper thinking.

Nystrand *et al.* (1997) identified three key features of dialogic talk:

1. 'Authentic questions': genuine questions to which there may be more than one answer and to which the teacher does not know the answer;
2. 'Uptake': where responses are a feature of subsequent questions;
3. 'High level evaluation': how the teacher validates and elaborates on a child's response.

In this dialogic exchange (Table 8.3), rather than just accept Jenny's answer, the teacher's feedback builds on what she has said. Jenny's response is rather like a fulcrum or pivot point to the teacher's follow-up or uptake. In a dialogic conversation, speakers need to be good listeners to respond in a way which keeps the dialogue going to explore

Table 8.3 Dialogic talk

Design Process	Dialogue	Type of Talk
Investigating/ Evaluating	**Teacher:** Which sandwich snack do you think is the most appealing?	authentic question
	Jenny: The duck and hoisin wrap	
	Teacher: Sometimes I order duck in hoisin sauce from the Chinese; I wonder what other Chinese dishes would be good in a wrap?	uptake elaborates on the response to previous question and poses another
		authentic question validating child's response
	Jenny: I like chicken chow mein . . . maybe chicken chow mein wraps would be good?	
	Teacher: The vegetables would make it crunchy	uptake elaborates on the response
	Jenny: Yes and the noodles feel soft in my mouth	uptake elaborates on response
	Teacher: Maybe you like food with different textures?	high level evaluation

an authentic question more deeply. The teacher's uptake response validates Jenny by confirming she also likes duck and hoisin sauce. The power of teacher modelling is exploited when she offers, 'The vegetables would make it crunchy'. Repeating the sentence idea, Jenny mirrors the model by describing how the noodles feel. The teacher elaborates in a reciprocal way, inviting the child to think creatively, build on what she knows, share her ideas and construct new understanding.

Dialogic talk requires skilful listening, quick thinking and an element of 'free-styling' or willingness to improvise on the part of the teacher; who may have to depart from the questions on her lesson plan. In a dialogic lesson, the planned questions become the jumping-off points for genuine dialogues: grappling with misconceptions or curious enquiry leading to deeper, more satisfying understanding and speculative, creative thought.

CLASSROOM IDEAS: HOW CAN WE FACILITATE EXPLORATORY TALK AND A MORE DIALOGIC APPROACH IN D&T?

Before expecting children to attempt talking in groups, something that can be beset with difficulties, children could devise a set of ground rules to guide their behaviour when talking and listening. They can easily devise these rules themselves and continually revisit and modify them.

Devising ground rules

Organise children to work in groups of ten; children pair up A and B.

A are talkers and, as a group, talk for a few minutes on a given subject.

B are observers/listeners and listen to the discussion, noting members' behaviour on post-its, for example, giving a reason, staying silent, interrupting, praising someone's idea.

Groups swap roles and repeat the activity.

They sort the behaviours described on post-its into two groups called Desirable Behaviours and Not Desirable Behaviours.

Groups compare behaviours and refine a set of rules written in child-friendly and positive language.

Planning for talk

With such a busy curriculum, it is often difficult to fit in activities just related to talk. A more time-efficient approach might be to link talk learning objectives to existing curriculum learning objectives. Since dialogic and exploratory talk skills take time and practice to develop, lessons could focus on promoting particular talk learning objectives over time.

Talk learning objectives:

■ to include everyone in the group
■ to share all ideas openly
■ to ask for and give reasons
■ to challenge what others say in a respectful manner
■ to sum up and come to an agreement
■ to request information and seek clarification
■ to constructively challenge and offer an alternative
■ to suggest a question for further discussion

You need to be good at listening if you are going to be a good talker.

Listening is not the absence of talking but the presence of active hearing. For children, D&T activity is often busy and noisy and it can be hard to listen to others when all you want to do is make. It might be easier for children to initially focus on developing good listening skills at the investigative and evaluative activities stage (see Chapter 1), since these are often discussion-based. Learning objectives linked to encouraging listening could be:

■ to listen to others' points of view
■ to repeat and elaborate on what a preceding speaker has said.

The following selection of ideas could be used to enhance thinking in the investigative and evaluative, focused tasks and design, make and evaluate stages of a unit of work.

INVESTIGATIVE AND EVALUATIVE ACTIVITIES

These activities call for children to investigate and evaluate a selection of designed and made products. When assembling collections of products, choose as wide a range as possible. For example, in a collection of toy vehicles, choose any that might constitute a vehicle. Choose vehicles made from different materials, for different users and purposes, with different axle and wheel arrangements and with different features. Seeing how designers answer a brief in so many ways encourages children to be creative in their own choices later on.

Including the phrase *'Do you think'* in our questions seeks to elicit children's personal response. It does not assume there is one right answer that the child must give, but implies it is what the child *thinks* that is important. A more dialogic exchange is encouraged as questions can be followed up with a genuine exploration of the child's reasons. To assess current understanding and allow children to build on prior knowledge, ask a starter question such as: 'Tell your partner anything you already know about these products?' Model, discuss and display the language you might hear. My research into children's talk when problem-solving in D&T suggested when children used conditionals such as 'might' and 'could', ideas were more readily accepted by group members as the language suggested tentativeness (Colfer, 2014).

The following questions are designed to draw children's attention to the specific features of a product that designers will have considered. Knowledge created through talking through answers to these questions is often bespoke to the distinctive nature of D&T lessons. However, it could be used in science and English; for example, an understanding of the design features of shoes will give a child many ideas to write about in his letter of complaint to the manufacturer about his faulty trainers.

Creating designerly questions (further discussion is in Chapter 3)

Talk learning objectives:

■   to request information and seek clarification
■   to suggest a question for further discussion.
■   to ask for and give reasons

Handle and talk about the different products you have collected together, for example, money containers, vehicles.

Write any questions, queries, puzzles you have about the products or any individual product on a post-it. Teachers explain that asking questions and seeking clarification is a talking skill.

> Requesting information and seeking clarification: I wonder if, how does it work, I would like to understand more about, I want to know, can you explain, can we find out if.

Display the questions on post-its asking children to sort them into similar groups. Label the questions; for example, questions about cost.

Asking designerly questions

Talk learning objectives:

■   to share all ideas openly
■   to challenge what others say in a respectful manner
■   to sum up and come to an agreement

Model language that children might find useful before asking them to discuss the questions. Encourage children to share their own ideas and opinions first and then come to a joint agreement.

Sharing ideas: I think, I feel, It seems to me that, I believe, I heard, this one might be the . . . because, you could say this one is the . . . as,

Challenging ideas respectfully: I hear what you are saying but I think . . . because, I disagree because, I have come to a different decision, the only problem with that suggestion is, one disadvantage of doing it that way could be, I can see what you mean but, have you considered another way of looking at this could be, perhaps if we tried,

Summing up and coming to a joint agreement: There are good reasons for both ideas but it seems that . . . has stronger reasons, our ideas are different but most seem to agree that, in conclusion we think, having thought about all our ideas and reasons we think . . . is the best because, we seem to have decided as a group that,

Cost: Which do you think is the most expensive, cheapest and why?

Aesthetics: Which do you think looks, feels, tastes, smells the most appealing?

Function/Fitness for Purpose: What job do you think each product does and how well does it do its job?

Ergonomics: How do you think the product has been designed to suit the users' physical size?

Quality: Which product do you think is the best made?

User: Who do you think each of these products has been designed and made for?

Environment: Which product do you think has used most of the earth's resources?

CAFÉ QUE is an acronym for the above groups. Ask children if they can think of another clever way to remember the groups of questions designers think about.

Sort!

Talk learning objective:

■ to share all ideas openly

Collect a range of products made of differing materials, designed for different users and purposes, for example, bags, snacks, vehicles.

Think of all the ways you can sort the products.

These are the same but this is different, what do you think?

Talk learning objective:

■ to ask for and give reasons

Choose two products that have one feature in common and one product where that particular feature is different and explain your reasoning. When a child has offered a suggestion, they encourage another by asking, 'What do you think, Jamie?'

Remembering CAFÉ QUE will prompt recognition of features.

Connections

Talk learning objective:

▓   to give reasons

Lay out all the products in two vertical parallel lines on a large sheet of paper. Children take turns to draw a line between two products that are the same in any way: for example, the organic cookie and the fair trade breakfast bar might be bought by people with more disposable income.

A child or teacher scribes the technical vocabulary generated in a list on the whiteboard. These can be discussed and referred to throughout the unit of work.

The activity can be adapted so children are asked to connect two products that are different: for example, the skateboard and fire truck are different because the skateboard has one chassis but the fire truck has two chassis joined together.

Top of the range or bargain basement!

Talk learning objectives:

▓   to constructively challenge and offer an alternative
▓   to repeat and elaborate on what a preceding speaker has said

In your opinion, which product do you individually think is the best and the worst? If you differ in opinion from someone in the group, show you have listened by repeating their opinion first, then offering your alternative opinion or idea. Alternatively, if you agree with what a previous speaker has suggested then repeat their idea, smile at them to acknowledge their suggestion, and then give a fuller explanation or reason why their idea is a good one.

Now decide which product is the best and worst overall? Teachers reassure children that it is fine to change their mind after listening to others' reasons.

Constructive challenge and offer an alternative: I can see the reason why you think this one is best but I think this one is better because, this one might be more aesthetically pleasing/ fun but that one does the job better, I agree with your choice for the best but this one is . . . and . . . so could be voted the worst, one problem with this one might be,

At first I thought . . . but now I have listened to everyone's opinions I think, I have been persuaded by . . . reasons, that is a good, logical reason, argument, explanation,

So, as a group it seems we favour, we have decided, we agree, we think,

The following activities could encourage any or all of the talk learning objectives.

Always, usually, sometimes, never

Decide if the following statements are always, usually, sometimes or never true.

a. Vehicles have four wheels and two axles.
b. The best shoes have grip on their soles.
c. Sandwiches are low in nutritional value.
d. Purses with zips keep your money safe.

Agree, disagree, unsure

Discussion of statements like these, before and after a unit of work on moving toys, could also help children clarify misconceptions and help a teacher assess understanding.

a. Cams control the speed and direction of movement.
b. It does not matter where the pivot is positioned in an eccentric cam.
c. Cams convert rotary movement into linear movement.
d. Cam followers move in a reciprocating way.

FOCUSED PRACTICAL TASKS

During this stage of a unit of work, children develop particular knowledge and skills that will help them carry out the design and make activity.

Market research

When designing a real product for a real user, it is helpful for children to conduct market research to collect information about what their clients' needs or preferences are. Although each of the following activities encourages aspects of exploratory talk, it is when designers collect and analyse all the market research that debate among the designers about how to meet these needs can encourage creative problem-solving. In this scenario, the group must create an agreed solution, so Mercer *et al.*'s (1999) exploratory talk, rather than Alexander's (2006) dialogic talk, best describes what we are hoping to achieve.

Hedonic table

A hedonic table () allows children, in their role as designers, to quickly survey a group of clients – for example, the netball team who want a healthy sandwich snack for after the game – and gather information as to the most popular choice of ingredient.

Ranking table

Clients: Taste the samples and place the bread choices in rank order (Table 8.5).
    If all members of the netball team complete the table with their preferences in order, the designers can start to see how to cater for their client's preferences.

■ **Table 8.4** Hedonic table

	Like a lot	Like	Neither like nor dislike	Do not like
Lettuce				
Red cabbage				
Celery				

■ **Table 8.5** Ranking table

	1st	2nd	3rd
Wholemeal pitta			
Seeded brown slice			
Wrap			

Devising design criteria and star diagrams

Designers: ask your clients to thought-shower ideas for the product they want made for them under the following headings:

Here's how an upper primary (10–11 years) netball team responded to the question: What words come to mind to describe the sandwich snack you would like us to make for you?

Design criteria

Clients decide on one of the suggestions offered in each category, giving their reasons and challenging or counter-challenging as they wish. Highlight the chosen word in each category on the design criteria chart (Table 8.6) and write it on the end of a point on the star diagram.

■ **Table 8.6** Design criteria chart

Cost	Aesthetics	Function	Ergonomics	User	Environment
luxury	shaped like a netball	energy boost	easy to eat on the go	likes healthy eating	locally produced ingredients
expensive	like a winner's cup	after-game snack	bite-size	growing	organic ingredients
value for money	colourful		big sandwiches	needs energy	fair trade ingredients

Star diagram

Designers: collect the design criteria chart to inform making
Clients: retain the star diagram to use when evaluating the product made for you.

Using market research to inform designing

Market research allows children to debate in a genuinely collaborative and exploratory way which ingredients, components and materials they could choose to answer the design brief. This is an excellent activity, facilitating all aspects of exploratory talk, as designers have to make genuine decisions and there will often be contention; for example, some designers may choose to ignore the preferences of their toddler clients and include fruit in the biscuits they make them for their teddy bears' picnic; designers may disagree about which ingredient to include that will meet their clients' specification for 'chewy', 'tasty' or 'luxurious'.

DESIGN, MAKE AND EVALUATE ASSIGNMENT

Children who have investigated and evaluated a range of products, have been taught the making skills and techniques and have collected market research about their clients' needs and preferences are now in a strong position to design, make and evaluate a creative solution to the design brief. Since we are hoping to encourage creative solutions through exploratory and dialogic talk, collaborative group work provides the greatest opportunity to achieve this.

Evaluating the processes and products

Encourage children to evaluate both the product and processes, with their group, as they make.

In the final evaluation, clients can evaluate the strengths and weaknesses of the product made for them; for example, the netball team can debate how luxurious their sandwich snack actually is and give it a mark out of five on their star diagram. Once they have tasted or tested their product, the star diagram can also help prompt feedback to the designers. Again, the contentious nature of evaluation and feedback will give rise to children disagreeing, justifying their choices with reasoning, challenge and counter challenge. As such, this is an excellent activity for encouraging exploratory talk skills in a safe, authentic and educationally productive way.

A FINAL THOUGHT

I am, at heart, a primary teacher, and a strong advocate of a broad and balanced curriculum and a holistic view of the child. A very exciting thing about focusing on exploratory and dialogic talk is that it is not just the prerogative of one subject area but a major arterial link between all subjects. More potent yet, if we can encourage the use of exploratory and dialogic talk in D&T, these talk skills will transfer beyond their pedagogical value in the classroom to successful communication in all aspects of life, work, society and relationships. Today's exploratory and dialogic talkers are tomorrow's designers, diplomats, architects, engineers, lawyers and leaders.

REFERENCES

Alexander, R. (2006) *Towards Dialogic Teaching: Rethinking Classroom Talk.* York: Dialogos.

Barnes, D. and Todd, F. (1977) *Communication and Learning in Small Groups*. London: Routledge.

Bruner, J. (1983) *Child's Talk: Learning to Use Language*. Oxford: Oxford University Press.

Colfer, C. (2014) 'Mechanisms employed by primary school children to establish and maintain collaboration and achieve exploratory talk to enable enhanced problem-solving', in Mercer, N. and Littleton, K. (eds) (2007) *Dialogue and the Development of Children's Thinking: A Socio-cultural Approach*. Oxon: Routledge.

Mercer, N. and Littleton, K. (eds) (2007) *Dialogue and the Development of Children's Thinking: A Socio-cultural Approach*. Oxon: Routledge.

Mercer, N. Wegerif, R. and Dawes, L. (1999) 'Children's talk and the development of reasoning in the classroom'. *British Educational Research Journal*, 13(1), 95–111.

Nystrand, M., Gameran, A., Kachur, R. and Prendergast, C. (1997) *Opening Dialogue: Understanding the Dynamics of Language and Learning in the English Classroom*. New York: Teachers College Press.

Piaget, J. (1977) *Sociological Studies*. London: Routledge.

Vygotsky, L. (1978) *Mind in Society: The Developmental of Higher Psychological Processes*. Cambridge, MA: Harvard University Press.

CHAPTER 9

CREATIVITY IN FOOD

*Suzanne Lawson and
Sue Wood-Griffiths*

INTRODUCTION

Through a variety of creative and practical activities, pupils should be taught the understanding and skills needed to engage in an iterative process of designing and making. Teaching food creatively in the primary classroom should not be about making different varieties of cupcakes or pizza. It is about children producing purposeful, functional, appealing products for themselves and other users based on healthy eating principles.

Creativity in food is also not about drawing or making extravagantly coloured food. Children need to work with food using a variety of tools and equipment to develop their skills (for example, cutting, shaping, mixing, combining and finishing). To do this, they need to select from a wide range of ingredients, understanding both their source and some of their working characteristics. To develop their evaluating skills, they might explore (try and taste) a range of existing products, as well as evaluating their own ideas and outcomes against criteria with a user and purpose in mind.

WASTE NOT, WANT NOT

The terms 'creativity' and 'food' can cause a tension when voiced together. On the one hand, we want spark and originality but on the other we want an edible product. If we are trying to avoid waste, perhaps creativity should be discouraged and replaced with a more dictatorial, functional approach to food education? When Dimbleby and Vincent (2013: 37) considered food in English schools, they noted that 'instilling a love of cooking in pupils will also open a door to one of the great expressions of human creativity'. Fautley and Savage (2007) observe that children who are encouraged to think creatively and independently become interested in discovering things for themselves; they try new things and are keen to work with others to explore ideas. The problem here is the definition of the term 'creativity' within the context of food.

Fautley and Savage (2007) explore the definition of the term, identifying key words such as 'doing' and 'action'. They suggest that the key to any 'active process' to make it truly 'creative' is the element of decision-making or choosing different paths at key points. Fautley and Savage then further clarify the definition to involve mental processes including actions within a domain that are purposeful and novel (to the individual). A design and technologist would interpret this process as constructing a specification to address. If this approach is applied in the classroom we can support children to work creatively and manage the tension of wasting food. The type of creativity we want to recognise and value is 'everyday creativity' and asking children to design within the boundaries of a value system can secure this.

The fact that creativity is not a simple process and cannot be defined as a unitary construct means that when teaching children about food we need to unpick issues associated with teaching creatively to ensure learning happens over time. We are not suggesting that creative learning is different or discrete; after all, learning should create new meaning for the individual and require them to 'think really hard'. What distinguishes creative learning, however defined, is that it is an active process, where the learner is engaged in and with the task (with a user and a purpose in mind), and where this engagement results in new knowledge. For creativity within the context of food education, this must involve food. For real learning to happen, the pupils cannot learn via video, worksheet, pictures, discussion, role play or imagination alone; they need to be 'doing' with food. Despite cost, availability, health and safety, resources or other challenges, teachers must ensure pupils have hands-on experience of working and problem-solving with food, which may require further creativity on the teacher's part.

IDENTIFYING A USER AND A PURPOSE IN FOOD

We do not necessarily need to set children artificial 'problems' (e.g. the Queen is coming to dinner so design her a pudding), but we do need to support pupils to develop strategies that will help them to think in a 'designerly' fashion (think through problems in the midst of designing and making). Davies and Howe (2009) note that, for a food technologist, designing a sandwich that will stick together, taste pleasant and not make the bread soggy presents a range of challenging problems. By providing children with a user and a purpose, we can ask them to design within the boundaries of a value system. These values could relate to healthy eating, sustainability, seasonality, cost, function or aesthetics, for example.

The user and the purpose should not be constraints on creativity. Davies and Howe (2009) note that the starting point (see others in Chapter 4) for creativity could be:

■ building on children's interests
■ identifying real opportunities
■ using relevant contexts.

For younger children, the starting point may be themselves. Designing a sandwich might have the starting point of a discussion about their particular preferences. The teacher may judge that it would be too demanding to think of the needs of others, at the same time as meeting the requirements to plan before making and to remember safe hygiene practices. As children move through the primary phase and become more confident working with food, there can be a scaffolded transition from egocentricity to awareness of the perspective of others.

One of the key findings of research into creativity (Howe *et al.* 2001) is the central importance of peers, supportive adults and role models. Involving food experts so that children are co-workers solves many organisational issues in the classroom and allows behaviours to be modelled and skills to be demonstrated. These experts could be a local baker, a chef or even a child's grandparent, depending on the context of the work. Visitors to the classroom can provide a genuine opportunity for children to 'bounce ideas' off each other and challenge formulaic thinking.

YOU ARE WHAT YOU EAT

When working alone or with others, children need to know about making good food choices, and this knowledge and understanding should be the basis of their creative work with food in schools. Public Health England (2015) suggests that adopting a whole school approach to food education across subjects such as science, personal, social, health and economic education (PSHE) and physical education (PE) can secure consistency of key concepts and healthy eating messages. Good food education is at the heart of the health and wellbeing agenda and if children can understand that they literally 'are what they eat', teachers are in a position to motivate a change in pupils' eating behaviour, for example, influencing the uptake of healthier school lunch choices, and encouraging them to try and work with a wider variety of foods. Within the context of teaching creatively, pupils should be encouraged to adopt an exploratory approach to working with food. We eat every day and so food provides great opportunities for everyday creativity.

KEY MESSAGES ABOUT HEALTHY EATING

When teaching children about healthy eating, teachers should be referring to current nutritional advice, and the British Nutrition Foundation website (www.foodafactoflife. org.uk), is a good point of reference for teachers around the world.

The UK's national food guide, updated in 2016, is the *Eatwell Guide* (Public Health England, 2016). This is a visual representation of the proportions of food required for a healthy diet for adults and children over 5 years old and is widely used by schools, health professionals and consumer organisations to convey a consistent message about healthy eating. Similar models prevail in the USA and Australia and now seem to be replacing other models such as the Healthy Food Pyramid, which has been another popular visual representation.

Teaching children to choose and work with a variety of foods within the four largest segments of the *Eatwell Guide* will add to the range of nutrients consumed. Using the *Eatwell Guide*, the following messages are central to promoting healthy choices for children:

▓ Eat plenty of fruit and vegetables
▓ Eat plenty of bread, rice, potatoes, pasta and other starchy foods
▓ Drink some milk and eat some dairy foods
▓ Eat some meat, fish, eggs, beans and other non-dairy sources of protein
▓ Avoid foods and drinks high in fat and/or sugar most of the time – these are not essential to a healthy diet and should be consumed only occasionally as treats and in small amounts
▓ Avoid adding salt to your food
▓ Drink plenty of water
▓ Always eat breakfast
▓ Requirements for food change through life

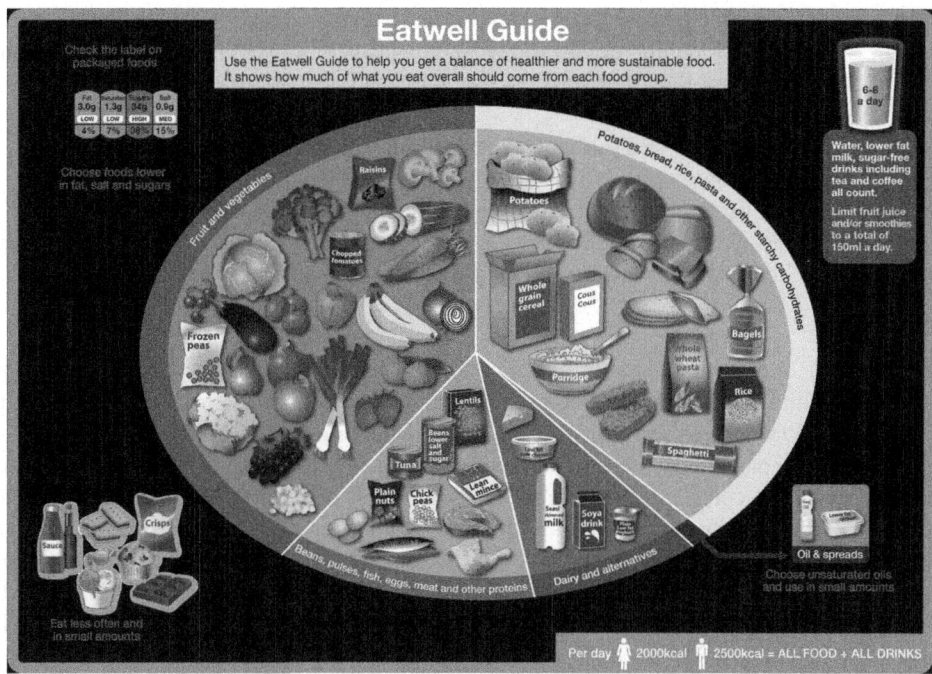

■ **Figure 9.1** Eatwell Guide (Public Health England, 2016)

This guidance should serve to help teachers plan their food activities and act as a guide to the foods children can work with. It is really important when teaching children about healthy food choices that foods are not demonised or banned and that children understand that their requirements for food change through life. They can make sweet things when the user and purpose requires this.

EXPLORE, DESIGN AND MAKE

How can we use these healthy eating messages to support children to explore, design and make with food and address curricula guidance? Throughout the UK and further afield, different curriculum guidance applies but recurring themes are that children should be taught how to design and make food products that solve real and relevant problems. As mentioned earlier, for younger children, the problem-solving often stems from building on their own interests in food and resolving any tension arising from a task initiated by their likes (or perceived likes). It is important that they are given a range of foodstuff to work with and to provide them with real choice. It is here that you can inspire them to be creative and to try new things. It is also important that the tasks they engage with are supported by suitable resources and equipment for their skill level. However, a lack of resources should never be an excuse for not working with food – children can develop a significant range of cooking skills (e.g. mashing, scooping, spreading, cutting, crimping) with basic table cutlery. If a school does not have a full-size cooker with a grill, hob and oven available, a combination microwave that can conventionally cook, microwave and grill enables pupils to undertake most cooking processes.

It is likely that the food work undertaken is integrated into other 'topic' work. Nevertheless, pupils' design and technology capability should be being developed through the food work they undertake. A useful pedagogical approach to adopt is to:

■ investigate and evaluate existing foods (products)
■ develop identified skills through focussed practical tasks (these are likely to focus on using equipment safely and developing basic skills)
■ design and make their own food products (where children are given the opportunity to make choices and plan and make their own ideas using the skills they have been taught).

Let us think how this might work in practice and how the same key messages about healthy eating might be explored. Assume we want to get across the message 'Don't skip breakfast'. There are many ways that this could be developed into part of a scheme of work.

For younger children (aged 3–5), this could start off by evaluating a selection of breakfast cereals. If permission was sought, this could start with tasting and testing. They could sort the cereals into the different grains (for example, wheat, oats, corn, rice, and so on) and explore where these cereal crops are grown. They could add some fresh fruit (using skills to hull fruit, pick grapes from a vine, mash fruit such as a banana with a fork, peel satsumas or bananas by hand). Further early years ideas are in Chapter 3. This could also link to a farm or shop visit or to an 'online field trip'. Chapter 11 has more on learning outside the classroom.

At the lower primary phase (aged 5–7), children could be challenged to design their own breakfast for themselves and a friend. To develop the task into a design and make opportunity, children could be provided with a selection of additional foodstuffs that they add to their cereal. This might include different grain cereals, a variety of fruits (dried, fresh and tinned) and a selection of unsweetened dairy products (milk, yogurt, fromage frais) to combine ingredients, thus creating their breakfast. Careful questioning can prompt them to think about how they will prepare the fruit (cutting, snipping, mashing, slicing, scooping), and the function of the ingredients they decide to include (adding sweetness, moisture, crunch). By carefully selecting the ingredients available to the children, they can be prompted to try new ingredients and to combine them in different ways.

Older pupils (aged 7–11) can use a wider range of equipment, making the same task more demanding. Again, permission for tasting and testing should be sought and note taken of any food intolerances. The pupils could start off by evaluating a selection of breads they could eat at breakfast, and they could explore the origin of the products. This could be developed, adopting some of the value decisions discussed earlier, considering how ingredients travel and the mode of transport. At this level, the design and make challenge might centre on making a topping for the bread. The pupils could be provided with a range of dairy products, eggs, vegetables and pulses to make their topping, or if a narrower brief was preferred, the pupils could be challenged to make the best baked bean topping using haricot beans, vegetables and a simple tomato sauce. As before, empowering children to select and combine the ingredients and think about how these might be prepared and cooked can support them to try out new ideas and understand how foods may be combined in different ways. This activity can also support pupils to investigate how food changes when it is cooked (for example, scrambled, poached or boiled eggs; melted cheese; softened vegetables) or how different flavours combine (beans and cheese, tomatoes and herbs).

Encouraging pupils to creatively combine ingredients in suitable proportions can promote creativity as they productively experiment with ingredients. The 'baked bean' activity could be a group spin-off challenge from the breakfast task, and pupils could develop a 'pitch' for their products, thinking about the user and purpose, and compare them to a leading brand as part of the evaluation.

These activities, while focusing on the same key message, provide opportunities to convey healthy eating. The activities have a clear sense of progression in terms of complexity, skills and designerly thinking, as well as moving children on to thinking beyond their own needs to meeting the needs of others.

DEVELOPING A COMPLEXITY OF SKILLS

The breakfast example above demonstrates the development of practical skills within a creative context. Spendlove and Wells (2013) note that many teachers want to provide creative opportunities but are unsure how to proceed and sometimes feel limited by the risks they can take in a culture that perceives performance in narrow terms. By considering progression in the complexity of skills, risk can be managed to suit the ability of the child. In the early years education breakfast example, the number of ingredients was limited and the associated skills included pulling, crushing and simple peeling (bananas and satsumas). As the children progress (aged 5–7), juicing, peeling (using a swivel peeler with adult support), spreading soft ingredients and simple shaping are proposed. Older pupils (7–11) might peel, juice, press, spread, shape and mould as indicated in Figure 9.2, published by the Design and Technology Association (www.data.org.uk).

Practical foods skills progression chart for pupils aged 3-11 years				
Food skills	Age 3-5	Age 5-7	Age 7-9	Age 9-11
	Pull - hull fruit, pick grapes from vine			
	Crush - soft fruit with a potato masher or fork, e.g. raspberries as a topping for yogurt or for a fruit drink	**Juice** - using a juicer to extract juice, e.g. orange	**Press** - using a garlic press	
	Peel - by hand, e.g. satsuma, banana	**Peel** - with a swivel peeler with adult support	**Peel** - with a swivel peeler with supervision	**Peel** - with a swivel peel to create food ribbons to be used in a dish, e.g. courgette/carrot ribbons with supervision
		Spread - soft ingredients, e.g. hummus	**Spread** - ingredients evenly over another food	
	Shape - foods by hand and with a rolling pin	**Shape** - with accuracy for a desired effect, e.g. basic bread roll - use a rolling pin	**Shape and mould** - to create visually appealing products e.g. mini cottage loaf or plait, wrap	

■ **Figure 9.2** Practical food skills progression chart (Design and Technology Association www.data.org.uk)

EXPERIMENTS AND INVESTIGATIONS

Experiments and investigations are a practical way to teach skills and technical knowledge and understanding in a practical context. Carrying out experiments and investigations with food helps children to understand the principles underlying some methods of food preparation, and supports teachers to make links between other areas of the curriculum. Food investigations can also create lots of opportunities for children to taste 'new' foods. To support pupils and teachers to be creative on a regular basis, an annual letter to parents requesting permission for pupils to participate in tasting sessions that requires them to make you aware of any allergies, intolerances or religious food constraints needs to be returned (an example is included at the end of the chapter).

There are some health and safety rules to consider in terms of food allergies and intolerances, and food hygiene (for example, pupils need to be trained not to 'double dip'). Once you have these rules in place, the opportunities to be creative are almost limitless. Teachers could set up a 'bushtucker trial' to encourage pupils to try new foodstuffs (primarily, but not exclusively, fruits and vegetables); children could try different festival food; they could taste their way through the alphabet or a rainbow.

Fruits and vegetables, the groups of food we need to eat most of, can provide opportunities for creative investigations in D&T and for pupils to engage in focused practical tasks and skill development.

Some examples might be:

Does it matter whether carrots are straight?
Pupils could work with a selection of carrots and prepare straight and wonky carrots in the same way to practise their chopping and grating skills, then taste the results.

What is the best way to prepare cabbage?
Pupils could try and compare different preparation methods using different pieces of equipment (e.g. tearing, cutting using scissors, slicing using a knife, grating with a manual or rotary grater). These investigations support young children to develop their skills and to be more creative and experimental when they next make a salad.

Why do old people have false teeth?
Currently there is much concern about the overconsumption of sugar and the links between this and childhood obesity and children's dental health. A story about an older person who only has false teeth could be the starting point for an inquiry. Activities might include experiments and investigations to explore how much sugar is present in popular foods and drink. Using a sugar lump to represent 2 grams enables a visual comparison to be made, or for older children, creating a comparison test to find out **'how low can you go?'** when making biscuits with reducing sugar contents might be an interesting exercise.

Experiments and investigations provide opportunities for evaluative work involving tasting that support pupils to make informed choices and develop their literacy skills. It is an activity that could almost take place on a daily basis with different foci. These activities can develop pupils' evaluative skills and use of language through speaking, listening, reading and writing.

USING STORIES

For younger children, picture books and stories can provide a starting point or context for work with food. The examples below illustrate some popular storybooks that could be used for this purpose.

Peas – it's not easy being peas-y by **Andy Cullen and Simon Rickerty** explores how a tiny pea gets from the peapod onto a plate – especially when they don't have legs and cannot walk.

How did that get in my lunchbox? The story of food by **Chris Butterworth** suggests that one of the best parts of a young child's day is opening a lunchbox and diving in. This story gives some healthy tips and a basic review of food groups that complete the menu. But how did that delicious food get there? From planting wheat to mixing dough, climbing trees to machine-squeezing fruit, picking cocoa pods to stirring a vat of melted bliss, this book provides vocabulary and inspiration for developing a range of practical skills in the early years setting.

Oliver's fruit salad by **Vivian French** is the story of Oliver who returns from a holiday with his grandparents. Unfortunately, nothing at home is quite as good as the home-grown produce from his grandad's house. This book, along with the sequel *Oliver's vegetables,* provides opportunities for experimental and investigative work as well as food provenance.

GROW IT, COOK IT, EAT IT

Exploring food provenance requires us to ask children 'where does food come from?' Pasta is an interesting starter. Does it grow on trees (spaghetti bushes, tagliatelle trees), can we dig it up (penne tubers) or can we make it? Making fresh pasta is fun and easy – 100 grams plain flour (yes, it should be a fine grade of flour but cheap supermarket flour works as well) and one egg. Pasta dough can be rolled with a rolling pin but a pasta machine is more fun. Asking your parent/teacher fundraising groups to purchase one is an option but experience shows that they are often unwanted Christmas presents, lurking in cupboards, with owners more than willing to donate or lend them to good causes. This fun activity allows pupils to select and use an appropriate range of small equipment safely and efficiently while also understanding where and how a variety of ingredients are grown, processed and then, using basic steps, produced into food.

If pasta is about 'making your own', then another good option is 'growing your own'. Raised beds make the growing easy to manage but a trough or even large pots can also serve the purpose. Spinach is an easy crop to grow: it can be cut and will grow again, and contains key nutrients including iron and Vitamin C. It also makes an excellent green paste to colour the pasta described above. A 10-year-old developed 'slugs and green worms' as a pasta product (spinach pasta and slug-shaped meatballs). For this pupil, the creativity in the concept inspired him to make, and eat, a healthy meal.

Whether growing in pots, troughs or raised beds, the variety of the produce that can be grown promotes creativity. Examples include growing runner beans, French beans (including different varieties – green, yellow and black), courgettes, marrows and potatoes.

The latter can be grown in potato sacks – harvesting is a wonderful experience when the 'potato treasure' is revealed. Cut-and-grow-again salad leaves can be grown on window sills, and tomatoes can be grown using yellow, red, orange, black and even tiger-striped varieties.

Using this own-grown produce to make a 'rainbow salsa' can develop skills as discussed earlier. With adult supervision, basic knife skills can also be introduced (see www.foodafactoflife.org.uk) using the simple claw and bridge techniques shown in Figure 9.3.

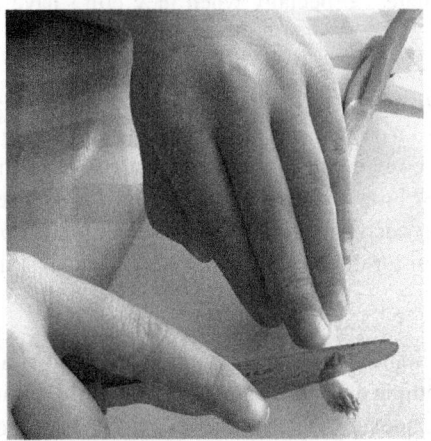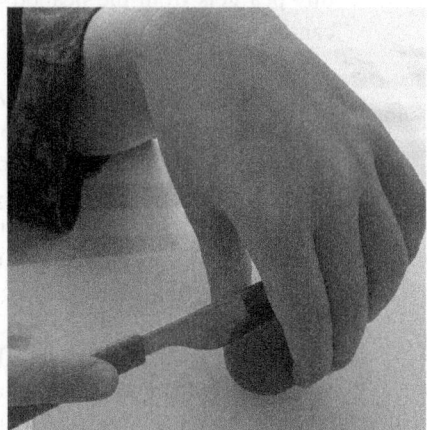

■ **Figure 9.3** The claw and bridge techniques

Spring onions can be cut using the claw grip, tomatoes cut using the bridge, basil torn with (clean) fingers, sun-dried tomatoes (that can also be produced in the classroom) snipped with (kitchen) scissors, lemons squeezed using a lemon squeezer and garlic peeled and then crushed with a garlic crusher. This activity has taught the children how to select and use an appropriate range of small equipment safely and efficiently. Taste testing with shop-bought varieties helps children to appreciate the superior taste of home-grown ingredients.

With several classes growing, cooking and eating their own foods, waste products can be recycled into composting bins, with the end product added to allotment areas to help plants grow better. About 20 per cent of an average school bin is food or garden waste, most of which can be composted. Setting up a compost scheme is an excellent way of introducing gardening and food growing in schools. It is wise to start small. Worm composting is another way of recycling kitchen waste. A worm bin is a container housing a colony of special worms, dendrobaenas, brandlings, tiger worms or redworms. Wormeries are ideal for schools with limited space, as they produce a limited quantity of compost and a liquid that forms a concentrated plant food.

There are thematic links to other subjects including science (finding out how plants need water, light and suitable temperatures to grow and stay healthy), mathematics (weighing and measuring) and English. *I will never not eat a tomato* by Lauren Child provides opportunities for the creation of fun names for strange or new food tastes. Can you match Child's 'orange twiglets from Jupiter' (carrots) and 'pointed peaks of Mount Fungi'? You will need to read the book to work this one out!

WHERE IN THE WORLD?

Links with geography provide an opportunity to explore foods from around the world, even when resources in the classroom are limited. Breads of the world can encourage children to taste a range of bread products, talking about and comparing the ingredients and textures of this staple food product. Breads such as tortillas, naan, focaccia, rye and soda bread are readily available and at a low cost. Pupils could make traditional bread; this provides opportunities to mix, prove, combine ingredients and shape the dough. For older pupils, the fermentation of yeast and the proving process offer links to science. Simple experiments can be set up with plastic bottles and balloons to investigate the conditions that yeast requires to work (varying the temperature of the water, using fresh or dried yeast, adding sugar, salt and so on). They could also explore adding ingredients to the dough for flavour (adding cheese, onion, dried fruit and so on). Where resources are limited, breads from different cultures can be made using just one cooker, for example, soda bread (oven), pitta bread (grill) and tortillas (hob).

Learning about food from local ethnic groups can promote creativity in the classroom. Children can learn about the role of foods in religious festivals such as Diwali, Eid, Hanukkah, Passover, Christmas and Easter. These events fall throughout the year and in a diverse community can offer opportunities for 'every day creativity'. However, the danger of tokenism needs to be addressed. A more holistic approach exploring carnivals and food festivals could offer opportunities for children to experience and taste a variety of street foods as an alternative context for exploring internationalism. Cooking egg noodles can provide children with an opportunity to try different new ingredients such as soy sauce, ginger, garlic, honey, grated carrots, shredded cabbage, fresh herbs and pak choi (which is also easy to grow). Low-cost noodle boxes can add to the experience, meaning that the children can take the food home or eat it outside of the classroom.

CONCLUSION

Creativity in food should instil a love of cooking so that children learn to cook and develop crucial life skills to feed themselves and their families. A creative approach must be mindful of not wasting food and ensure that the principles of eating a healthy and varied diet are followed. Teachers need to develop a range of skills in children, starting with simple techniques using a limited range of ingredients and equipment. This should move quickly on to developing more independence and a wider range of cooking skills that develop values including the consideration of sustainability, seasonality, cost and health. Children need to understand where food comes from, including where and how a variety of ingredients are grown, reared, caught and processed. This should not come from watching videos or colouring worksheets but from hands-on practical experience working with food inside and outside the classroom. By helping children to be creative with food, we are helping them to engage, become interested, discover for themselves, work together and question what they do and eat.

Having 'good ideas' is fundamental to creativity. Food is a resource that should be appreciated and not wasted, so children must be supported to produce edible outcomes. Carving a car with vegetables is not food technology but using the vegetables to make a healthy soup is. By 'good ideas', we refer not only to inventing new products but, more commonly in food, it is about exploring new ways of looking at things and presenting ideas. As 'food designers', we want children to come up with a number of possibilities, and then evaluate them before proceeding. We do not want children to say 'I can't think of anything' or proceed with the first idea that occurs to them, nor do we suggest that every child should come up with three ideas and choose 'the best one'. This approach is too formulaic to encourage reasoned decision-making. When working with food, children need time to think and plan before they proceed – this should not be a drawing or written exercise. Instead, it will involve them in tasting, researching, testing and evaluating, and using this information to formulate an idea and a plan.

FURTHER ACTIVITIES AND IDEAS

You are what you eat
Hold a tasting party. Prepare a range of bite-sized familiar and less familiar foods (breads, vegetables and fruit). Let each child choose the sample they would like to try. Use this to launch a mini project using the new foods.

Where does food come from?
Make butter in a jam jar. You need a carton of double or single cream (250 ml), one jam jar with a lid or a plastic container for younger children and a strong pair of arms.

Make soft 'acid curdled' cheese.
You need 2 litres of whole milk and the juice of a lemon. The lemon will curdle the milk into curds and whey (most children will have heard of curds and whey but few know what it means or is). Strain it through a sieve (it is best if this is lined with a clean 'j-cloth' or cotton muslin) with a weight on top to accelerate the draining. The resulting soft cheese can then be flavoured and made into a dip (add some snipped chives, tomato paste or garlic) or used to make a cheese sandwich or a cheesecake.

If this process is carried out with soya milk you can also make tofu.

The whey (which contains protein) from the process can be used instead of butter-milk to make soda bread, reinforcing the message not to waste food (it would go nicely with the butter!)

Make yogurt in a thermos flask.
You need 500 ml whole milk and a tablespoon of natural 'live' yogurt. Warm the milk to 'body temperature', no hotter than just warm. Add one tablespoon of yogurt. Pour into a clean flask (it is a good idea to flush it with some boiling water, although not essential). Leave overnight and the next day you will have a flask full of yogurt. Pupils can then experiment with flavouring this with fresh fruit (mashed or chunks).

The same or different?
Corn on the cob, sweetcorn (canned or frozen), cornflakes and popcorn tasting is another idea. This activity can support children to understand that food has a primary source that is processed in different ways. Following the tasting activity, children could be challenged to make something using corn (in any of its states).

Grow it, cook it and eat it

Plant potatoes – companies will provide schools with free seed potatoes that can be grown in sacks, buckets or plant pots. Alternatively, they cost very little from garden centres. Salad potatoes (first earlies) work better for the academic year as they can be planted in March and harvested in June.

Cut-and-grow-again salad leaves or herbs (parsley and cress are the easiest) can be grown all year round in plastic pots on a window sill.

Courgettes – these take about 10 weeks to grow. Start by planting in early spring in pots, then after about 4 weeks, transfer to an allotment area. If the children do not like courgettes, try using a spiraliser to produce fine ribbons. They can even be grated and made into savoury muffins.

REFERENCES

Davies, D. and Howe, A. (2009) 'Creativity in primary design and technology', in Wilson, A. (ed.) *Creativity in Primary Education*. Exeter: Learning Matters.

Design and Technology Association (2016) Practical food skills progression chart (for pupils aged 3–11 years). www.data.org.uk/resource-shop/lgp-are-you-teaching-food-in-primary-dt/ (accessed 19 May 2016).

Dimbleby, H. and Vincent, J. (2013) *The School Food Plan*. www.schoolfoodplan.com/ (accessed 5 April 2016).

Fautley, M. and Savage, J. (2007) *Creativity in Secondary Education*. Exeter: Learning Matters.

Howe, A., Davies, D. and Ritchie, R. (2001) *Primary Design and Technology for the Future*. London: David Fulton Publishers.

Public Health England (2015) *Food Teaching in Primary Schools- a Framework of Knowledge and Skills*. www.gov.uk/government/publications/food-teaching-in-primary-schools-knowledge-and-skills-framework (accessed 5 April 2016).

Public Health England (2016) *The Eatwell Guide*. www.gov.uk/government/publications/the-eatwell-guide (accessed 5 April 2016).

Spendlove, D. and Wells, A. (2013) 'Creativity for a new generation', in Owen-Jackson, G. (ed.) *Debates in Design and Technology Education*. Oxon: Routledge.

Useful Websites

Children's Food Trust: www.childrensfoodtrust.org.uk/

Core competences for children and young people aged 5–16 years: www.nutrition.org.uk/foodinschools/competences/competences.html

Design and Technology Association: www.data.org.uk

FACE: Farming and Countryside Education www.face-online.org.uk – a useful source for organising visits to farm and food producers.

Focus on Food: www.focusonfood.org – offers teaching, training and support to help schools, individuals and communities across the UK benefit from hands-on, practical cooking sessions through the cooking bus.

Food – a fact of life: www.foodafactoflife.org.uk/

Jamie Oliver Food Revolution Day: www.foodrevolutionday.com/schools/

National Curriculum (England): www.gov.uk/government/collections/national-curriculum

Tesco 'Eat Happy Project': www.eathappyproject.com/

EXAMPLES OF BOOKS WITH A FOOD THEME:

Gregory, the terrible eater by **Mitchell Sharmat**

Gregory's parents would like him to eat trash – tyres, cans and t-shirts – but he much prefers fruits, vegetables, eggs and fish. In this book of silly role reversals, children will be able to identify what is healthy, which can be a launch into a topic on this subject area.

It's disgusting and we ate it! True food facts from around the world and throughout history by **James Solheim**

This book is a fun way to introduce foods from around the world. By the end of the book, even the pickiest of eaters will think that meatloaf and mashed potatoes are a good option.

The boy who loved broccoli by **Sarah A. Creighton**

Meet Baxter – the boy who loves broccoli. This superfood gives Baxter superpowers, allowing him to jump over mountains, splash through lakes and perform superhero deeds. However, when he convinces others to eat his super food they too gain superpowers. This might get Baxter into a spot of trouble.

Green eggs and ham by **Dr. Seuss**

Aimed at slightly older pupils, this classic book is a great introduction to eggs. Eggs are the ultimate fast food and can be poached, scrambled, boiled and even pickled. They can be used as a coating with breadcrumbs, added to cakes, made into pancakes and whisked into meringues. They can also be eaten with ham!

APPENDIX

Annual permission letter

This annual permission letter is recommended to ensure that you are fully aware of food allergies, intolerances and religious food constraints.

Name of School/Logo/Address

Dear Parent/Carer,

I am writing to let you know that class _____ is planning to run food activities regularly throughout the year to support learning in design and technology, PHSE and science. In our lessons, we will be designing, making and tasting different foods. The school will supply the range of foods, all of which will be suitable for the class to eat and share.

To ensure that we can include everybody safely, I would be most grateful if you could complete and return the consent slip below by _____.

Please do not hesitate to contact me at school if I can be of any further help.

Best wishes

Ms A Teacher

Class Teacher

CONSENT SLIP   Pupil Name:

I give/do not give my permission for my child to take part in tasting food and cooking work at school.

My child has an intolerance/is allergic to the following food ingredients:

My child cannot eat the following foods due to our religion/culture/belief:

Signed: _____ Date: _____

LINKING DESIGN AND TECHNOLOGY AND COMPUTING TO PROMOTE CREATIVE LEARNING EXPERIENCES

Sally Hardman and Pam Maunders

INTRODUCTION

We often want pupils to engage in creative projects where they take responsibility for a real challenge. One solution is to 'bring a story to life' through the creation of an interactive storyboard. This provides the opportunity for a collaborative project between design and technology (D&T) and computing, allowing for the integration of the two subject areas to promote creative learning experiences.

PUTTING D&T AND COMPUTING INTO CONTEXT

Historically, computer control has always been an exciting and innovative area in D&T but has tended to be regarded with a degree of fear and apprehension by teachers. It has often been presented as the final frontier – something to aspire to but never quite achieve. However, information and communication technology (ICT) is beginning to develop a much broader remit and computing is now a more ambitious subject that allows for invention and resourcefulness. Pupils are expected to relate their learning to real-world systems and to the creation of purposeful outcomes in an engaging supportive environment. For example, both in the English National Curriculum (Department for Education, 2013) and the Australian Curriculum (Australian Curriculum and Assessment Reporting Authority, 2014), it is no longer acceptable to just focus on productivity software and the digital skills of using computer systems.

The nature of D&T means that it initiates opportunities for pupils to be involved in technical and practical education. Its creative role allows pupils to make products, encouraging them to develop higher level cognitive skills by giving opportunities to develop designs, synthesise ideas and evaluate the outcomes. In the same way that D&T fosters

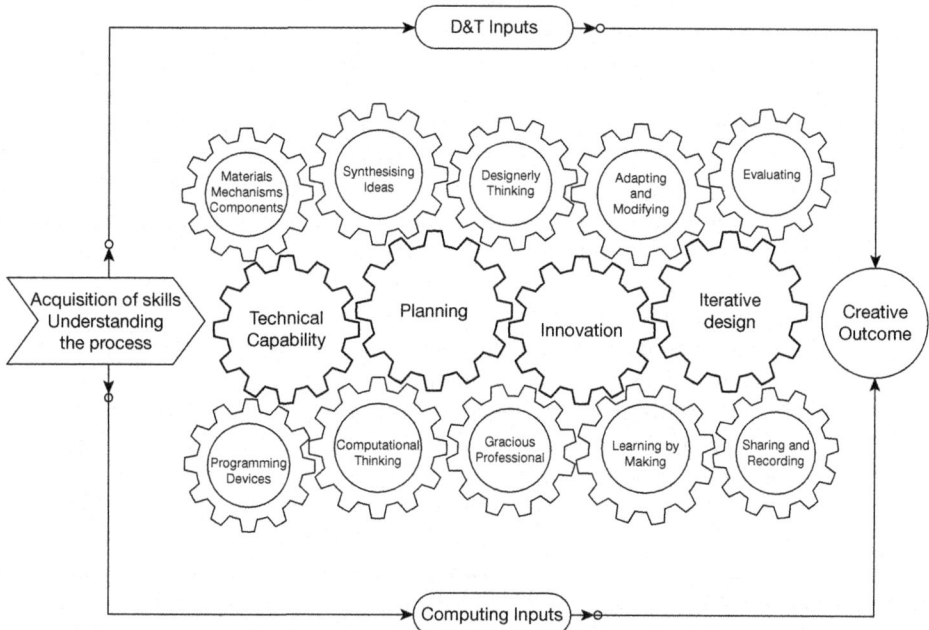

Figure 10.1 A representation of how computing and D&T interact to produce a creative outcome, created by Hardman and Maunders

these principles, computing focuses not only on the skills of programming but also on the concepts associated with computational thinking. This involves pupils in considering a problem and thinking of ways that it can be solved. There may be several different methods to solve the problem; this open-ended approach gives the pupils opportunities to develop their own learning and ask meaningful questions that will help them reach an inventive solution. More on questioning in Chapters 3 and 8.

There is a great deal of synergy between the practical areas of D&T and computing as both subjects place an emphasis on the area of control. D&T requires pupils to be able to apply their understanding of computing to program, monitor and control their products. To be successful at computing, pupils should be able to design, write and debug programs that accomplish specific goals. This should include control or simulation of physical systems and problem-solving by decomposition into smaller parts (Figure 10.1).

These natural overlaps in the subject areas create the ideal opportunity to establish cross-curricular activities without affecting children's learning and progression in either subject. They also offer the possibility of introducing innovative learning experiences by enabling pupils to develop their own ideas and take ownership of the process.

TEACHING CREATIVELY

A design and make activity which both exploits the natural links between D&T and computing and provides a cross-curricular structure that underpins the values of both subjects is ideal for teaching creatively. However, Pimley (2012) suggests that for children to receive a good-quality experience across the curriculum, the integrity of each subject needs to be maintained. With this in mind, careful attention should be given to the teaching input, ensuring that the nature of both subject areas is not lost within the cross-curricular approach.

Initially, the storyboard activity was designed for trainee teachers with the view that it could be explored, developed and ultimately taken into school to use with their pupils. Trainees often lack the experience and expertise to teach elements of D&T, such as computer control, in a way that stimulates creativity and curiosity, even though this is often their goal. Indeed, Spendlove and Wells (2013) note that at the start of their training the majority of students aim to engender creativity in their pupils; however, this aspiration is often not as prevalent at the end of their training.

To develop confidence and understanding of the use of technology to support the development of pupils' creativity, teachers need to be encouraged to consider their own attitudes and approaches to technology. Emphasis should be placed on the use of technology to solve problems rather than just learning about the technology. This is in line with the belief that 'prospective teachers who are trained in thinking and teaching creatively and in creative problem-solving will be better prepared to value and nurture the same creative characteristics in their classrooms' (Abdallah, 1996: 52). The Office for Standards in Education (Ofsted) (2003) suggests that some features of teacher training in England contribute towards the confidence in trainees to teach creatively by emphasising mastery of subject knowledge, freeing them to 'take risks' in the classroom. Without this mastery, there is an unwillingness to allow pupils to solve their own problems without teacher invention.

PRODUCING AN ENGAGING AND PURPOSEFUL PRODUCT

Careful thought needs to be given to the choice of an activity that can provide ample opportunity for the appropriate use of control techniques to ensure that the desired product functions effectively. A product that incorporates movement and light, and also requires the planning and implementation of a control system, guarantees that computers and digital devices are an integral part of the whole process. A meaningful context for developing relevant technical skills is required and the use of a tablet computer by older primary school pupils to take notes, video and photographs to record the stages of the design process can ensure that the computing element is not diluted.

Attention should be given to the user and the purpose of the activity in order that the pupils have a clear idea of who they are designing for and what is required. It is also important that the product should be authentic and have a genuine context in order that it is meaningful and real (National Curriculum Expert Group, 2013). This ensures that pupils are as engaged as possible in the process and more likely to use their own original thoughts and imagination to produce an innovative and creative product.

A STORYBOARD ACTIVITY

A target audience of young children aged 4–5 years old can provide an excellent context, which is easily accessible in school and is real to the pupils. There is security in the school setting and the purpose is easy to define; in addition, the user is often already known so their demands are easy to predict. The storyboard activity is based on this audience and its aims are illustrated in Figure 10.2.

 To explore simple movement

 To produce an appealing product incorporating mechanical, electrical and computer control

 To program creatively in order for the product to function effectively

 To use a table computer as a means of recording the process and evaluating the product

■ **Figure 10.2** Storyboard activity framework, created by Hardman and Maunders

The task is for a small group to design and construct an interactive storyboard to appeal to younger children. Requirements are that it has to incorporate a selection of materials, include moving parts and provide electronic and computer control opportunities. Every stage of the design process can be recorded on a tablet computer. A short film and e-book can be produced at the end of the project recounting the process undertaken and finally telling the story acted out on the storyboard in an animated form.

The activity is designed to promote and facilitate the learning experience by providing the conditions for intervention rather than providing ready-made knowledge. This emulates the view that pupils should be active participants in the learning process rather than passive recipients of facts (Prince, 2004). Active participation is far more likely to initiate creative ideas leading to pupils 'pushing the boundaries' and developing originality in their thinking.

Through the learning-by-making process, opportunities are presented to co-construct knowledge and become actively engaged in learning. This in turn draws out creativity by encouraging experimentation and risk-taking and promoting 'what if'?' questions. Encouraging pupils to learn independently, solve problems and ask questions, think flexibly and self- and peer-evaluate enables them to focus on the learning process, not simply on the result. Pupils should also be introduced to the idea of being 'gracious professionals', highlighting the importance of respect for individuals in a team project. This team approach can enhance the collaborative vision by providing the supportive climate needed to freely express ideas where pupils are secure in the knowledge that their ideas will be valued.

Sessions can be organised as a series of enquiry-based lessons drawing on the principles of designerly thinking and learning by making (more in Chapter 3), with an expectation that collaboration would help to:

- establish joint goals
- make joint decisions
- solve emerging problems
- construct and modify solutions
- evaluate the outcomes through dialogue and action.

Designerly thinking encourages pupils' ideas to grow, allows them to be playful with purpose and enables them to spend time in useful fun (McLaren, 2011). Through engaging in the process of constructing a meaningful product, participants test out their plans, learn from each other and solve problems as they progress. Abstract ideas and concepts become concrete and are situated in real-life contexts (Wheeler, 2012).

INVESTIGATING QUALITY PRODUCTS

In line with the designerly thinking approach, it is useful to create a prototype that exemplifies successful attributes of the product (Figure 10.3) . This will not only help the

▪ **Figure 10.3** An example of a storyboard for exploration, created by Hardman and Maunders

teacher to consider possible misconceptions before setting pupils the task, but it also creates a starting point for the pupils' initial ideas and is an indication to the teacher of the pupils' existing knowledge.

Pupils should be encouraged to explore the movement and identify opportunities for electrical and computer control. Product analysis is an important part of the design and make process, allowing pupils to understand the function of the product and the possibilities for movement. It is often useful to disassemble a product in order to explore it fully, so as teachers we need to be prepared for exemplars to be examined, even though this can be detrimental to the original product as it is pulled apart and investigated by many inquisitive fingers. Although an exemplar can influence the outcome of the activity and possibly direct pupils' thoughts, for this type of activity that has a series of fairly complex requirements it is useful to provide an idea of a possible product. There are still ample opportunities for creativity and providing the rough framework helps to give pupils a focus.

AN OPEN-ENDED APPROACH

An open-ended approach has many benefits when aiming for a creative output, but it should also be recognised that it may have some limitations. Studies have shown that some pupils respond positively to the more open-ended brief, but others can feel quite insecure with less direction (Chin and Kayalvizhi, 2005). This could lead to less positive views of the two subject areas and engender a negative view of the design and make experience; therefore, it is important that adequate support is available throughout the activity. Often, this will depend on the group of children, their age and most importantly their previous experience.

Jarvis and Pell (2004) suggest that, as many teachers also feel insecure in the field of D&T, they prefer closed lessons, which are easier to manage practically with a limitation on the technical demands. The storyboard activity is designed to support creativity in both D&T and computing, and to give teachers the experience to teach in a way that stimulates creativity but is also manageable in the classroom environment.

Consideration of the design brief is one of the most important elements of the design process; a more open brief generally leads to a greater variety of products and more opportunities for the incorporation of creative and imaginative ideas. For example, if pupils are requested to simply 'design a storyboard', they have the potential to produce products that are large or small, colourful or monotone, three-dimensional or flat, moving or stationary. They can use any combination of resources and base them on any number of ideas. If the brief becomes more closed, then the variety of products is likely to decrease and possible opportunities for creativity will decrease in line with this. If pupils are required to 'produce a moving storyboard based on the story of Cinderella which is A2 in size and uses a sliding mechanism and is red and pink', then the outcomes are likely to be more or less identical. For the teacher, however, this situation is easier to manage from both the technical aspects and the resource implications. It is achieving this balance between the level of freedom and the ability to manage the practicalities that is often the challenge.

USING A FAMILIAR CONTEXT

Using stories in the primary classroom is widely recognised as a powerful method of teaching many aspects of the curriculum (see Chapter 4 for more discussion). Recounting stories is an important skill for children to develop and using a stimulus that has a familiar structure can create a supportive context for learning about the writing process. It enables pupils to build background knowledge of the setting and scaffolds the creation of original stories. Producing moving stories gives the opportunity to analyse the narrative and visualise telling a story by using pictorial representations. The creation of the storyboard encourages interaction and computational thinking by decomposing the story (Berry, 2014) into component parts and choosing the key incidents to be sequenced in the storyboard. Benson and Mantell (1999) stress the benefit of linking language development with D&T in order to create a relevant context to apply appropriate language.

Initially, a period of time will be required to clarify ideas about the story; pupils are likely to interpret the ideas of a story quite differently and creatively, depending on their own interests. Time needs to be dedicated to allowing pupils to talk through and clarify their ideas with the group and it is important that all participants are listened to. There are likely to be many options available and the decision as to which story to choose can have a substantial impact on the success of the project. The focus of the story may relate to a particular classroom topic or it may be that any type of story genre can be used; again, this will impact on the teacher's role. If pupils are given a completely free choice, it may be necessary to intervene to support the final decision as a simple storyline will be required. Examples could be:

■ Recounting a familiar tale, Rapunzel or Cinderella
■ The life cycle of a butterfly, linking with science
■ A seasonal theme
■ An interesting place, under the sea or in the jungle

SIMPLIFYING A STORY

The first stage is to deconstruct the story into a series of smaller steps (Figure 10.4), dealing with each one separately. Illustrating these steps with simple drawings or using a sequence format can be very challenging for pupils. In preparation for the design and make task, support activities could be carried out, for example, encouraging pupils to draw or photocopy composite pictures of familiar stories and highlight particular parts of the story that could include movement or electricity. In response to the challenge of deconstructing the story into steps, it may be useful to offer examples to illustrate the expectations, again depending on the confidence level of the group. This has a supporting and scaffolding role and can help the pupils to clarify their ideas further.

Some children may need the reassurance of a familiar story or a traditional tale while others will be happy to construct their own stories. Comments made at this point in our project included:

'Using a children's book was great as the ideas are already there – none of us are very imaginative.'

'It's a good idea to have a Christmas theme as it is topical at the moment.'

'We want to link it to science and telling a story like a life cycle would be engaging.'

'We have lots of ideas; it's difficult to choose just one that we can make in the time.'

■ **Figure 10.4** A step-by-step representation of the stages of the story source, created by Hardman and Maunders

VISUALISING THE STORYBOARD

The next step involves transferring the ideas about the story into a single frame that has the potential to be controlled in order to recreate the stages of the story. A possible approach to producing the storyboard could be to consider the background and main feature of the story; think about the foreground and then look at the series of contributing events in a sequence Figure 10.5 demonstrates this.

USING A TABLET COMPUTER

An important part of this activity is to record the journey, so pupils need to be reminded to take pictures of their planning and possibly make audio recordings of the process. This has a dual purpose; it enables the pupils to clarify and record their own thoughts and ideas and also enables the teacher to collect evidence of the process involved. For a teacher, it can be challenging to build awareness of the whole design and make process, especially about contributions from individual members of a team. Involving the pupils in recording their own journey can provide a valuable source of information, which can also be useful for assessment purposes.

Having clarified ideas about the stages of the story and decided on the parts that need to be included, pupils will need to plan their whole board together. This is likely to take the form of a rough sketch, probably depicting movement using arrows (Figure 10.6). Encouraging the pupils to indicate the direction of movement and possible flashing lights using rough sketches helps to define their thoughts and ensures that they have started to address the idea of incorporating mechanisms and electricity.

Story	Main Feature/ Background	Foreground	Storyline	→	→	→	Final Scene
Rapunzel	Castle with princess	Prince, witch, horse	Prince arrives	Princess lets hair down	Prince climbs hair	Witch flies away	Broom and eye flash
The life cycle of a butterfly	Garden with flowers	Caterpillar	Caterpillar moves	Eats leaves	Turns in to pupa	Sun rotates	Butterfly emerges, lights up, wings flutter
Christmas	House at night with decorations	Child at window	Child waves	Sleigh pulled by reindeer with nose flashing	Presents drop down chimney	Flashing lights on house	Santa leaves
Jungle story	Tiger in a bush	Crocodile, giraffe, hoverfly, monkey	Coconut falls on crocodile	Crocodile jumps	Giraffe raises head	Hoverfly's wings rotate	Tiger's nose flashes

■ **Figure 10.5** Planning the components of the storyboard

■ **Figure 10.6** A sketch of the jungle story indicating possibilities for movement and electrical control

BUILDING THE TECHNICAL KNOWLEDGE

Although the intention is for pupils to take ownership of the activity, a vital part of the process is to diagnose the prerequisite skills. By evaluating pupils' knowledge at the start of the project, it should be possible to assess the amount of guidance necessary to provide the knowledge and practical capability required to employ these skills flexibly in the design process. In order for pupils to be freely creative, they must have access to the practical skills necessary to complete a project and truly turn their visions into appealing and satisfying quality products.

Experience of particular skills and techniques enables the effective use of more challenging tools and interesting materials, resulting in more opportunities for creativity within the design process (Hope, 2004). However, in the classroom, there will always be a balance between the extent that independent learning can occur and the supervision required to ensure that the learning environment is safe.

D&T requires pupils to understand and use mechanical systems in their products as part of their technical knowledge. There are many interesting and age-appropriate resources available to support this technical requirement and to help develop pupils' understanding. Animated resources can be used to explore how simple mechanisms function and how levers and linkages can be assembled to make mechanisms. In choosing to use an animated resource, it is possible to focus specifically on the type of movement created by a particular mechanism and it is this aspect that is very important for pupils to appreciate. It can be

■ **Figure 10.7** Prototype mechanisms to explore and investigate, created by Hardman and Maunders

useful to create a range of prototype mechanisms to describe simple movement and encourage pupils to practically explore how they work (Figure 10.7).

Lucas *et al.* (2014) identified six engineering habits of mind, which describe the way engineers think and act. These are:

▪ systems thinking
▪ adapting
▪ problem-finding
▪ creative problem-solving
▪ visualising
▪ improving.

The storyboard project demands that pupils begin to think like engineers, they are required to visualise the way they wish their story to be told and make the storyboard work effectively by considering how to produce the movement and electrical output required. In this way, they are also addressing systems thinking, the process of understanding how components fit together in the final product. The more confident pupils become with this type of approach, the more creative they are able to be; with confidence in the process comes the flexibility to be more inventive and original (Education Scotland, 2013).

RESOURCING IMAGINATIVELY

A more interesting and appealing selection of resources is likely to produce a wider variety of creative products. There is often a tendency to present resources that the pupils are used to, but it is interesting to introduce materials that are less familiar as these are often the catalyst to producing something more original. It is important that pupils are given plenty of time to freely explore the resources available. It is tempting to leave resourcing until later, as this step inevitably involves time to prepare; however, pupils must be aware of the selection available before they embark on the making process. This is in line with real-world situations where a true project would never be introduced without a complete awareness of the resource implications.

▪ **Figure 10.8** A selection of creative resources

In order to enhance the appeal of products, resources must be selected carefully and pupils should be aware of their various characteristics and suitability for purpose. Pupils can focus on colour, texture, flexibility, ability to join and strengthening properties. Knowing the characteristics and properties of a wide range of resources immediately enables pupils to incorporate a more interesting selection of materials into their products (Figure 10.8). The storyboard activity gives opportunities for many different materials to be used, even incorporating a more three-dimensional aspect by including reusable materials such as egg boxes and plastic pots.

Resources for the storyboard project could include:

■ corrugated plastic board and a choice of paper and card of varying thickness
■ brass fasteners and paper clips of different sizes
■ a wide selection of coloured tissue paper
■ coloured lollipop sticks
■ felt, fur, fabric and feathers
■ thick and thin coloured pipe cleaners
■ wool, cotton and cotton wool
■ bright buttons and sequins.

UNDERSTANDING THE COMPUTING ASPECTS

As part of the planning process for the storyboard, pupils should be encouraged to think computationally and be introduced to the correct computing terminology. This demonstrates the strong relationship that computational thinking has in a cross-curricular activity. Three elements of computing are addressed through the storyboard activity. These are:

■ computational thinking
■ programming using digital devices
■ using tablet computers to document the process of making and recording the finished product and to recount the story.

Computational thinking is a thought process that encompasses logical reasoning; it concerns the creation of solutions to problems. Pupils will be required to analyse what needs to be done and decide on the steps required to complete the task. There are a number of ideas that pupils will need to understand. These include:

■ the ability to recognise patterns, by quickly solving new problems, building on prior experience – asking questions such as 'Is this similar to a problem I've already solved?' and 'How is it different?'
■ the ability to decompose what they are designing into component parts, making the designing and making less complex – asking questions such as 'Can I break down the problem into smaller parts?' and 'Can I explain the different parts of this problem and solution?'
■ the ability to abstract all the unnecessary elements of the design – asking questions such as 'What information do I actually need?' and 'Have I made this more complicated than I need to?'
■ the ability to think algorithmically, solving the problem by following a set of instructions – asking questions such as 'What are the steps I need to follow to make this work?'

The more familiar pupils become with these ideas, the more adept they will be at using computational thought. Ultimately this will enable them to produce more complex products with a more demanding technical remit. Their ability to visualise and recreate their ideas will become more advanced and they will have more opportunities to produce imaginative and innovative products.

CONTROL DEVICES

Often, schools will already have a variety of control boxes associated with programming; these could include CoCo, Deltronics, Junior Control It, Flowol, TTS Egg Boxes and Data Harvest LEARN & GO. The leads and software must be compatible with the modern laptops and desktops purchased in recent years, so it is important to ensure everything works before introducing the equipment to the children. The type of equipment is not as important as understanding the process of using the device to control inputs and outputs. The programming aspects of the process are likely to be very similar whatever equipment is available in school. During this project, Data Harvest LEARN & GO and TTS Egg Boxes were introduced, both of which work without the need for a computer interface and are moderately priced.

USING A SIMPLE CONTROL BOX

Pupils need to understand how to control elements of their story by using a simple control box to sequence a set of instructions in order to achieve a specific outcome. The storyboard activity requires pupils to understand the principles of controlling mechanisms and apply these. This process involves:

- **finding out** how simple systems work
- **making changes** to systems by altering their properties
- **developing** systems by making changes.

As a starting point, it can be useful to ask pupils to consider everyday devices such as traffic lights and flashing Christmas tree lights to discuss how they rely on simple control features to make them operate. Referring to an everyday context helps to develop understanding of sequences involving timing.

To begin with, pupils can build simple electrical circuits which turn on and off. However, most control boxes have the ability to learn the order in which switches are pressed and this allows creative sequences to be developed. The programmed sequences can be played back from memory, meaning that a series of flashing lights or a sequence of lights can be included in the storyboard.

A simple sequence of commands is likely to involve:

- connecting components to the output ports – either bulbs, buzzers or motors
- creating a sequence using commands
- saving the sequence
- running the stored sequence to control the output components.

COMPUTER PROGRAMMING

More challenging and ultimately more interesting control tools will enable older pupils to explore programming in more depth and produce far more capable and innovative products. Once pupils have mastered the idea of simple programming and have understood the underlying ideas, they can be introduced to more capable and demanding tools, allowing motors and lights to be controlled via a computer interface (Figure 10.9).

The computer interface has several output components, which can be incorporated productively into the storyboard. The motor can be attached to an object and by simply dragging blocks onto the script area, the motor is activated and the object will rotate. The ability to control parts of the storyboard to this extent can add interest to the final product. As pupils become more adept and inventive with their programming skills, research suggests that they develop independent learning skills and perseverance, and are able to create some extremely complex and technically demanding creative products (Serafini, 2011).

Example 1: Learn and Go instructions	Computer interface instruction
Press the LEARN button	when ⚑ clicked
Press the Output 1 button	turn motor on
Press the Output 1 button	turn motor off for ❶ secs
Press the Output 1 button	turn motor off
Press the LEARN button	

▨ **Figure 10.9** An example of control instructions using a computer interface

ADAPTING AND MODIFYING

As pupils progress through the storyboard activity, it is unlikely that they will adhere completely to their initial designs. While they will have a rough idea of their desired outcome and a hazy idea of the appearance of their storyboard, many changes are likely to be made during their journey. In line with the iterative approach to the design and make process, pupils will be modifying and adapting their ideas throughout the making stage (Kimbell *et al.*, 1991).

The initial gathering of resources tends to happen in the first stages of an activity, but pupils will need to access resources at all times. It can be useful for pupils to create prototype mechanisms to test out specific techniques and processes in order to identify suitable mechanisms that will produce particular outputs. It is vital that pupils are given

■ **Figure 10.10** Examples of some completed interactive storyboards

enough time to dedicate to this process, as this is often where the skills of designing and making become much more developed. As confidence and capability increases, pupils are able to employ these skills to produce more intricate and interesting ideas that are refined and modified in order to fulfil specific purposes.

As final details are added to the developing storyboards, it is important to remind pupils that the quality of the product is important as well as the process involved. In order to be completely satisfied with their finished storyboard, pupils must have fully engaged with the making process, and often adding the finishing touches can make the difference between an unsatisfactory product and an appealing and pleasing outcome (Figure 10.10).

CREATIVELY EVALUATING THE PROCESS AND THE PRODUCT

Using the tablet computer to plan, carry out and analyse the creative process enables the teacher to gain access to the various iterations of the developing product and this provides useful evidence to prove that pupils are engaging in the stages of a design and make process. Pupils can plan the design, share pictures of resources, write about the process and make a prototype. This process is more adaptable than more formal approaches to evaluation as pupils can record their learning journey themselves, making it easier for those pupils who find written recording challenging.

Although there are many applications that could be used, an eBook generator is the most accessible as it allows pupils to import different media – pictures, video, sound as well as recording. Pupils can use the camera built into the tablet computer to take pictures and chronicle the making of the storyboard, in addition to presenting the finished product that tells the story.

CONCLUSION

The interactive storyboard activity provides excellent opportunities for developing the links between D&T and computing, and creative outcomes are promoted by the design brief. There are possibilities for the incorporation of a variety of mechanical and electronic components, which can be fairly simple or more complex, depending on the capability of the children. Scaffolding an open-ended activity facilitates creative approaches from both the computing and the D&T perspectives.

■ **Figure 10.11** Exploring and investigating a storyboard

When the project was trialled, the participants reflected on the outcomes. They commented that when the project was first outlined to them, they felt it would be very complicated; however, they were amazed at their own creativity and ability to design and make an interactive storyboard without difficulty. They had not realised that programming was so simple and could be used in such a cross-curricular manner. They were proud of their finished products and were really excited at the prospect of taking this activity into school.

Developing confidence in areas such as the effective use of resources, tools and materials and understanding of programming all contribute to pupils' ability to produce quality products. This is often where true creativity is achieved, as pupils are not confined by their practical capability and are able to bring their initial visualisations and imaginings to life.

Ultimately, the success and appeal of a product is determined by the audience it is designed for; the young children who investigated the finished products were able to tell some amazing stories, using the interactive features to stimulate their imagination (Figure 10.11).

REFERENCES

Abdallah, A. (1996) 'Fostering creativity in student teachers'. *Community Review*, 14, 52–58.

Australian Curriculum and Assessment Reporting Authority (2014) *Foundation to Year 10 Curriculum: Language, Language for Interaction.* www.australiancurriculum.edu.au. (accessed 6 May 2016).

Berry, M. (2014) *An Open Mind: Computational Thinking in Primary Schools* http://milesberry. net/2014/03/computational-thinking-in-primary-schools/ (accessed 5 April 2016).

Benson, C. and Mantell, J. (1999) *Developing Language Through D&T.* Wellesbourne: D&T Association.

Chin, C. and Kayalvizhi, G. (2005) 'What do pupils think of open science investigations? A study of Singaporean primary 6 pupils'. *Educational Research*, 47(1), 107–126.

Department for Education (2013) *The National Curriculum in England: Key Stages 1 and 2 Framework Document.* London: DfE.

Education Scotland Creativity across Learning 3–18 (2013) www.educationscotland.gov.uk/ Images/Creativity3to18_tcm4–814361.pdf. (accessed 6 May 2016).

Hope, G. (2004) *Teaching D&T 3–11: The Essential Guide for Teachers (Reaching the Standard).* London: Continuum.

Jarvis, T. and Pell, A. (2004) 'Primary teachers' changing attitudes and cognition during a two-year science inservice programme and their effect on pupils'. *International Journal of Science Education*, 26(14), 1787–1811.

Kimbell, R., Stables, K., Wheeler, T., Wozniak, A. and Kelly, A.V. (1991) *The Assessment of Performance in Design and Technology.* London: SEAC/HM.

Lucas, B., Hanson, J. and Claxton, G. (2014) *Thinking Like an Engineer: Implications for the Education System.* London: Royal Academy of Engineering.

McLaren, S.V. (2011) 'Technologies in Scotland's Curriculum for Excellence: time for change', (eds.) Kay Stables, Clare Benson & Marc de Vries, *PATT 25 Perspectives on Learning in Design and Technology*, Goldsmiths London University, 285-293.

National Curriculum Expert Group (2013) *School Curriculum Principles for D&T.* Wellesbourne: D&T Association.

Ofsted. (2003) *Expecting the unexpected: Developing Creativity in Primary and Secondary Schools.* HMI. http://dera.ioe.ac.uk/id/eprint/4766 (accessed 12 February 2016).

Pimley, G. (2012) *Making Cross Curricular Links.* www.teachprimary.com/learning_resources/view/making-cross-curricular-links (accessed 12 February 2016).

Prince, M. (2004) 'Does active learning work: a review of the research'. *Journal of Engineering Education*, 93(3), 223–232.

Serafini, G. (2011), 'Teaching programming at primary schools: visions, experiences, and long-term research prospects', *Proceedings of the 5th International Conference on Informatics in Schools: Situation, Evolution and Perspectives.* Berlin and Heidelberg, Springer-Verlag, p. 143.

Spendlove, D. and Wells, A. (2013) 'Creativity for a new generation', in Owen-Jackson, G. (ed). *Debates in D&T Education.* London: Routledge.

Wheeler, S. (2012) *Learning by Making.* http://steve-wheeler.blogspot.co.uk/2012/09/learning-by-making.html (accessed 23 January 2016).

CHILDREN LEARNING OUTSIDE THE CLASSROOM

Louise Milne

INTRODUCTION

Learning outside the classroom has the potential to extend a child's technological knowledge and promote design solutions to real-world problems. When a visit involves making a chocolate gift to celebrate Mother's Day, there are lots of opportunities for creative and original ideas that consider personal interests and the pupils' aspirations for creating a gift for their mother or relative.

BACKGROUND

The original study, from which this chapter is drawn, comprised a qualitative, case-study approach. The context, and the nature and age group of the participants, required an examination of literature from three areas of study: design and technology (D&T), education outside the classroom (EOTC), and the nature and the characteristics of 5-year-old children. This provided the principles that underpinned a planning framework co-constructed by myself and the two teachers of the new entrant classes. Over a 6-month period, data was gathered during three phases of the study: first, preparation for the visit outside the classroom; then the visit to the chocolate factory and the subsequent development of the chocolate gift in the classroom; and finally exploring the children's enduring understandings that resulted from the visit. Data was gathered through a series of interviews with the children and their teachers, observations and the analysis of the children's work. In addition, the focus of this chapter required an examination of literature that explored creativity and how this may be fostered with young children. Further discussion is in Chapter 3. Interestingly, the key ideas of this investigation merged closely with the pedagogical approach employed to support the children in their technological practice and problem-solving.

Enhancing creativity

The origin of the term 'creative' has a long and constantly evolving history, and today there is widespread acceptance that 'creativity' is a difficult concept to define (Carter, 2004).

Bruce (2011: 111) believes that 'creativity in everyday life lifts living to levels of fulfilment, satisfaction, effective, deep and rigorous practical thinking which are in a different league to pedestrian, boring and commonplace living'. Being creative problem-solvers is apparent in many of the activities we carry out in our day-to-day lives, but interestingly, in the technology community of which I have been a part, there has been little commitment to untangling notions of creativity from what we understand to be the nature of technology and technology education. It could be said that in some regard there has been no need as they appear indivisibly connected, one overlapping the other. To borrow from the analogy of Gibbons and Johnston (1974) in which they described the relationship between science and technology, creativity, I believe, provides a pool of skill and talent from which the technologist can fish.

International curricula for primary-aged children generally support cultivating and supporting children's developing creativity. How then does this manifest in the 5-year-old's classroom? Bruce (2011) has written extensively on the subject of cultivating creativity with very young children. She argues that there is evidence to suggest that children born into families where they are exposed to music, dance or the visual arts from an early age, will experience an impact on their brain development. However, she also dispels the myth that creativity 'is a gift with which only some people are born' (Damasio, 1999: 1) and that young children can be helped from an early age to be 'courageous learners with a sense of adventure, able to take risks, dare to make mistakes and have a go, try alternatives, rearrange what they know or try out new ways of working' (Damasio, 1999: 7). A key element in this development is undoubtedly teacher knowledge – knowledge of how to nurture creative learning, how to build an environment in which children feel emotionally safe, willing to take risks, make mistakes and to break the rules of engagement (Bruce, 2011).

Howkins (2001) identifies five elements that he sees as integral to creative thinking – review, incubation, dreams, excitement and reality checks. However, the application of these to the learning of 5-year-old children in D&T offers another level of complexity to teacher planning. For example, it is likely that these children engage, possibly for the first time, in a technological problem that is proposed by their classroom teacher. Their early childhood experiences are likely to be individual or group activities that are supported, rather than directed, by the teacher, where the teacher/child ratio is lower and there is greater opportunity for children to pursue their own interests.

An example of the cognitive limitations these children experience is explained in Piaget's description of the 'intuitive sub-stage' child, the 4–7-year-old child, who is more likely to make decisions based on intuition rather than logic, who may develop representational skills of language, mental imaging and drawing to view the world, but only from his/her own perspective (Piaget, 1954). This may cause the child to ignore important information if tackling a technological problem, which concerns a person other than him/herself. The challenge for the teacher, therefore, is to plan and facilitate a technology project that is age-appropriate, has a limited number of variables for the child to consider, and involves a context that is of high interest (Chapter 4 has more on starting points).

TEACHERS' PLANNING OF D&T

A 13-year-old student who participated in an early D&T research project once stated that 'technology is having ideas and making them' (Ministry of Education, 1997). This is a simple and reasonably accurate description of what technology education is for young children, but for the technology teacher, a deeper understanding is required to inform their planning and their pedagogical practice.

There are four widely accepted categories for examining technology: technology as objects or artefacts, technology as knowledge, technology as activity, and technology as volition (de Vries, 2012; Jones *et al.*, 2013). The category most relevant in this instance is 'technology as activity'. Here we see the first clear connection with creativity and creative response through design. de Vries (2012) identifies three components of 'technology as activities': designing, making and using and/or appreciating processes (De Vries, 2012: 22). Design and the process of designing a product is a key component of D&T. It is defined in a number of ways and may describe a preliminary drawing for something that is to be made; it may describe a period of time, for example, the Arts and Crafts movement of the late 1800s; or it may describe a process of product development from initial concept through to its final realisation.

'Technology as activity' is presented in D&T in a number of curricula throughout the world. Of interest in this discussion is how this is addressed when working with new entrant children, the 5-year-olds. D&T naturally draws knowledge and skills from other curriculum areas. Five-year-old children are at an early stage of language development, and within a technology unit most activities will include discussion, supported planning and investigations, with limited expectations for independent reading and writing. The duration of a technology unit, often positioned as part of other learning, is typically spread over one to two weeks. Within this period, the children would develop an understanding of the technological problem to be solved, and importantly, who was to receive their final solution. With the help of their teacher they would create a plan, and begin to investigate the context and the possible design solutions for their final product. An important goal is to produce an outcome that is fit-for-purpose and this often requires the children to carry out some simple market research – typically employing simple text, images and emoticons (Ministry of Education, 2010).

Pedagogically, there are a number of challenges that teachers face when teaching D&T to 5-year-old children; for example, their design capabilities and their limited understanding of the continuous process required to complete a final outcome. It is recognised by a number of researchers investigating primary children's technology that their understanding of the purpose of a technology brief can easily be lost in the multitude of activities in a busy classroom programme (Moreland and Cowie, 2011). Moreland and Cowie (2011) discuss this in terms of maintaining a sense of continuity and connectedness when teaching technology to this younger age group. These children are known to have difficulty recognising that each phase of their work is not an end-point in its own right but rather one step in a more extensive process. Their design drawings are a good example of this. Young children may complete their drawn designs and then either disregard them when constructing a final outcome or take them home to share with the family, rather than keeping them at school and using them to help in the construction of their product (Rogers and Wallace, 2000). Fleer (2000) noted that young children do not understand the purpose of design drawings, what information they should contain or how they should be constructed. Rogers and Wallace (2000) emphasise the need for children to understand the difference between drawings that explain, as in a plan, and drawings that depict, as in a piece of art work. This research suggests that where children are able to conceptualise the difference between the two, the task of creating a design drawing is more likely to merge with the process of technological development and give it greater meaning and purpose.

ALEX'S PICTURE

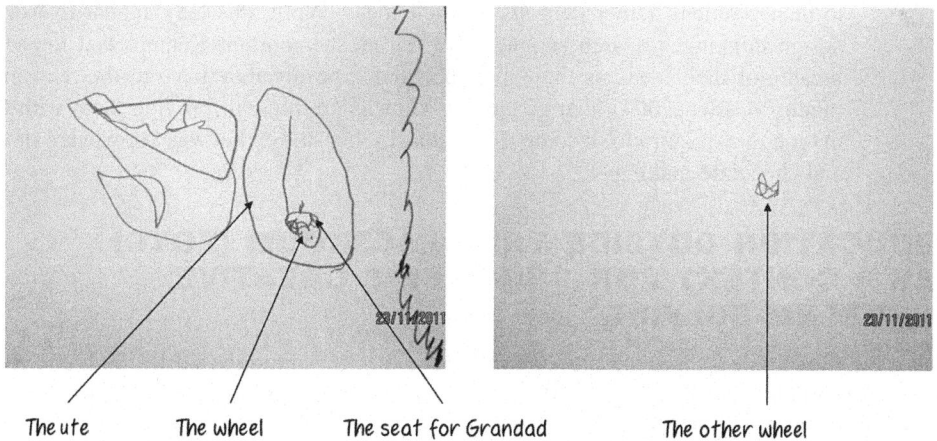

The ute   The wheel   The seat for Grandad   The other wheel

Mama: What are you drawing?
Alex: I drew a ute, there's a seat for Grandad and a wheel. But where do I put the other wheel?
Mama: What do you mean?
Alex: The one you can't see. I know. (Alex turns page, draws wheel, and smiles) There!

NB: Imagination required to make out all aspects of the picture! (Like the vertical grass!)

Figure 11.1 A pre-schooler's drawing showing her awareness of 3D

However, a further challenge for young children planning a three-dimensional structure is their inability to draw in three dimensions. While there is evidence that young children are aware of the three-dimensional nature of structures, they have difficulty expressing this through their drawings (Jolley, 2010). An example of this is shown in a drawing by Alex, a 3-year-old attempting to draw her grandfather's farm vehicle (see Figure 11.1). After drawing the body of the vehicle, she was unsure where to draw the wheel that was on the other side of the vehicle but which she could not see. Her solution was to turn the page over and draw the wheel on the back of the paper (A. Milne, personal communication). Further discussion on drawing is in Chapter 6.

The expectation for young children to include design drawings in their D&T projects has been extensively challenged by researchers. Their ability to translate a three-dimensional structure into a two-dimensional drawing requires higher-level thinking and abilities, and this is generally beyond the capabilities of the 5-year-old child. As a means of resolving this issue, the early research carried out by Golomb (1989) suggests that children's design thinking can be enhanced if they are encouraged to communicate their design ideas by using a three-dimensional medium such as clay or plasticine. This avoids the constraints of managing a two-dimensional medium in order to communicate a three-dimensional structure, particularly as it relates to planning, positioning and alignment.

In general, the technological process of 5-year-old children is one that lies somewhere between the exploration goals of their early childhood experiences and the achievement goals of their primary school curriculum. The children's practice will tend to focus on one solution and generally lack iteration or review. Design drawings can be encouraged, but left alone, children are most likely to experiment with materials in order to find a solution to their problem, rather than sketch their ideas. While this may appear to hamper their design thinking, research suggests that the most important element that impacts on the breadth of their ideas, is the experience and exposure they have to the relevant field of inquiry (Carter, 2004), that is, gaining knowledge that will provide them with the information they require to develop a solution. In this study, this was knowledge of chocolate and chocolate-making.

EDUCATION OUTSIDE THE CLASSROOM (EOTC) AS A CONTEXT FOR CHILDREN'S CREATIVE PROBLEM-SOLVING

EOTC is a generic term used to describe the curriculum-based learning and teaching in schools that extends beyond the four walls of the classroom. Ideally, these experiences should provide links between children's classroom studies and the real world in which they live. They should include activities that are hands-on, interactive and have the potential to enrich the learning opportunities provided in the classroom (Ministry of Education, 2010).

Falk and Dierking (2000) describe learning experiences outside the classroom as 'a whole-body, whole-brain, whole-experience activity' (Falk and Dierking, 2000: 10). They developed the Contextual Model of Learning, which consists of three overlapping contexts: the personal, the socio-cultural and the physical (Falk and Dierking, 2000). When planning a visit, the personal context highlights the motivation and expectations of the children, understanding something of the children's prior knowledge, their interests and beliefs, and providing levels of choice and control in the direction that the study will take. The socio-cultural context includes within-group socio-cultural mediation and facilitated mediation by the teachers, site staff and parent-helpers. The physical context includes the children having knowledge of how the visit will be organised, what to expect when they get there, and teaching time given to reinforcing events and experiences after the site visit (Falk, 2004). A fourth dimension of 'time' was also added to the Contextual Model, as further research indicated that random events could occur during a visit, which interrupt the experience and were likely to impact on the quality and quantity of visitor learning. Here we can see a direct overlap of ideas described in the earlier section where creativity and the 5-year-old child was discussed.

The type of learning most commonly associated with learning outside the classroom is informal learning. Falk and Dierking's concept of 'perceived choice' (Falk and Dierking, 2002), instead of informal learning or free-choice learning, resonates well with the visit that was enacted as part of this study. While a set of predetermined learning intentions from the curriculum was selected by the teachers, the participants were motivated by a 'need to know' factor (Lambert and Balderstone, 2000), that is, the children needed to find out how to make a chocolate gift for their mother. They were also motivated by a very predictable interest in the chocolate-making context. It was anticipated that the children might approach the visit with a sense of freedom to select or take note of items that appealed to them and processes they thought would have relevance to their task of making a chocolate gift. In effect, they were to decide when, where and what to learn.

The early work of Falk and Balling (2001) describes the most valuable and memorable learning experiences outside the classroom as 'novel' experiences – those that are new, and of high interest. In their research on the long-term memories of visitors to world expositions, Anderson *et al.* (2003) argue that 'memories were overwhelmingly dominated and mediated by the socio-cultural identity of the individual at the time of the visit' (Anderson *et al.*, 2003: 407). The lens through which the experience is viewed strongly influences what is noticed and remembered. For example, the interests of five-year-old children will have an effect on what attracts their attention and what is ignored. This may not relate well to the learning intentions identified by the teachers. Also aligned with the success of an experience outside the classroom is the children's enjoyment of the visit. Interestingly, by experiencing an emotional connection with the experience – that is, excitement, wonderment, amusement and even shock – it is likely that the children's memories of the event will be increased (Anderson *et al.*, 2003).

In order to maximise children's learning opportunities at sites away from the classroom, there are a number of key features to consider. Falk and Balling (2001) refer to settings that should be of appropriate novelty. Sites should provide children with new, interesting and clearly discriminable events or activities, without the distraction of irrelevant stimuli or overly lengthy visits. Not all sites will suit all age groups and so it is important that teachers select sites for children that offer an age-appropriate experience. Falk and Balling (2001) suggest that young children may gain value from very short forays away from the classroom, rather than the usual 'day trip', if learning is to be the primary intent of the day. A teacher's reason for taking children on a visit can be viewed as *the* most important decision when planning a learning experience outside the classroom (Rennie and McClafferty, 1996). Similarly, the children's understanding of why they are going on the visit is equally important, as this will impact significantly on their learning outcomes.

Selecting a suitable context for the children to experience D&T is best achieved by finding design opportunities that emerge from their everyday lives, at home, at school or from within their community. Being familiar with the context enables the children to engage in it with greater confidence, to understand more about the requirements of the user and to critique their final outcomes. Table 11.1 shows some possible examples.

The following section describes how the elements of D&T, EOTC and nurturing children's creativity were incorporated into the fourth D&T unit listed in Table 11.1. Two classes of 5-year-old children participated in the unit during which they investigated, designed and then created a chocolate gift for Mother's Day.

■ **Table 11.1** Real-world opportunities for teaching D&T

D&T Focus	*Education Outside the Classroom*
Designing and making pop-up cards to celebrate a special occasion, e.g. the teacher's wedding	A visit to a local greetings card manufacturer
Designing and making fruity muffins to welcome the children on their visit from the local pre-school	A visit to a local bakery
Designing a new piece of equipment for the junior school playground	A visit to a local playground with the playground engineer
Designing and making a chocolate gift for Mother's Day	A visit to a local chocolate-making factory

NURTURING THE CREATIVE RESPONSES OF CHILDREN TO TECHNOLOGICAL PROBLEM-SOLVING

Planning a teaching unit that incorporated EOTC and D&T reflected the cognitive apprenticeship model that is associated with teaching D&T – the concept of working alongside an expert in order to respond to a technological problem. The D&T unit developed by the teachers and me comprised three phases: preparation for the visit to the chocolate factory, the visit to the factory and follow-up tasks, and finally the design and construction of the children's gift for Mothers' Day. Each of these phases is described in a table (see Tables 11.2–11.4) with an accompanying paragraph to explain how the plan was drawn together so that it reflected the key components of each of the identified domains, the characteristics of the 5-year-old children, D&T, EOTC and children's developing creativity.

Prior to examining the detail of the plan, a general observation is that, while the disposition of individual children impacts significantly on how they will respond to any given situation, the pedagogical approach of the teacher and his/her ability to create a nurturing learning environment will have significant bearing on how a child engages with the opportunities available to them. Bruce (2011) referred to this type of environment as

■ **Table 11.2** Teaching sequence phase one

1. Establish scenario and guide discussion regarding Mother's Day being celebrated shortly and chocolates often given as a gift.

2. Establish problem, e.g. 'How can we make chocolates for a gift that are safe to eat and that are Mum's favourite?'

3. Establish what children need to know in order to solve problem. This should lead into need to find an expert or visit an expert, e.g. Candyland.

4. Establish what children would like to know about chocolates.

5. Find out what children's existing knowledge is about the chocolate-making process – draw a small sequence of pictures showing how they think chocolate might be made.

6. Brainstorm what children know about the different types of chocolate, e.g. dark chocolate, milk chocolate, coloured chocolate, shapes and fillings. Chart these for reference later (see Figure 11.2).

7. Teach the chocolate-making process from the fruit of the cacao tree to the production of large blocks of bulk chocolate for use in factories.

8. Brainstorm/teach children about the different types of chocolate you can buy. Taste-test a range of chocolate flavours.

9. Discuss how chocolates might be designed, e.g. adding colour.

10. Think about what they would like to make and how they might do that. This should lead into deciding what questions they will need to ask at Candyland.

11. Explain the programme for the visit to children, e.g. the chocolate-making presentation, the lollipop-making presentation, and the investigation in the shop of the different types, shapes and colours of chocolates.

Andrew

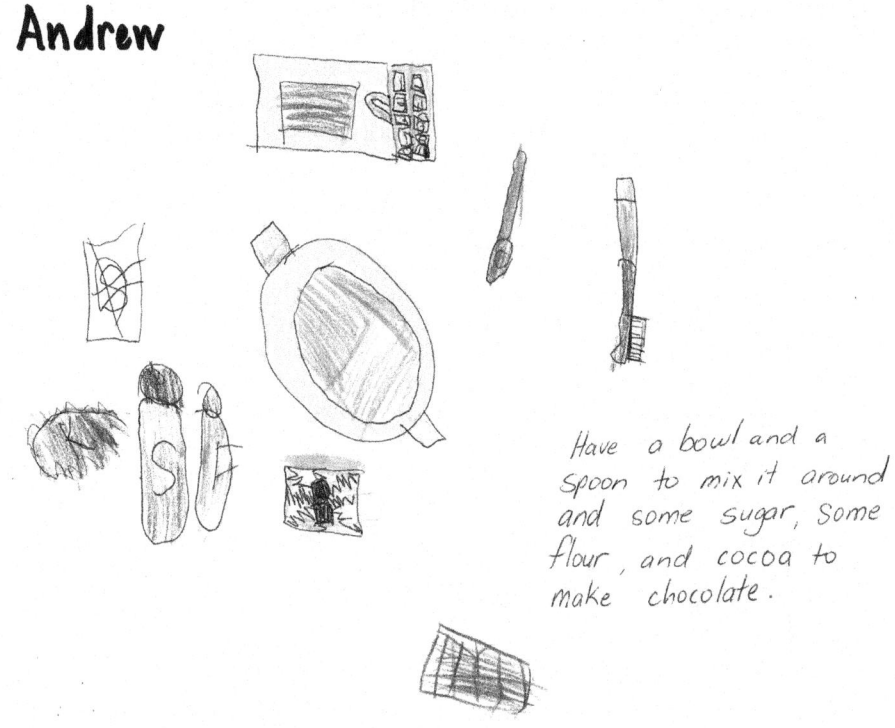

Have a bowl and a spoon to mix it around and some sugar, some flour, and cocoa to make chocolate.

■ **Figure 11.2** An example of a child's prior knowledge of making chocolate

one that creates 'courageous learners', the children who feel supported, emotionally safe to take risks and demonstrate a willingness to try new ways of doing things (Bruce, 2011: 7). The research teachers in this study were adept at creating an environment that was both engaging and empowering.

(i) Preparation for the visit

Carter (2004) reminds us that, in this context, knowledge of chocolate and chocolate-making is not sufficient in itself to assure a creative response to the children's problem. However, this information-gathering phase of the teaching plan was critical. It introduced the context, presented the problem to be solved and established the purpose of the visit to the factory. It provided an opportunity for the teacher to understand something of the children's prior experiences in relation to the context, and enabled her to build on these experiences so the children had ideas and experiences to draw on when creating their design solutions. This was the phase that incorporated Howkins' (2001) stages of creative thinking during which children review, incubate, dream and gather excitement as they begin to consider how they might create their chocolates for Mother's Day. They built an extensive knowledge of chocolate and chocolate-making by taste-testing different types of chocolate, reading stories and viewing video clips of where the cacao bean is sourced. The language of chocolate-making was emphasised and the children understood something of how the beans were collected, ground, mixed and made into the bulk chocolate that they would see being used at the factory. As a result of the preparation they experienced, the children generally understood the purpose of the visit and were able to go to the factory understanding that there was a job to do – as Lambert and Balderstone state (2000), the children were armed with a 'need to know' focus, and the 'incubation' phase (Howkins, 2001) of their creative design ideas was in motion.

(ii) The visit to the factory and follow-up

This phase of the children's technology project can be likened to Howkins' 'reality checks' in which the children see for themselves the process of making chocolate, the extensive

---

■ **Table 11.3** Teaching sequence phase two

---

1. Children organised into small groups with one parent-helper to supervise. Travel to venue.

2. Children and parent-helpers assemble outside Candyland for morning tea. Children move through factory visit with parent-helper. Parents interpret activities and emphasise key points. Endeavour to keep children focused and on-task – e.g. finding out how to make a chocolate gift for Mum.

3. Prompt children to ask their prepared questions and any others that may arise.

4. After the chocolate-making demonstration, parent-helpers take children to the retail shop to look at the different types of chocolates. Use the correct terms and encourage children to look at labels. Talk about how the products have been made, e.g. adding colouring or flavouring.

5. Look at the moulds available in the shop. (This is important as the children will need to consider these when they design their own chocolate gift.)

6. After the visit, talk about the chocolate-making process the children observed at Candyland using a sequence of photographs to support their ideas. Ensure the language of the experience is used, e.g. the ingredients, the processes, the machines, the stages of production, e.g. syrup, moulds, etc. Spend time re-sequencing the activities so they understand that a specific process is important.

7. Children draw a picture showing what they learnt about the chocolate-making process. Encourage them to talk about their drawings and, if they can, draw simple labels showing the names of the equipment and ingredients.

8. Discuss hygienic practices and the reasons for this. Link to the visit, mentioning the hand washing, use of gloves and other special clothing. Maybe share stories of food poisoning?

9. Brainstorm all the possibilities for the look (and filling) they have for their chocolates. Do this on separate charts or in separate sessions.

10. Discuss how the children will find out what their mothers like best when choosing chocolates and how they could remember her ideas, so they can design their chocolate gift. Introduce the simple questionnaire for them to fill in for homework.

11. Brainstorm/teach children about the different fillings that you can put inside chocolates. Carry out simple taste-testing with a range of chocolates and fillings as background knowledge for them – remembering who they are making the chocolates for.

■ **Figure 11.3** An example of chocolates on display

range of possibilities and a glimpse of what the limitations might be when they attempt to fashion their own designs in their classroom. The role of the parent-helpers who accompanied the children on their visit was very influential. They were responsible for keeping the children focused on their task, reiterating the language of chocolate-making, and ensuring that key phases of the chocolate production observed in the factory were not overlooked in the excitement of the visit. This increasingly enabled the children to talk about and better understand each of the development phases they viewed during the tour.

The retail shop had a key role to play in extending the children's design ideas, and the parent-helpers spent a good portion of time encouraging the children to examine the shapes, colours, fillings and toppings as well as the equipment that was needed to create a chocolate design. The laughter and excitement that reverberated around the room as they peered into the display cases (see Figure 11.3) confirmed the high level of engagement and interest being experienced by the children. It was also an effective way of extending the possibilities for the children's design ideas for their gift.

(iii) The design and construction of the gift for Mother's Day

The impact that the visit to the factory had on the children's design ideas was significant. A comparison of the data gathered prior to the visit and the children's drawings and models

■ **Table 11.4** Teaching sequence phase three

1. In small groups, discuss/'analyse' the data they collected from their questionnaires.

2. Discuss the purpose of making a drawing or model of their chocolate gift, i.e.

   (i) to help them decide what their chocolate gift might look like, and
   (ii) to show the teacher what they want to make so equipment and ingredients can be prepared.

3. Using clay or other 3D medium, experiment with shapes, sizes and patterns which would be appropriate for Mum's chocolates.

4. Develop a procedural chart as a class to show how the children will make their own chocolates. Discuss the use of moulds and a safe way they could fill them with the warm chocolate. (Refer to technique used at Candyland).

5. Discuss how children might add in extras, e.g. a filling or topping (piece of flake or swirl, etc.)

6. Teacher prepares equipment and space for the chocolate-making. In small pre-arranged groups, children prepare to make their chocolate gift (hygienic practices . . .), discuss their designs, revisiting their models and questionnaire, and then pour their moulds. Add extras. Try to keep the children as involved as possible in discussions and make sufficient chocolates for them to taste-test themselves, show the class and still leave some for Mum! Keeping to plans is not critical.

7. In groups, children taste-test their finished products and draw their chosen emoticon on a chart. Writers can add a written comment. Encourage them to think about their 'data' regarding Mum's preferences and whether they think they achieved it. If they think they didn't achieve it, what might they need to do another time – a simple reflection of the intended outcome and an opportunity to problem-solve outcomes which were not as they intended.

8. Package chocolates in a simple cellophane bag or similar, to take home for Mum.

9. Follow-up discussions to review and reflect on their achievements.

revealed the extensive broadening of ideas that had occurred over the three weeks of the unit.

While the children's first interviews and drawings generally described chocolate as brown rectangles, their drawings and the clay and plasticine models created after the visit displayed a spectacular range of colours and shapes (see Figure 11.4). These included several hearts, a sun, a flower, a butterfly, a number of balloons, a worm, a fish, an ice-cream and, interestingly, a pair of red chocolate sunglasses!

While the final outcomes created by the children were very satisfying and well received by their mothers, they did not necessarily reflect the data that was collected in their questionnaires, for example, the mother's preferred flavours and colourings. These outcomes emphasise one of the difficulties 5-year-old children experience when creating a product for someone other than themselves. The 4–7-year-old child in the 'intuitive sub-stage' may struggle to view the world from the perspective of others (Piaget, 1954), creating products that they like themselves but willingly give to others. In saying that, the expansion of the children's design ideas is clearly evident, and the memory of the experience continued to be discussed by the children for the remainder of the year.

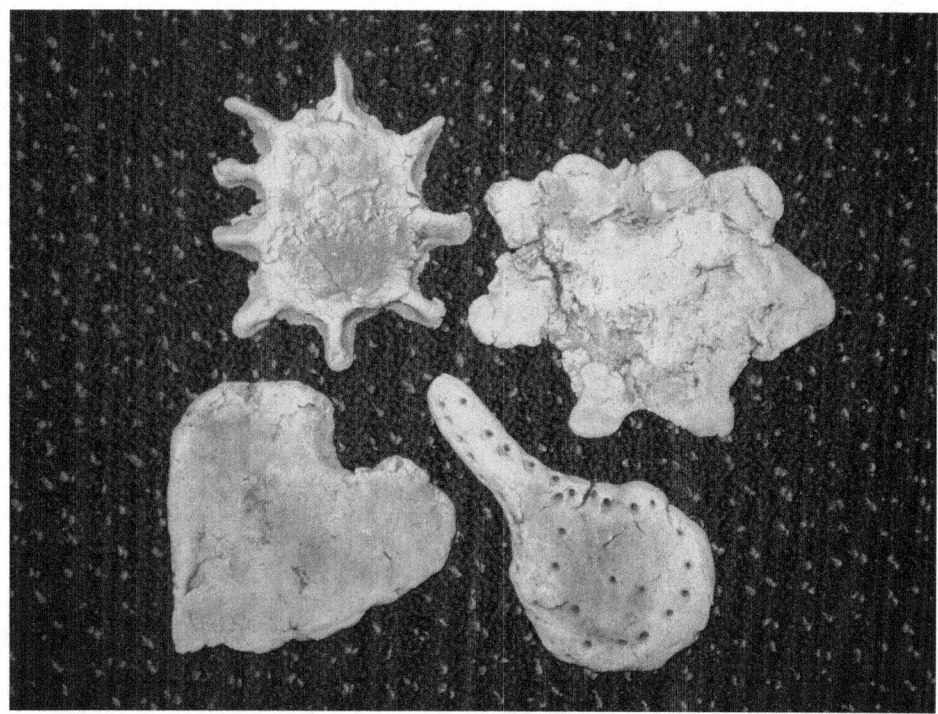

■ **Figure 11.4** Examples of the children's clay models

CONCLUSION

Nurturing the creative thinking of 5-year-old children is fittingly summarised in Bruce's statement that 'creativity doesn't come from nowhere. It feeds off our experiences. It depends on the experience of life in order for creative ideas to develop' (Bruce, 2011: 78).

The literature of EOTC supports the notion of real-world contexts and real-world experiences, which, when linked to children studies within the classroom, can significantly impact on their learning (Dierking *et al.*, 2003). This study, where the children investigated the practice of expert chocolate-makers at the factory, aligns with this philosophy. The context-specific language developed over the time of the teaching unit was robust, and where the children experienced repeated exposure to vocabulary after the event, the new language was retained as part of their everyday repertoire. The time given to preparing the children for the visit was validated by the confidence with which they engaged with the experience, and the relative ease with which they drew on and utilised new knowledge and design ideas. The children's ideas in this study broadened significantly from perceiving chocolate as small, brown rectangles, to chocolate as any colour or shape imaginable! An experience outside the classroom that is planned specifically for the 5-year-old child, and where time is given to both preparing them for the visit and following up the experience, has the potential to inspire an exciting, and at times surprising, array of creative ideas and satisfying technological outcomes.

REFERENCES

Anderson, D., Thomas, G.P. and Ellenbogen, K.M. (2003) 'Learning science from experiences in informal contexts: the next generation of research'. *Asia-Pacific Forum on Science Learning and Teaching*, 4(1).

Bruce, T. (2011) *Cultivating Creativity for Babies and Children* , 2nd Edn. London: Hachette.

Carter, R. (2004) *Language and Creativity: The Art of Common Talk.* London: Routledge.

Damasio, A. (1999) *The Feeling of What Happens: A Lifewide Foundation.* London: Heinemann.

de Vries, M.J. (2012) 'Philosophy of technology', in Williams, P.J. (ed.) *Technology Education for Teachers.* Rotterdam: Sense, 15–34.

Dierking, L.D., Falk, J.H., Rennie, L., Anderson, D. and Ellenbogen, K. (2003) 'Policy Statement of the "Informal Science Education" ad hoc committee'. *Journal of Research in Science Teaching*, 40(2), 108–111.

Falk, J.H. (2004) 'The director's cut: toward an improved understanding of learning from museums'. *Science Education*, 88(1), 83–96.

Falk, J.H. and Balling, J.D. (2001) 'The field trip milieu: learning and behaviour as a function of contextual events'. *Journal of Educational Research*, 76(1), 22–28.

Falk, J.H. and Dierking, L.D. (2000) *Learning from Museums.* New York: Alta Mira Press.

Falk, J.H. and Dierking, L.D. (2002) *Lessons Without Limits: How Free-choice Learning Is Transforming Education.* Walnut Creek: AltaMira Press.

Fleer, M. (2000) 'Working technologically: investigations into how young children design and make during technology education'. *International Journal of Technology and Design Education*, 10, 43–59.

Gibbons, M. and Johnston, R. (1974) 'The roles of science in technological innovation'. *Research Policy*, 3, 220–242.

Golomb, C. (1989) *The Child's Creation of a Pictorial World: Studies in the Psychology of Art.* Berkeley, CA: University of California.

Howkins, J. (2001) *The Creative Economy: How People Make Money from Ideas.* London: Penguin Press.

Jolley, R.P. (2010) *Children and Pictures: Drawing and Understanding.* Chichester, UK: Wiley.

Jones, A., Buntting, C. and de Vries, M.J. (2013) 'The developing field of technology education: a review to look forward'. *International Journal of Technology and Design Education*, 23(4), 191–212.

Lambert, D. and Balderstone, D. (2000) 'Fieldwork and teaching', in *Learning to Teach Geography in the Secondary School.* London: Routledge/Falmer.

Ministry of Education (1997) *Towards Teaching Technology: Know How 2.* Wellington, New Zealand: Learning Media.

Ministry of Education (2010) *Te Kete Ipurangi.* www.tki.org.nz/ (accessed 27 February 2009).

Moreland, J. and Cowie, B. (2011) 'A matter of time: a temporal focus on teaching and learning primary technology', in Stables, K., Benson, C. and de Vries, M. (eds) *PATT 25: CRIPT 8*, London, UK: Goldsmiths, 302.

Piaget, J. (1954) *The Construction of Reality in the Child.* New York, NY: Basic Books.

Rennie, L.J. and McClafferty, T.P. (1996) 'Science centres and science learning'. *Studies in Science Education*, 27, 53–98.

Rogers, G. and Wallace, J. (2000) 'The wheels of the bus: children designing in an early years classroom'. *Research in Science and Technological Education*, 18(1), 127–136.

CREATIVITY THROUGH CONVERSATION

Wendy Fox-Turnbull

INTRODUCTION

Active learning through talk allows teachers and children to collaborate throughout all stages of learning: planning, deciding the context of study, establishing the intended learning, developing or co-constructing associated success criteria and critically engaging in analysing learning. Classroom talk is a critical component of this process (Clarke, 2008). Learning needs to be interactive and flexible enough to change direction if children's interests dictate it and if curriculum coverage is not compromised.

When preparing explicit learning objectives for children, the separation of the learning objective from its context ensures that children and teachers are clearly focused on learning. This facilitates teacher clarity when talking to children about their learning. Clarke suggests that this can have a dramatic effect on teaching and learning. Context, the activity or 'vehicle' through which learning occurs (Clarke, 2005; 2008; 2014), is, however, vitally important. Examples of context-free learning objectives in D&T are given below in Table 12.1 (Fox-Turnbull, 2012). Context-free learning objectives assist teachers and children in the giving of focused feedback. By making the learning objective and the context separately explicit, students are better able to transfer skills and knowledge through to other contexts within and across curriculum areas (Clarke, 2008).

Active learning aligns with an inquiry model of learning discussed later in the chapter. Inquiry learning and D&T are perfect partners (Snape and Fox-Turnbull, 2011; Fox-Turnbull, 2012). Clarke (2008) suggests that to ensure maximum impact on motivation and achievement, schools need to make their curriculum creative and flexible. When assessing D&T, teachers need to consider children's creativity, originality, imagination, innovative approaches and artistic abilities (Gunter and Gunter, 2015). The process of giving children critical guidance and feedback to enhance learning opportunities involves ongoing classroom talk (Black and Wiliam, 1998).

A CASE FOR CLASSROOM TALK IN D&T

Many curricula worldwide, including New Zealand, England and Australia, encourage creating a supportive learning environment, encouraging reflective thought, enhancing the relevance of new learning, facilitating shared learning, making connections to prior learning

WENDY FOX-TURNBULL ■ ■ ■ ■

■ Table 12.1 Learning objective with context separated

Learning objective Children are learning to . . .	Context
design an innovative dwelling	A home for my future life
develop food dishes to welcome people from a range of cultures and religions	Meals for 'International Week' at school
understand how the physical and functional nature of an outcome impacts on performance	Puzzles for young children
understand the role 'mocking-up' has on the quality and creativity of final outcomes	School senior ball

and experiencing sufficient opportunities to explore and create to enhance children's learning (Ministry of Education, 2007: 35). These strategies are all a natural part of quality classroom D&T practice. Talk is a significant component of all of them. We can surmise, therefore, that D&T is well placed to motivate and engage children and that classroom talk plays a significant role in the successful implementation of effective teaching and learning.

Talk plays a significant role in cognitive development (Clarke 2003; Mercer and Hodgkinson, 2008). Children learn through talk and their development is related to cultural practices and the circumstances of the communities within which they develop (Fox-Turnbull, 2013a). This was exemplified by the pair who were talking about their task of stuffing their fish with paper to give it a three-dimensional effect before papier maché was applied. Both children had experienced fishing with their families.

> *Ellis*: Yeah, like we're actually putting all the salmon into the fish.
> *Anne*: All the meat into the fish and not all meat out of the fish.

Child development occurs through participation in everyday life and reflects the relationship between the child and its surroundings. Dialogue between the child and an adult will assist children towards independence in tasks they are learning (Daniels, 1996). However, as anyone who has experienced a 2-year-old will know, individuals often experience conflict of opinion or come up against differing views to their own. This challenge to what a child thinks he or she 'knows' can spark cognitive development because in any conversation the listener perceives and understands meaning while simultaneously developing an active response to it, either agreeing or disagreeing, partially or completely, augments it, applies it and prepares for its execution.

Talk is essential in D&T, especially when children are working with a range of people including their peers, teachers and potential stakeholders. During D&T practice, children are highly likely to experience points of view both similar and different to their own, ultimately leading to new and varied understandings, especially as they come to grips with the reality of collaboratively developing single technological outcomes.

EFFECTIVE CLASSROOM TALK

Mercer and Littleton (2007) suggest that educational success and failure may be explained by the quality of educational talk, rather than simply by considering the capability of individual children or the skill of their teachers. So, what is effective classroom talk? Effective talk and thinking together are an important part of life and have long been ignored or actively discouraged in schools (Mercer and Littleton, 2007). For two people to communicate effectively, both participants need to contribute to the conversation. To enable equal contribution, both must have a common understanding of the exchange that is taking place or is about to take place and have respect for the views of others', even if different from their own.

Engagement in effective classroom talk involves trust and some degree of relationship between the people involved. When people work together in problem-solving situations as in D&T, they do much more than just talk together – they 'inter-think'. This involves combining shared understandings and their intellects in creative ways so that they often reach outcomes that are well above the capability of each individual. Problem-solving situations involve a dynamic engagement of ideas with talk as the principal means used to establish a shared understanding, test solutions and reach agreement or compromise. Shields and Edwards (2005) suggest that this type of talk can bring moments of intense connection between participants with feelings of remarkable openness, which can be deeply affirming and highly exhilarating. It is therefore argued that teachers need to engage children in quality classroom talk to help them make sense both cognitively and experientially of the world in which they live and work (Shields and Edwards, 2005; Mercer and Littleton, 2007).

Effective talk is a key classroom component, but it cannot happen if one person treats the other person disrespectfully; instead it requires all participants to be treated with 'absolute regard'. Frequently, in the classroom, children are not given time to think about what they are doing in relation to the wider situation or previous learning and experiences. Much adult interaction with children is about management (of behaviour, resources, time and movement, etc.) rather than learning, and results in lost learning opportunities. High-quality interactions are best exemplified when teachers engage the philosophy that all children are unique individuals, have the potential to learn and have a contribution to make to their learning (Fleer, 1995; Clarke, 2008).

INTER-COGNITIVE CONVERSATION

One tool that can be used to facilitate effective classroom talk is the use of inter-cognitive conversation (Fox-Turnbull, 2013a). Inter-cognitive conversation involves relating to others, being open to new ideas and working with others to develop new understandings and outcomes. During inter-cognitive conversation, all participants learn through interaction and associated reflections. In D&T, when children are learning in and about a common context and engaged in constructive talk, they assist each other. In doing so they also advance their own knowledge in and about technology (Fox-Turnbull, 2013a; Fox-Turnbull, 2016). This was exemplified in D&T when higher-level questions and discussion were used to assist three children, Teddy, Mandy and Jay, to determine the difference between antique and replica antique radios without actually telling them the answer. It also occurred when Mandy later contributed the idea of using bracing to join trellis timber to assist the construction of their radio. Teddy and Jay learned about the concept of bracing while all three learned about the functional nature of the bracing when combined with trellis wood.

Debate and disagreement also assist children's understanding in D&T, but only when participants are open to change and new ideas. In situations where conflict arises, and because in D&T children are often collaboratively developing a single outcome, they have to find a single solution. This means either they accept others' ideas or combine and blend ideas until a compromise is reached (Fox-Turnbull, 2013a). An example of this occurred when Dougal and Alan's views about suitable designs for the microphone stand forced Dougal to consider his design critically and somewhat reluctantly agree that Alan's was the better. Another example was when Rex identified that working with others was difficult as his group of three always fought and couldn't agree; however, he later stated that working with Debbie and Issy had been good and that together they had achieved more than he could have by himself. In response to my question 'If you were working by yourself, would your fish be as good as the one that you finally made?' Rex, Issy and Debbie answered 'No', then Rex added 'because then we can actually, work really, really hard. We wouldn't . . . be able to make it all by ourselves'.

Through the use of child-to-child inter-cognitive conversation, children are able to take their knowledge and skill development further than they would have been able to do individually. Talk is a vital component of this process. Teachers need to plan for and teach children to talk constructively, to use debate and discussion as a tool for advancing understanding. During the initial stages of a project, children also need to be taught how to listen to and accept others' ideas without necessarily agreeing with the ideas presented. Teachers may further need to assist children to understand that, although their own ideas are not always accepted, their contribution is still important. Conflicting ideas and opinions force all members of the group to question and justify their decision-making, thus making stronger connections to key concepts and knowledge, resulting in a better-informed outcome (Fox Turnbull, 2016).

THE ROLE OF CONVERSATION IN DEVELOPING CREATIVITY

As already stated, there is a considerable body of knowledge on understanding how conversations between children can enhance their learning (Alexander, 2008; Fox-Turnbull, 2013b). Conversation allows people to communicate and share experiences and ideas, therefore allowing the transformation of experiences into cultural knowledge and understanding (Mercer, 1995).

Torrance (1972) suggests that the inclusion of opportunities for interaction between children, teachers and peers is a most successful strategy for enhancing creativity. During interaction, children construct their worlds. Talk provides both the process and the product for cognitively focused interactions. As oral communication takes place, children are involved in the process of constructing and reconstructing themselves. The construct of language is not a system of set meanings to which everyone agrees; it is uniquely individual. Single utterances may mean different things to different people, implying that there is potential for conflict and disagreement (Burr, 1995). Within design, Oak (2011) states that face-to-face talk between all the participants is essential to the collaborative process of design and should occur in tandem with other design strategies such as sketching, mind mapping, mood boards and modelling. This is especially the case in the D&T classroom with children.

STRATEGIES FOR DEVELOPING CREATIVITY IN D&T THROUGH TALK

Classroom talk can be used to assist children's creativity and facilitate learning in D&T. Specific strategies can contribute to a classroom learning culture that places children at the centre of learning. Useful strategies foster critical and independent thinking, both of which are key elements in the fostering of creativity. Engaging children in these strategies also offers opportunities for them to engage in inter-cognitive conversations in D&T, including strategies such as debate and challenging of design ideas, thus the potential for increased creativity. As children's thinking is challenged, compared and contrasted to that of others, children can be encouraged to be open to new ideas and thinking.

There are a number of strategies to engage children in creative and higher-level thinking that are assisted by classroom talk. In D&T, projects should be interesting, unique and authentic. The strategies suggested in this chapter are a few of many that offer opportunities to develop creativity and assist children to think 'outside the box' when designing technology outcomes. These strategies include: inquiry learning, ideation, and divergent and convergent thinking. I also describe some other strategies that value the role of talk in learning and that I have found to be particularly successful in D&T. These include: No hands up, Talking partners, and Questions as statements – agree or disagree.

INQUIRY LEARNING

Inquiry learning (IL) is one tool that can facilitate an open-ended approach and is perfectly suited as a method of delivering D&T (Snape and Fox-Turnbull, 2011). Inquiry learning includes open-ended pursuits undertaken by children and can draw on knowledge and skills not otherwise used in school (Lewis, 2009). It facilitates higher-level thinking and problem-solving very successfully as it encompasses a wide range of skills and processes in active learning, leading to a much broader understanding of the world. When learning through inquiry, children are encouraged to develop skills, knowledge and understandings within their own cultural framework, enabling them to take responsibility for their learning. This approach focuses on the facilitation of independent knowledge-based learning and reflects the belief that, for children, active involvement in construction of their knowledge is essential for effective learning. In short, IL facilitates learning through social interaction with others, through the identification and research of learner-owned questions and the solving of associated problems. Conversation is an integral part of the inquiry learning process, as teachers and peers share and discuss findings as they occur, consider their significance and identify the next steps of the inquiry. Inquiry learning is exemplified when a group of 10-year-olds were asked to develop a futuristic space station. Early 'emersion' lessons included videos of people in space, email interviews with astronauts, and identification of current and potential issues for Earth. In groups, the students identified a specific need that they wanted to address with their space station. At the unit conclusion, modelled space stations included: the Earth's prison, a holiday resort and the Earth's hydroponic vegetable garden among others.

IDEATION

Ideation is the taking of a single idea in a variety of directions with the aim of creating something new and original. It is a strategy used by designers and D&T teachers to assist children with their creative thinking (Ormrod, 2012). Ideation is not about coming up with lots of ideas, but rather coming up with one big innovative idea. Ideation includes a number of techniques, all of which assist children to develop creativity and innovation in their design. Matimore (2016) identified several of particular interest for use in the oral context within D&T.

The 'Worst Idea Technique' is a technique in which children call out their worst possible idea. The example Matimore gives is 'think of the worst idea for soup'. This strategy values creative thinking and assists children's thinking of really wacky ideas, which further down the track may assist them in the articulation of other creative ideas. The 'Questions Assumptions' technique facilitates the collaborative design process by questioning potential assumptions. For example, a typical assumption when asked to design a new chair is that it will be sat on. Although assumptions do have their place and can save considerable time, it is useful to question basic assumptions at times. 'Idea Hooks' is a technique that uses associated metaphors as jumping-off points for new ways of thinking. Although not only an oral exercise if combined with inter-cognitive conversations, children are encouraged to look at things in different ways. An example I witnessed was the use of projection of nature through exploring the form of armadillos, snails, turtles and tortoises to assist in the design of a holiday home. During this approach, students start sketching aspects of natural forms which, over a series of steps, they transform into another form. Although this strategy most prominently uses drawing, D&T teachers should couple this activity with inter-cognitive conversation to assist children to gain insight into their 'designerly' thinking and concepts.

CONVERGENT AND DIVERGENT THINKING

Another technique that is particularly useful for promoting creativity in D&T is convergent and divergent thinking – a sub-set of ideation. Divergent thinking (Figure 12.1) encourages children in D&T to start with an idea and to branch out in as many different ways as possible. Brainstorming is a foundational aspect of divergent thinking that is essentially oral, with ideas from everyone recorded for all to see. Children can be encouraged to think from a variety of perspectives. For example, when thinking about a potential new toy, one perspective may be from that of a young child, or a cat or dog, or from a retailer's viewpoint. When doing this in a collaborative situation and to facilitate the success of divergent thinking especially during the brainstorming stage, there are a few simple rules that need to be established:

1. Defer judgement of unusual ideas
2. Avoid ownership of ideas
3. Respect others
4. Be open to learn ideas from others

Once a range of ideas is identified, children might either select one to take further, combine the thinking of two or more options or each group member may develop one

Multiple New Ideas to Explore

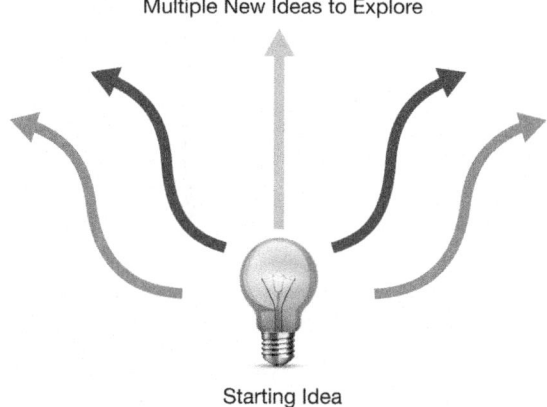

Starting Idea

■ **Figure 12.1** Divergent thinking (Ormrod, 2012, modified by author)

idea, not their original contribution, to explore further (Baer and Garret, 2010). Divergent thinking is exemplified in the following activity.

The task is to design and mock-up a new piece of playground equipment because the children are moving to a new school site. Each group of children is given a picture of an existing piece of playground equipment. The teacher then asks the children to draw their piece of equipment multiple times by making the following modifications:

- Add a new aspect to make it more fun
- Take away a part and add another
- Change the materials that a part of it is made of
- Increase the size of one aspect of the equipment and decrease another
- Make a change so as to encourage 'old people' to play on it
- Change it to look futuristic, or like a cat

As a result of this activity, the children come up with a range of divergent design ideas.

In convergent thinking (Figure 12.2), the same rules apply but children start with a variety of ideas or objects, such as those identified in an Idea Hook session. Collaboratively children critique existing designs, discuss and modify their ideas until they merge into that of a new and innovative technological outcome. This is exemplified by an activity I do with my primary student teachers but which is equally suitable for a primary classroom. In groups of six, the students are given four or five different peelers to explore to identify their physical and functional features. Then they produce annotated sketches detailing various aspects. As a group, they then identify a potential target audience for whom they design an innovative peeler. Detailed designs are drawn and a mock-up produced. This activity can be completed with any small device or tool that has a range of varieties or types, such as pens or drink bottles. When undertaking this activity, children use convergent thinking by considering a range of outcomes and ideas, which then converge to a new and innovative outcome to meet specific needs.

Varied Starting Ideas

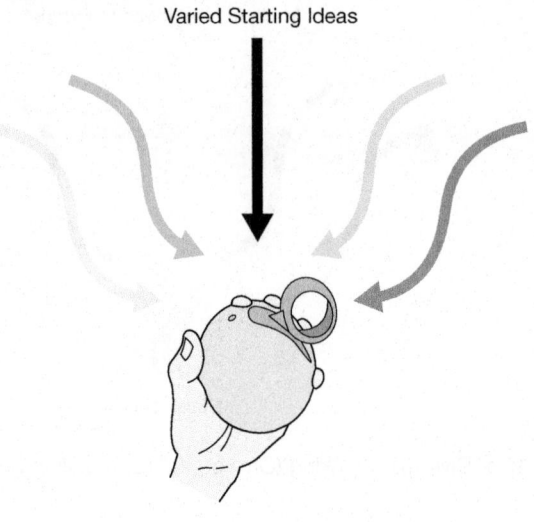

Innovative Product

■ **Figure 12.2** Convergent thinking (Ormrod, 2012, modified by author)

NO HANDS UP AND TALKING PARTNERS

No hands up

Typically, in the classroom teachers begin a session with a quick recall of prior learning through a question-and-answer session, resulting in the same few children responding to the questions. Teachers usually have a correct answer in mind and continue until the correct answer is obtained. Clarke (2005) found that even when an open question is asked, children begin thinking but stop as soon as the first hands go up. Many children experience this so frequently that they eventually stop trying to think about the answer because of the constant interruption, and they develop the belief that they are less able than their peers. In a *No hands up* classroom, children move towards a solution (Clarke, 2008). When implementing this strategy, all children are asked questions as before, but they are told that anyone maybe called on to answer the questions. To avoid the 'I don't know' response, teachers are best to avoid recall questions, aiming to ask open questions or questions about children's opinions or feelings, which avoid the right or wrong scenario (Clarke, 2005). After time to think, children are asked randomly for their thoughts. The children understand that any child might be asked at any time, but rather than being asked about what they individually think, they may be asked to comment on the conversation they add with their talking partner if given the opportunity to discuss question with a peer before answers or thoughts are shared.

Talking partners

Often paired with *No hands up*, *Talking partners* is an effective way to instigate discussion with a range of questions for children to respond to. After the asking of the question and before responding publicly, children are asked to talk to a randomly pre-selected talking partner for thirty seconds to one minute. The answers are then gathered from pairs using *No hands up* with one of the pair being the spokesperson; an emphasis is placed on a pair response rather than an individual response. This strategy allows children to think and articulate their understandings before speaking in a public domain such as to the whole class. It also enables shy, less confident children to have a voice when in traditional settings they may not have the opportunity or feel confident to do so.

These strategies can be particularly successful with shy (Issy) and dominant (Ellis) children. During an interview I undertook with Fleur, a classroom teacher, about her experiences with these two strategies, she indicated: 'Issy was a different student who had begun to contribute to whole class conversation, something she did not do in the past.' In response to the question 'What most impacted on the students' learning?' Fleur responded: 'Their [her children] thinking, and the questioning, their questioning techniques and I'm still using your no hands up.' I also observed that Ellis didn't dominate classroom conversation as much after the implementation of the strategies. He was always given the opportunity to talk his ideas through, if not to everyone in the class.

The organisation and training of talking partners is essential, regardless of age. Clarke (2005) suggests a number of guidelines and rules for *Talking partners*:

1. *Talking partners* have to be set and changed regularly to ensure children experience different ideas and personalities. She has also found that random pairs seem to be the most effective.
2. A typical time slot for talking partners is about three weeks. When picked, the children will sit next to their new talking partner. If they are working in ability groups, then they obviously need a talking partner within their group; for example, they may have three talking partners at a time, one for maths within their group, one for reading within their group and one for all other times.
3. Teachers need to ensure children know who they are talking to. They need to check for absences and make sure all children are included. For junior children, an imaginary 'magic spot', a pre-designated spot in the classroom for each pair, helps cement who they are working with.
4. Teachers should model how to talk with their talking partner with an assistant or another child and create a set of class rules from the demonstration.

Suggested rules for talking partners include:

1. Look at your partner when they are talking
2. Look interested, nod occasionally
3. Don't fidget or let other things distract you
4. Let your partner express his or her views
5. Think about what your partner is saying
6. Sometimes 'let go' of what you want to say if you think your partner's train of thought is interesting

7. Stay focused, try to be clear about what you mean when you speak
8. Say more than one or two words
9. Be prepared to compromise or constructively persuade (Clarke, 2005).

By establishing a classroom climate where children's and teachers' views are respected equally, the above two strategies are a perfect tool for exploring ideas. Creativity can be enhanced as children are encouraged to explore and articulate all their ideas without judgemental comments being made.

QUESTIONS AS STATEMENTS – AGREE OR DISAGREE

In this strategy, questions are turned into statements to which the children are asked to discuss and either 'agree' or 'disagree'. They are then asked to justify their response. Prior to the children presenting and justifying their responses, they are given an opportunity to talk about their thinking with their talking partner. When given a statement to reflect upon, children defend or explain their point of view, facilitating high-quality child-to-child interaction.

In a recent D&T research project that I undertook, this strategy was used to assist 6-year-old children to understand the desirable attributes for props in a school play. The children had previously undertaken a range of activities and co-constructed with the teachers a set of desirable attributes for stage props. Statements were read to the class one at a time. Each pair discussed the statements to identify whether they believed them to be true or false and why. The statements included:

1. Props need to be small
2. A thimble is a good prop
3. A banana cannot be a prop
4. A pencil sharpener as a prop needs to be small.

After *Talking partner* discussions, the children shared their ideas with the class. On one occasion, different pairs successfully justified opposite opinions. The first pair identified 'props need to be small' as true because of the size of related props in the scene. A large pencil sharpener next to a pencil would look ridiculous. Another group argued the statement to be false because small props were difficult for the audience to see. This response recalled what the props manager from a local theatre company had said. This is exemplified in the example below:

Teacher: A pencil sharpener as a prop in a play needs to be small. Agree or disagree?
Child 1: Agree because if you had a big pencil sharpener you would need to have a big pencil.
Child 2: Disagree because if it was small the audience would not see it.

This illustrates the flexibility and critical thinking involved in such an activity. The children learned that opposing views can be argued as correct depending on the position of the stakeholder or other people involved. This strategy has the potential to assist creativity, as it gives children an increased awareness that a range of points of view and design ideas can be successful while decreasing the likelihood of children coming to D&T classes with the mindset that they are going to design and make 'one correct answer'.

CONCLUSION

Effective classroom talk through the planned and structured delivery of strategies to engage children in higher-level thinking and paired with collaborative practice has the potential to greatly enhance abilities and creativity in D&T. Engaging children in activities such as those outlined above can facilitate higher-level thinking of ideas with applications to new situations. This is particularly useful in D&T when children are designing innovative technological outcomes. Teaching strategies that facilitate learner-focused conversations enable children to articulate ideas in a low-risk environment before sharing with a wider audience, to assist children's ability to draw from a range of views and to enhance their design ideas.

REFERENCES

Alexander, R. (2008) *Towards Dialogic Teaching: Rethinking Classroom Talk.* Cambridge: Dialogos.

Baer, J. and Garret, T. (2010) 'Teaching for creativity in an era of content standards and accountability', in Beghetto, R.A. and Kaufman, J.C. (eds) *Nurturing Creativity in the Classroom.* Cambridge: Cambridge University Press, 6–23.

Black, P. and Wiliam, D. (1998) *Inside the Black Box: Raising Standards Through Classroom Assessment.* London: King's College.

Burr, V. (1995) *An Introduction to Social Constructionism.* London: Routledge.

Clarke, S. (2003) *Enriching Feedback in the Primary Classroom.* Oxon: Hodder Murray.

Clarke, S. (2005) *Formative Assessment in Action: Weaving the Elements Together.* Oxon: Hodder Murray.

Clarke, S. (2008) *Active Learning Through Formative Assessment.* London: Hodder Education.

Clarke, S. (2014) *Outstanding Formative Assessment: Culture and Practice.* London: Hodder Education.

Daniels, H. (1996) *An Introduction to Vygotsky.* London: Routledge.

Fleer, M. (1995) *Staff-child Interactions: A Vygotskian Perspective.* Canberra: Australian Early Childhood Association Inc., 1.

Fox-Turnbull, W. (2012) 'Learning in technology', in Williams, P.J. (ed.) *Technology Education for Teachers.* Rotterdam: Sense Publishers.

Fox-Turnbull, W. (2013a) *The Nature of Conversation of Primary Students in Technology Education: Implications for Teaching and Learning.* PhD., University of Waikato, Hamilton, NZ.

Fox-Turnbull, W. (2013b) *Themes of Conversation in Technology Education.* Paper presented at the International Technology and Engineering Educators' Association Conference, Columbus, Ohio.

Fox-Turnbull, W. (2016) 'The nature of primary students' conversation in technology education'. *International Journal of Technology and Design Education*, 26(1), 21–41. Retrieved from http://dx.doi.org/10.1007/s10798-015-9303-6 (accessed 27 June 2016).

Gunter, G.A. and Gunter, R.E. (2015) *Teachers Discovering Computers: Integrating Technology in a Changing World.* Boston: Cengage Learning.

Lewis, T. (2009) 'Creativity in technology education: providing children with glimpses of their inventive potential'. *International Journal of Technology & Design Education*, 19(3), 255–268. doi:10.1007/s10798-008-9051-y, (accessed 9 February 2016).

Matimore, B. (2016). Ideation techniques. Retrieved from http://www.technologyforge.net/enma/6020/6020Lectures/Ideation/ENMA291IdeationReferences/ENMA291Ideation Techniques.pdf

Mercer, N. (1995) *The Guided Construction of Knowledge: Talk Among Teachers and Learners*. Avon, UK: Multilingual Matters Ltd.

Mercer, N. and Hodgkinson, S. (eds) (2008) *Exploring Talk in School*. London: Sage Publications Ltd.

Mercer, N. and Littleton, K. (2007) *Dialogue and the Development of Children's Thinking: A Sociocultural Approach*. Oxon: Routledge.

Ministry of Education (2007) *The New Zealand curriculum*. Wellington: Learning Media.

Oak, A. (2011) 'What can talk tell us about design? Analyzing conversation to understand practice'. *Design Studies*, 32, 211–234.

Ormrod, J. (2012) *Human Learning*. Boston: Pearson Education.

Shields, C. and Edwards, M. (2005) *Dialogue Is Not Just Talk: A New Ground for Educational Leadership*. New York: Peter Lang Publishing Inc.

Snape, P. and Fox-Turnbull, W. (2011) 'Twenty-first century learning and technology education nexus'. *Problems of Education in the 21st Century*, 34, 149–161.

Torrance, E.P. (1972) 'Can we Teach Children to Think Creatively'. *The Journal of Creative Behaviour*, 6(2), 114–143.

CREATIVITY – FUTURE CHALLENGES AND REWARDS

Steve Keirl

INTRODUCTION

For our journey of teaching design and technology (D&T) creatively, it is helpful to remember that both the subject (D&T) and the phenomenon (creativity) can be thought of *holistically*.

D&T's very name implies something rather richer than simply a body of knowledge or a traditional 'subject'. For a start, 'design' is both noun and verb and, educationally, we are interested in both *processes* and *products*. Meanwhile, Technology (big 'T') alludes to a *field of human enterprise* embracing multiple technologies (small 't'). In the classroom, we do not give attention to any one technology all of the time. Rather, we move among them according to our educational purposes.

I would also like to suggest that it helps to think of creativity holistically rather than as a single concept or phenomenon. Because creativity is such a rich, personally and socially beneficial educational concept, it cannot usefully be approached from a narrow interpretation. There are many ways of looking at creativity, and the term is used in different ways in different contexts.

By keeping these holistic approaches in mind, we can better celebrate D&T's wonderful partnership with creativity, and we can discover rewards and challenges that we might not have anticipated in our work. Through our D&T teaching, we introduce children to opportunities for working creatively as well as to ways of understanding themselves and their ability to act on, and change, their worlds. We can also develop professionally in how we look at the curriculum and how we work creatively with colleagues. In turn, schools enhance their creative cultures as a direct result of a rich spectrum of D&T creative activity.

Taking a holistic approach, we can consider D&T's special contribution to creativity in three ways: *for* creativity, *through* creativity and *about* creativity. Put simply, D&T can educate *for* creativity on the assumption that we are supporting the advancement of *creativity itself* as a societal good for the future. Helping children be creative (and all that this entails) becomes a contribution towards desirable futures. Educating *through* creativity is to suggest that there is a particular kind of learning that D&T education delivers through its creative practices. Here, D&T serves as a sophisticated tool to advance learning in ways that are special to the field. Education *about* creativity involves D&T helping children understand the multiple, valuable facets of creativity-as-practice. Here, children step back from creative practice to reflect on what creativity is, how it works, how to put it to work and how to critique it.

When D&T adopts this holistic approach to creativity education, it is fulfilling its role as a powerful and unique form of education and as a key contributor to general education. While some of the general education aspects of creativity may appear else-where in the curriculum, when D&T integrates all three ways of addressing creativity it is doing so uniquely as a form of *design and technological literacy*, that is, as education of value to every child no matter where in the world and regardless of the talents they hold. When this happens, teachers are indeed (to reflect on this book's title) teaching D&T creatively.

SEEING CREATIVITY THROUGH D&T

How then might we view creativity in ways that alert us to new challenges and bring us new rewards? How might we develop our special sense of D&T creativity for the benefit of the primary classroom? As this book shows, creativity is not a tangible entity – something we can touch, readily describe or even agree upon; it is a concept better understood educationally from a range of perspectives. In this next section, I explore some of the ways we can see creativity through D&T.

CREATIVITY AS A PERSONAL AND COLLECTIVE GOOD

When teachers are helping children be creative, they are first and foremost supporting the individual – the person – but they are also contributing to an important social good that is of broader cultural benefit. (Of course, they will be nurturing the occasional creative genius too.) All researchers and scholars of creativity agree that creative capacities lie within everyone to some degree. Our educational challenge is the fostering of the individual's creativity – whether that is a matter of confidence-building, evocative questioning, playing games or harnessing mischievous minds.

The significance of creativity to the individual, to their identity and to their personal development is so important – not least because creativity can be understood as an aspect of consciousness, of expressing one's being. As Lubart puts it: 'Being creative is, in part, a philosophy of life, which is acquired through childhood experiences' (Lubart, 2004: 12). It is part of who we are and we have a sense of purpose when we behave creatively. Creativity matters to us as persons. It is at the personal level that creativity is both challenging and rewarding, and, in this, D&T can play a major role.

Mumford (1934) argued creative activity to be a necessity of human fulfilment, which should be socialised through education. That is, by helping pupils realise their creative potential they can also understand its benefits to others. Parnes (1963/1970) argued that creative activity amounts to a fulfilment of the highest of Maslow's needs – that of self-actualisation. We certainly know this from students' delight when they come up with ideas and products which, to them, are original – of their own creation. Yet, as we know from our personal experience as teachers and adults (which we bring to our pedagogy), being creative can also be demanding, risky and emotionally challenging. To paraphrase Lubart (2004: 12), creativity both *gives* to the person and *asks of* the person.

Through their designerly activities, children learn that creativity is a disposition, a behavioural tool that they can choose to use at will. When, as teachers, we treat creativity as we would literacy or numeracy, it becomes part of life-as-usual, having benefits that are of rich educational value to our pupils. Better still, pupils educated about their personal and collective creative potential can apply their creativity as a *social good* for individuals, communities, societies and humankind alike. Like Mumford, Koestler (1964/1975) saw the creative life as a social one and he talked of *creative contagion,* of how creativity stimulates creativity – a concept of real value to our D&T teaching.

Florida (2003) presents his own sense of creative contagion when he witnesses the rising social significance of creativity through *the creative age, the creative economy* and *the creativity index*. When he describes an emergent *creative class* with two major sub-components of a 'super-creative core' and 'creative professionals' he includes educators (unsurprisingly) in the former group – a rewarding professional salute but also perhaps another expectation of teachers in changing times.

THE SIGNIFICANCE OF DESIGNERLY AND TECHNOLOGICAL CREATIVITY TO HUMANITY

As a species, we cannot *be* without technologies, or they without us. Our *being* is as much technological as it is human. However, we must remember that all technologies are the result of human *design*, which is implicitly creative. Remarkably, we still do not have a parallel education for these incredibly significant circumstances. However, D&T creativity education does open up multiple possibilities for teachers to explore ideas with children about evolution; how creative acts brought about life- and society-changing technologies; the place of designed technologies in historical events; and, equally, how innovations often bring new problems. Any product analysis game opens up the whole connected web of issues around who brought products into being, how they were made, who was affected by them and what the consequences are (always a mix of the positive and negative here).

In reflecting on the history of technologies and designs, I am reminded of classroom discussions where children consider the differences between discovery and invention (a contribution to understandings of why technology is not science). Similarly, when children discuss the differences between accident and design, they are engaging in (although they may not know it) philosophical explorations of determinism, free will and questions of choice – all significant to humanity. In turn, when they are being creative they are weighing up the competing values that will constitute their design choices. They are critiquing or questioning *what are the best decisions* and, importantly, they are considering *why*. When such considerations emerge, creativity is celebrated in, for and through D&T. What is interesting is how these begin in the primary classroom yet can have far-reaching benefits – which is education at its best!

ALL CREATIVE AND DESIGN ACTS ARE INTENTIONAL ACTS

Creativity always has an intentional orientation – towards the future – whether that future is the immediacy of thought or a distant outcome. By whatever definition, it is about *bringing into being* ideas, designs or actual products not yet existing. Creativity is the oxygen of design activity and descriptions of creativity invariably embrace some sense of *originality*, that is, a lack of prior existence. Therefore, designing is often described as acting with intention on the world or changing one set of circumstances into another. Lubart (2004) talks of *conation* – the drive to act purposefully. Put differently, we entertain *motives*. Understanding creativity-as-intention celebrates D&T's special contribution to educating children to apply their thinking and to enact change. In turn, we can reflect on Hannah Arendt's observation that: '. . . the moment we turn our mind to the future, we are no longer concerned with "objects" but with *projects* . . . And just as the past always presents itself to the mind in the guise of certainty, the future's main characteristic is its basic uncertainty' (cited in Mitcham, 1994: 254).

Bound up in the intentional perspective is the recognition that to design is to resist determinism – the view that all events are determined by prior events. Creativity and designing are actions of the will – intentional acts to reshape what exists into another condition. There are plenty of popular manifestations of technological determinism, for example: that technologies are 'inevitable', that we have no say in their introduction and effects and that 'that's progress'. So when children have opportunities to be creative, whatever the design project, we can invite them to reflect on the fact that they were the decision-makers in the process, that they can change their design decisions and that they can also legitimately question the design decisions that others have made in their products.

By engaging in reflections on their creativity as both process and behaviour, children come to understand design as a form of empowerment in which their own decisions bring design responsibility. They understand that design is what makes change happen in the world and that this is how the future can be engaged. Pupils' education about creativity is richest when they learn that they are consciously asserting their own will and imagination through creative, designerly acts. Furthermore, through such self-expression, risk-taking and exploring uncertainty, their personal identity is shaped.

ALL CREATIVE AND DESIGN ACTS INVOLVE VALUE JUDGEMENTS AND THE CONSIDERATION OF CONSEQUENCES

Because it is not possible to talk of 'being human' or 'human being' without considering the intertwined nature of ourselves and the technologies we have (creatively) designed and developed, we have to accept that, while we might say that 'we' did not personally design this or that technology, we are largely responsible for adopting technologies into our lives. Humanity is where it is today (personally, socially, politically, environmentally) because of our technologies and people's creative acts of design. However, it is important to know that our circumstances today are quite different from those of our forebears. We have ever-deepening awareness of our power to design, of the potential consequences of our designs and of our potential to shape the future not just locally but globally – for better or for worse!

What does this mean for the primary classroom? As children learn that the processes and behaviours of creativity and designing are more than just 'having different ideas' (as invaluable and essential as this is), they understand that all such activity is about choice–making. Choices are made to design this way, not that; even to initiate a design; and these choices are invariably dealing with questions like 'What is better, or worse, here?'

By weighing up design variables, children commit to value judgements. 'Costs' might be financial, personal, social, human, environmental, aesthetic and so on. Designing is eternally about compromise, and children soon learn that not everyone or every criterion can be satisfied. So, in deciding to act this way or that, when invited to explain their decisions they have to articulate their thinking in ways that, sooner or later, are ethical in nature (Keirl, 2011). They are formulating ideas about what counts as right, where 'right' has multiple senses. The value judgements that are forever arising in creative designing are interwoven with ideas of good–bad, better–worse and the consideration of alternatives. Here we have creativity in its rich D&T sense extending into the moral world and, with this, imagination, critical thinking and reflection are all developed. Along with good D&T creativity comes the recognition of a spectrum of consequences – from meeting a brief to imagining differing kinds of effects and outcomes. When we (and children) understand that we are all part of ongoing change, we are the future we contribute to and that we are choice-makers, then we understand something of identity, of responsibility and of shared futures (McLaren, 2012).

CREATIVITY IN D&T: SOME INHIBITORS

Just because we might accept and advocate creative D&T as an educational good, that is no guarantee of its ready acceptance into the curriculum. It would be naïve not to proceed without bearing in mind the kinds of things that can inhibit our good intentions.

I will start by asking that we remember that there is a political context to our work as teachers. I am under no illusions whatsoever about the pressures under which many teachers are expected to work and that any curriculum innovation can seem daunting. Ours is a profession forever full of contradictions and tensions, and many of these come from beyond our classrooms. In countries such as England, teachers are constrained in their work by bureaucratic demands and testing regimes that induce particular professional and school cultures. These demands and regimes do not just happen. They are themselves intentional political acts – designed technologies. They are telling of how schools are viewed and of how some believe children should be treated. In 1972, the seminal work of Paolo Freire illuminated a major contradiction in the ways in which children were seen by educational systems. He offered a creative curriculum analysis that resonated globally and continues to remind us of educational alternatives today. His landmark pedagogical critique famously contrasted 'banking education' (system-centred with education intentionally restricted to facts and prescribed knowledge) with 'problem-posing education' (pupil- and teacher-centred with education as engagement with the world).

> Banking education treats students as objects of assistance; problem-posing education makes them *critical thinkers*. Banking education *inhibits creativity* and domesticates (although it cannot completely destroy) the *intentionality of consciousness* by isolating consciousness from the world, thereby denying people their ontological and historical vocation of *becoming more fully human*. Problem-posing education bases itself on *creativity* and stimulates true *reflection* and *action upon reality*, thereby responding to the vocation of *persons as beings* only when engaged in *inquiry* and *creative transformation*.
>
> (Freire, 1972: 56. my italics)

I hope the spirit of this rich quotation is evident. For our subject, the 'design' in D&T is ever in danger of being marginalised as simply drawing and reproductive skilling (a particular challenge for secondary school colleagues), or it is rendered invisible by educationally divisive trends such as STEM (a shelf-ready acronym for neatly packaged, humanities-marginalising science, technology, engineering and maths). Meanwhile, the 'technology' in D&T meets the banking formulation when the subject is reduced to making children only passively aware of technologies and how to use them, that is, enculturation into the uncritical acceptance of technologies. In the circumstances I describe here, creativity is seriously inhibited.

When there is a dominant bureaucratic climate (which takes professional judgement away from teachers) and testing (rather than *assessment*) regimes, then it is the system's needs that are being privileged. Creativity and creative teaching cannot flourish in such climates. My point here is that, whatever our sense of 'creativity', it can be compromised by educational straitjackets. Thus, probably our single greatest challenge regarding education for, through and about creativity is how to enact it. Perhaps we can help usurp the status quo by taking up our book's invitation to *teach design and technology creatively*. At least, for now, D&T can enjoy life outside of testing regimes, even though as a consequence of the pull on resources that the regimes demand, D&T loses its educationally defensible place in a rich and necessary curriculum for all primary pupils.

Thus, there can be organisational challenges for teachers' intent on celebrating creativity in the classroom. Here, I am referring to the fact that it is very hard for a few teachers to try to teach creativity and to teach creatively when the school as a whole does not (or cannot) celebrate creativity. For creativity and creative contagion to flourish, a *culture of creativity* is needed and this is a matter of leadership and whole-school commitment. Florida (2003) observes that '. . . perhaps the biggest issue at stake in this emerging (creative) age is the ongoing tension between creativity and organization' (Florida, 2003: 21–22). Such is the case for schools.

Just as there are human traits relating to creative behaviours and cultures, so there are organisational ones too. Creative organisations facilitate creativity positively. Others pay only lip service to creativity, feel threatened by it or actively discourage it. Creativity can thrive when: risk-taking is welcomed; negativity and blame are combated; bureaucratisation and administrivia are minimised; vision is maintained; and spoon-feeding is avoided. In other words, professional independence and judgement allow for imagination and creativity to flourish. However, while there are some serious systemic issues to consider when seeking to enhance creativity in primary schools, we need not be pessimistic on the D&T front.

Interest in creativity 'for productivity', with an accompanying educational agenda, boomed massively in the 1960s – not least as a result of one international superpower feeling it was technologically 'falling behind' the other. At that time, Parnes (1963/1970) reported research predicting that, in teaching, '. . . there will be less emphasis on memory and more on creative thinking'. Commenting on the rapid expansion of knowledge and increasing pace of change (even then!), he noted the impossibility of predicting what knowledge would serve society best in a decade's time. Consequently, he advocated the development of '. . . the attitudes and abilities that will help (people) meet *any* future problem creatively and inventively' (Parnes, 1963/1970: 351). Despite this earnest foresight and considerable growth in creative education in schools through the 1970s, nearly 50 years on, this hope remains unfulfilled in today's content- and test-driven curricula. However, history and optimism both tell us that creativity and creative education are ripe for renaissance in our primary schools, and it is possible that we are witnessing the cusp of change for the better right now. The (political) curriculum pendulum may well swing back and D&T can rightfully contribute to the momentum.

CREATIVITY'S CO-CONSPIRATORS

While we can see how richly creativity-through-D&T plays into the general curriculum as well as being a distinct subject, we should also consider a group of concepts that relate to, or qualify, our sense of creativity. I mention these because I believe they are suggestive of possibilities when teaching creativity through D&T. While we can think of creativity as design's oxygen, it does not equate design (which can be noun and/or verb). Besides, creativity is just one of many approaches that design embraces for its purposes.

Some concepts such as idealism, empathy, curiosity, apathy (as a social condition) and boredom (a personal one) can provide an entry point for creativity and can inform creative practices. Much in life can be lived with an orientation toward *the ideal* that is perpetually sought-after, never-to-be-attained and ever reimagined yet ethically defensible. For me, democracy is an example of this. *Empathy* is something about which children learn, that contributes to their development, and from such a trait come creative design opportunities.

Curiosity has ever inspired creativity and can be considered one of life's motivators, raising questions that beg invention, new thinking and alternatives – remembering that Pandora's curiosity left us with innumerable problems too! Creativity can serve as reagent to *apathy* and *boredom* and, for children, builds both agency and confidence. In the classroom, we can often witness mischief as a behaviour of the intelligent, creative, yet bored, child.

Differently, creativity's major co-conspirator is *imagination*, whether imagining big picture as in future possibilities (the foresight of Prometheus or the invitation of John Lennon's 'Imagine') or in the detailed workings of the mind's eye when 'building' something inside the head. We are also witnessing the emergence of *critiquing* as a powerful component of D&T practice. The South Australian curriculum of 2001 led the way with this innovation but its educational power must be well managed. Critiquing is an invaluable practice in the weighing of value judgements in design decision-making and in questioning design intentions. However, it must never be allowed to inhibit the imagination (Keirl, 2004). It helps to remember that, while creativity and designing are *proactive* (they look to the future), critiquing is *reactive* – something (a thought, event or act) has to have happened before it can take place.

D&T AS CREATIVITY IN ACTION – REWARDING CHILDREN, TEACHERS, SCHOOLS *AND* SOCIETY

Having explored some of the many ways that creativity interplays with the designed and technological world, how might we consider its rewarding relationships with D&T in the primary classroom?

For D&T to realise its potential as a mainstay of creativity education, it should, I argue, be seen as *both* design- and technological-literacy *and* as a subject of special and unique educational focus. The former celebrates D&T's well-recognised capacities for integrating the primary curriculum and to act as a catalyst for all kinds of learning. We have long known that almost any learning style or (multiple) intelligence, no matter whether head, hands or heart, can be 'hooked' and enhanced through D&T. The situation regarding creativity is no different.

D&T education, with the rich creativity it facilitates, is of value to children everywhere. Wherever they live, children are born into a particular set of technological circumstances and a good D&T education helps them see that those circumstances are transient and malleable. For D&T to flourish, I would like to suggest we remember that:

- we think of creativity holistically, that is: *for* advancing creativity in general; *through* creativity as an agent of design practices; and, *about* creativity as a topic of learning itself
- there is a symbiotic arrangement between creativity and D&T – through their practice, each enhances the other
- creativity is viewed not as a singular entity or process but always as part of a greater context
- creativity is viewed ethically for the value judgements that are made during the creative process and for the consequences of its products
- creativity is for all – whether as personal fulfilment or as societal good (or ill!)
- a creative classroom environment is essential and a creative school culture is very important. Creativity must be seen to be valued by all in the school.

D&T TEACHERS AS CREATIVITY'S CO-CONSPIRATORS

Clearly, where an imbalanced or heavily tested curriculum drains resources (human, temporal and other) and a school finds it challenging to celebrate creativity (for whatever reason), then it's not easy for teachers to do so either. However, because D&T enjoys a symbiotic relationship with creativity, so long as it maintains its place in the curriculum then it will fly creativity's flag. Thus, as ever, the teacher is pivotal to the successful engagement of children's creativity. What professional assets do we have to counter the challenges?

First, we can champion D&T's huge educational potential a) for all learners no matter the learning preference; b) as a curriculum integrator to bring meaning to learning through design activity and practical engagements that contextualise other fields; c) as a forum for action-on-the-world and of identity formation; d) as a forum for the expression and realisation of designerly thinking; e) as a forum for debating and critiquing existing technologies and products; f) as a special way of seeing and understanding one's world and those of other cultures and communities; and g) as a place for considering futures and change positively and with optimism. D&T can be thought of as a way of doing, thinking, knowing, creating and being. If it is fostered and celebrated by schools, then the school's creative culture will blossom too.

In a perverse way, we can also take strength from the fact that, because D&T is not encumbered (at least directly) by testing regimes, it is reasonably free to get on with its very special form of education. Whatever the situation, D&T has excellent educational credentials *of its own right*. Whoever seeks to marginalise it is usually coming from a particular, narrow and/or dated educational stance. Many curriculum decision-makers have not had the benefit of a rich D&T education, so are ill-equipped to make those decisions.

Second, we can act collegially. Freire (1972) saw curriculum as a dialogue to be created and re-created. It helps to remember that we educators inhabit curricula and that we can modify our environments – that is the way of things, to design and to redesign as an articulate professional group. I see curriculum as I see democracy – as an ideal always in need of re-creation and reconceptualisation – and the required ongoing dialogue occurs better in 'professional learning communities' than in 'performance training sects' (Hargreaves, 2003). There is a need to resist having to work alone and to work in the immediate (two deliberate pressures on the profession in many jurisdictions). Working together and with vision facilitates stronger change than seeking isolated quick fixes as curriculum development.

Third, teachers' professional judgment is a double strength – collectively and individually. Collegial action can be political (small 'p') in that it is both strategic and enables resistance to the 'schools should' brigade – all those 'experts' who 'know' what we should be doing – especially regarding creativity. If teachers are to be role models for creative learners, then their understandings both of creativity and of their students need to be rich and carefully integrated as research-informed pedagogy. 'Creativity as personal fulfilment' can come to children and teachers alike, even when competing values have to be met and resolved as part of the pedagogical journey. Teachers can indeed celebrate their worth as members of Florida's (2003) 'super-creative core' of the creative class.

When Lubart (2004) reports his UNESCO research, he is reporting on the creative curriculum *in general*, noting that teachers:

> ... encourage independent learning, have a co-operative teaching style, motivate students to learn (useful facts as a basis) for divergent thinking, encourage flexible thinking, delay judging students' ideas until they have been fully considered, promote self-evaluation of ideas, take students' questions and suggestions seriously, offer opportunities to work with a variety of materials in varied conditions, and help students to cope with frustration and failure in order to build the courage to pursue new ideas.
>
> (Lubart, 2004: 13)

What is interesting (and ironic) here is that this is business as usual for D&T education. It cannot be emphasised too strongly that if teachers and schools are practising good D&T education, then they will be delivering good creativity education. Teachers of D&T are celebrants of designerly behaviours; they seek creative contagion in their children and their schools. Fun plays a key role in the learning. Multiple intelligences are well celebrated through D&T learning, and multiple creativities can be too. Mischief can play a part, as can anarchic thinking. Here, children can articulate imagination; be creative; bring ideas into reality; think and work towards preferred futures; creatively critique their work, the work of others, and the designs and technologies that constitute their worlds; gain fulfilment and develop identity; celebrate and explore the interdependence of people and technologies and cultures; and learn about value judgements and ethics.

Having done all such things and more, children have learned *for* creativity, *through* creativity and *about* creativity. They, too, are creative co-conspirators for better worlds – a journey affording nothing but continuous challenges and rewards.

REFERENCES

Florida, R. (2003) *The Rise of the Creative Class: And How it's Transforming Work, Leisure, Community and Everyday Life*. North Melbourne: Pluto Press.

Freire, P. (1972) *Pedagogy of the Oppressed*. London: Penguin.

Hargreaves, A. (2003) *Teaching in the Knowledge Society: Education in the Age of Insecurity*. Maidenhead: Open University Press.

Keirl, S. (2004) 'Critiquing and designing as keys of technological literacy: matters arising from the meeting', in Middleton, H., Pavlova, M. and Roebuck, D. (eds) *Learning for Innovation in Technology Education: Proceedings of the 3rd Biennial International Conference on Technology Education Research*, 2, 91–98, Surfers Paradise, Australia, 9–11 December 2004.

Keirl, S. (2011) 'Primary design and technology education and ethical technological literacy', in Benson, C. and Lunt, J. (eds) *International Handbook of Primary Technology Education: Reviewing the Past Twenty Years*. Rotterdam: Sense.

Koestler, A. (1964/1975) *The Act of Creation*. Picador edn. London: Pan Books.

Lubart, T. (2004) *Individual student differences and Creativity for Quality Education*. Paper commissioned for the Education for All Global Monitoring Report 2005, The Quality Imperative. Paris: UNESCO. http://unesdoc.unesco.org/images/0014/001466/146667e. pdf (accessed 17 April 2008).

McLaren, S.V. (2012) 'The role of technology education in transformational change', in Williams, J. (ed.) *Technology Education for Teachers*. Rotterdam: Sense 231–260.

Mitcham, C. (1994) *Thinking Through Technology: The Path between Engineering and Philosophy*. Chicago: University of Chicago Press.

Mumford, L. (1934) *Technics and Civilisation*. London: Routledge & Kegan Paul.

Parnes, S.J. (1963/1970) 'Education and creativity', in Vernon, P.E. (ed.) *Creativity*. London: Penguin.

Further reading

Csikszentmihalyi, M. (1997) *Creativity: Flow and the Psychology of Discovery and Invention*. London: HarperPerennial.

Davies, T. (2000) 'Confidence! Its role in the creative teaching and learning of design and technology', *Journal of Technology Education*, 12(1). http://scholar.lib.vt.edu/ ejournals/JTE/v12n1/davies.html (accessed 17 April 2008).

Department of Education, Training and Employment (DETE) (2001) *South Australian Curriculum Standards and Accountability Framework* (SACSA). www.sacsa.sa.edu.au (accessed 17 April 2008).

Gardner, H. (1983) *Frames of Mind: The Theory of Multiple Intelligences*. London: Fontana.

Gardner, H. (1993) *Creating Minds: An Anatomy of Creativity Seen Through the Lives of Freud, Einstein, Picasso, Stravinsky, Eliot, Graham and Gandhi*. New York: BasicBooks.

Keirl, S. (2004) 'Creativity, innovation and life in the lily-pond: nurturing the design and technology family while keeping the alligators fed – DATA international keynote address'. *Journal of Design and Technology Education*, 9(3), 145–160.

Keirl, S. (2007) 'The politics of technology curriculum', in Barlex, D. (ed.) *Design and Technology – For the Next Generation: A Collection of Provocative Pieces, Written by Experts in Their Field, to Stimulate Reflection and Curriculum Innovation*. London: Nuffield Foundation.

Keirl, S. (2015) 'Global ethics, sustainability, and design and technology education', in Stables, K. and Keirl, S. (eds) *Environment, Ethics and Cultures: Design and Technology Education's Contribution to Sustainable Global Futures*. Rotterdam: Sense.

INDEX